Re-Mapping
Realities and Metaphors in Irish Literature and History

THE DOLPHIN

General Editor:
Tabish Khair

34

THE DOLPHIN
34

Re-Mapping Exile
Realities and Metaphors in Irish
Literature and History

Edited by

Michael Böss
Irene Gilsenan Nordin
Britta Olinder

Aarhus University Press, Denmark

AARHUS UNIVERSITY PRESS
Langelandsgade 177
DK–8200 Aarhus N, Denmark
Fax (+45) 8942 5380
www.unipress.dk

White Cross Mills
Hightown
Lancaster LA1 4XS
Fax (+44) 1524 63232

Box 511
Oakville, Conn. 06779
Fax (+1) 860 945 9468

Editorial address:
THE DOLPHIN
Department of English
University of Aarhus
DK–8000 Aarhus C, Denmark
Fax (+45) 8942 6540

This volume is published with financial support from the Aarhus
University Research Foundation and the Danish Research Council
for the Humanities.

Contents

INTRODUCTION
Re-Mapping Exile

Michael Böss and Irene Gilsenan Nordin

Political exile and economic emigration once formed a nexus that played a significant role for the construction of Irish patriotism and nationalism. But it was not until 1985, when Kerby Miller published his book *Emigrants and Exiles: Ireland and the Irish Exodus to North America* that the mental, cultural, and ideological connectives were empirically demonstrated. Miller challenged nationalist orthodoxy in so far as he showed how 'exile', far from simply denoting political banishment, was a social construct with multiple cultural meanings and connotations. Miller concluded that ordinary 'exiled' 18th-century emigrants to North America were victimized more by pre-modern cultural determinants, nationalist propaganda and a modernising economy than by British rule and alien, evicting landlords.

Miller's conclusions fed into the resuscitated debate on 'Irishness' in the 1980s and 1990s. However, it took relatively long for this debate to affect Irish literary criticism. As Patrick Ward correctly points out, most literary critics and editors up to then had either wholly disregarded the subject of exile or dealt with it in a rather incidental and vague way (3). The only systematic monograph so far on this topic from a literary point of view is Ward's own *Exile, Emigration and Irish Writing*, which is an investigation of thematic configurations of exile in the work of Irish writers since the Middle Ages. Ward examines the history of notions of exile in medieval, Gaelic tradition and demonstrates how they contribute to the formation of new meanings in the context of Irish nationalism, modernisation, and nation building in the 19th and 20th centuries.

Re-Mapping Exile: Realities and Metaphors in Irish Literature and History, ed. Michael Böss, Irene Gilsenan Nordin and Britta Olinder, *The Dolphin* 34. © 2005 by Aarhus University Press, Denmark. ISBN 87 7934 010 5.

Some of the essays in the present collection are broadly inspired by Miller and Ward's critical inquiries in that they combine historical, cultural, and literary analyses in their treatment of aspects of exile in Irish writing. The theoretical perspective of exile in these essays is 'structuralist', understood in the political and/or individual context, where exile is seen from a structuralist predominance of negativity, in the sense that exile is understood as a physical state of being, often associated with absence, into which an individual willingly or unwillingly enters. Other essays in the volume are inspired by a 'poststructuralist' perspective, where exile is considered in the light of postmodernist and psychoanalytic concerns. In this respect the narration of exile is understood as a celebration of playful transgressiveness, of hybridity, diversity and otherness, of simulacra and simulation, as a prototype of a split, fluid subjectivity that leaves behind a linear mode of thinking, in favour of 'a sense of identity that rests not on fixity but contingency' (Braidotti 31). This type of exile moves away from a political, cultural, economic idea of exile to an understanding of exile in a wider existential sense.

The volume is the product of a group of Irish Studies scholars in the Nordic countries. It presents readings of Irish literature, history and culture that reflect some of the historical, sociological, psychological and philosophical dimensions of exile in the 1800s and 1900s. We have been particularly interested in discussing 'exile' in a wide range of texts including literature, political writings and song-writing, either in works of Irish writers not normally associated with exile, or in which new aspects of 'exile' can be discerned. Works by the following authors have been examined in order of arrangement in the collection: Hubert Butler, Thomas D'Arcy McGee, Rosa Mulholland, James Joyce, John Hewitt, Van Morrison, Eiléan Ní Chuilleanáin, as well as a number of other Irish women poets, Roddy Doyle, and John Banville. The book is a collaborative joint venture in so far as it emerges from a series of interdisciplinary workshops and seminars held in the period 2001-2004. During these work-in-process sessions, the participants, although each responsible for his or her own contribution, have been subject to collegial scrutiny and encouragement, as well as the occasional ignorant question, which may be seen as both the burden and blessing of interdisciplinary collaboration. The latter was our experience, however. We fully enjoyed producing scholarship in a way which we consider is far too rare within the humanities. We regard the plurality of approaches represented here not as a flaw, but rather as a source of strength, because it reflects our general view that the historically changing meanings of 'exile' evade rigid and narrow definitions.

The individual authors of the essays have not been asked to strive towards any theoretical unity, but instead to apply the methods and theories that were found most relevant for their approach and the texts chosen for study. The first essay by Michael Böss, 'Theorizing Exile', outlines some general observations on theoretical and historical approaches to exile and suggests areas and topics for future research. This essay offers a systematic and critical discussion of a number of definitions and major theories of exile within contemporary sociological and literary studies. Böss draws on new insights from a variety of academic disciplines and demonstrates how they may contribute to developing a new, general understanding of exile as a multidimensional and 'bilateral' phenomenon. With reference, for example, to recent biblical scholarship, contemporary sociological theory and, especially, Hispanicist Paul Ilie's theory of 'inner exile', Böss suggests that a new 'sociology of exile' may open up for a fresh approach to the study of the role of exile in Irish history and literature. Finally, he discusses how new notions and meanings of exile developed in 20th century philosophy and literature, as a result of the experience of economic modernization, mass migration, extended warfare, and the breakdown of traditional notions of individual belonging and social order.

Billy Gray, in his essay '"The lukewarm conviction of temporary lodgers": The Anglo-Irish and Dimensions of Exile in the Work of Hubert Butler', examines how differing concepts of exile can be applied to Hubert Butler's perception of the Anglo-Irish experience after the Act of Union. As this essay demonstrates, Butler argues that within the confines of a comparatively short historical period, the Protestant Aristocracy, who had been the original progenitors of Irish nationalism, came to view themselves as exiles within their own country. Gray's contention is that by applying the ideas of exile theorists such as Joseph Wittlin and Jan Vladeslav – particularly those concepts which elucidate exilic experiences pertaining to 'communal trauma' and 'powerlessness' – it is possible to illuminate Butler's views on what he refers to as 'the withdrawal of a whole historic class'.

In 'Exiles no More: Ethnic Leadership and the Construction of the Myth of Thomas D'Arcy McGee', Michael Böss argues that these two leading Irish writers and publishers in 19th-century North America (McGee and Sadlier) contributed significantly to the acculturation of Irish Catholic immigrants in Canada and the United States from the middle of the 19th century. By virtue of their shared sense of mission as leaders of the Irish Catholic communities of North America, they helped especially famine immigrants adjust to life in North America. In particular, it is demonstrated how McGee – a former Irish revolutionary nationalist who later became a socially conservative prophet of Canadian nationalism – served Catholic Irish immigrants in Canada, by divesting them of reasons for maintaining a separatist and exilic identity. He taught them, instead, to see themselves as Catholic Canadians of 'Celtic' ethnicity. The argument rests on the assumption that McGee's own 'conversion' to Canadianness occurred at a time of his life when he had learned to accept and respect the role of the Catholic Church in the New World.

The concepts of the stranger and the returning exile, quite common motifs in nineteenth and early twentieth-century Irish literature, are addressed by Heidi Hansson, in her essay, 'From Reformer to Sufferer: The Returning Exile in Rosa Mulholland's Fiction'. According to Hansson, the difference between these two concepts is that the stranger's function is mainly to be the vehicle through which an author can educate readers about the positive aspects of Irish life, whereas the returning exile is more often used to convey social critique. The returning exile sees the need for reform and change, while the stranger is usually shown to finally embrace the initially foreign Irish society as it is. Because the returning exile belongs to both Ireland and the place of exile – usually America or Australia – the return 'home' is often shown to result in a sense of hybridity. This becomes particularly clear when it is a woman who returns. A man who comes back is often shown to return in triumph, but when the protagonist is a woman, the return is often described as problematic.

Ida Klitgård's essay, '(Dis)Location and Its (Dis)Contents: Translation as Exile in James Joyce's *A Portrait of the Artist as a Young Man* and *Finnegans Wake*', argues that James Joyce makes use of a poetics of translation as a metaphorical means of expressing states of exile in two of his major works: *A Portrait of the Artist* and *Finnegans Wake*. A voluntary exile himself, James Joyce was deeply influenced by travel and multiple languages. This experience became the impetus of his life-long literary revolt against British reign in Ireland. This essay situates itself within a poststructuralist framework by questioning topics of philosophical, translation theoretical, and literary interest in a reading of Joyce. In a demonstration of how Joyce relies on a poetics of translation in his works, the essay questions conventional boundaries of what is perceived as the essence of original language – exemplified in the Tower of Babel myth, boundaries of conventional ideas of translation as mere ethnocentric transformation of languages, and boundaries of conventional literary style in usually one language.

In 'John Hewitt at Home and in Exile', Britta Olinder discusses the complications of roots and rootlessness in the works of the Northern Irish poet and autobiographer, John Hewitt. Not only does Hewitt deal with the discomfort felt by the early colonizers in exile from England, and the stories of family members who emigrated to America, but also with his own alienation, even from his friendly Catholic neighbours in the Glens of Antrim, or his inner exile among conservative Protestants in power in his province. This last turns into dissent as exile, felt most keenly during the war when he is, however, also acquainting himself with so far unknown parts of his home ground. In his fifteen-year actual exile in Coventry, Hewitt finds ample opportunities to ponder the advantages and drawbacks of his situation and occasions for feeling at home and simultaneously as a stranger in other foreign countries.

Representations of Celtic roots and Irish diaspora identities in three 1980s albums by the Belfast born singer/songwriter, Van Morrison, are examined by Bent Sørensen in 'The Celtic Ray: Representations of Diaspora Identities in Van Morrison Lyrics'. Morrison's music, it is argued, is based on a mixture of North American forms (rhythm and blues/jazz and folk/country) and traditional Irish folk inspiration. The 1980s saw Morrison return more explicitly to Irish roots, and a trilogy of albums from that period express Celtic longings, culminating in a full-length album collaboration with The Chieftains (*Irish Heartbeat*, 1988). The essay shows how the songs *Celtic Ray* and *Irish Heartbeat* thematize tensions between longing and belonging in a conflict that, according to Sørensen, is typical of diaspora texts. As the songs reappear in full Celtic-style arrangements on the 1988 album, they form a seamless part of a whole suite of songs on migration (usually figured as 'roving') and exile, describing an arch in the singer's personal development of identity. The essay concludes with a discussion of Morrison's notions of Celtic brotherhood as a hybrid between American New Age philosophies (individualist) and Irish identity positions (collectivist), a duality which is further mirrored in Morrison's internal and external exile positions.

From a poststructuralist, philosophical point of view, Irene Gilsenan Nordin examines exile as an existential state of being, and an expression of the essential human condition, in her essay entitled '"Between the Dark Shore and the Light": The Exilic Subject in Eiléan Ní Chuilleanáin's *The Second Voyage*'. The essay traces the related metaphors of homelessness and home in Ní Chuilleanáin's *The Second Voyage*, and shows how images of fixity, such as those of the house and land, are contrasted with those of fluidity, seen especially in Ní Chuilleanáin's use of water and the sea. Gilsenan Nordin argues that images of home can be seen in terms of the restricting linear mode of intellectual thinking, versus those of homelessness, the contrasting semiotic images of unconscious desire, which are liberating and empowering forces. These juxtapositions are explored in light of the idea of the speaking subject as exilic, one that is constantly moving between contrasting states of being. Gilsenan Nordin compares this with what the philosopher Rosi Braidotti calls the nomadic subject, one that continually moves across 'established categories and levels of experience: blurring boundaries without burning bridges'.

By way of comparison and complement, Britta Olinder in her essay 'Washed up on Somebody Else's Tide: The Exile Motif in Contemporary Poetry by Women' shows, indeed, that exile has many faces, as many as those in exile. It is 'bitter, sharp-tongued, mournful and/or delicious', sometimes at one and the same time. If one cannot or will not regard the new country as one's own, the distance, the accepted alienation in the new situation, becomes a fact. Exile then becomes a life-style. The exiled person turns into a continually fugitive soul who can never find peace. These and other attitudes to exile can be found in poetry written by Irish women. Most aspects such as homelessness, the bitterness over conditions that left exile the only option, the feeling of being dispossessed, and comparisons with biblical exile, are also dealt with by male poets, while the daughter's obligation to follow her father into exile or marriage experienced as an exiled state, are experiences specific to women. The essay also examines the role and importance of language and dialect to the person in exile.

Åke Persson's essay, '"The culchies have fuckin' everythin'": Internal Exile in Roddy Doyle's *The Barrytown Trilogy*', argues that Doyle's Barrytown Trilogy is most fruitfully understood if placed against and within the dominant socio-political and economic realities of post-Independence Ireland. Persson sees the Trilogy as being in dialogue with traditional Ireland governed by a rigid system of exclusion. In other words, the Trilogy must be read in a historical context. This essay draws on a range of insights from history and sociology as well as socioeconomic and physical geography to open up the texts, and the author's reading of Doyle can best be described as materialist, although not necessarily Marxist. It might be argued that it comes close to New Historicism/Cultural Materialism. The essay argues that Doyle's works are a product of and a response to the cultural and political webs of a particular society and must be understood in relation to those webs.

Filtering John Banville's novel *Shroud* through a raster of certain postmodern ideas, Hedda Friberg, in her essay, 'John Banville's *Shroud*: Exile in Simulation', examines what she sees as an exilic condition present in the novel. Reading *Shroud* through Jean Baudrillard's early writings on contemporary culture, through his vision of an age of simulation, an 'implosive era of models' – especially as expressed in his *Simulacra and Simulation* – Friberg sees Banville's novel as engaged in a dialogue with Baudrillard's text. Friberg suggests that the novel's protagonist, Axel Vander, can be seen as moving in a state of exile in simulation. Exile is here used both in its original sense of banishment, and in the sense of alienation, or estrangement. Vander's exile is triple-levelled: he is exiled from his people and, through a process of falsification, from their history; he is exiled from the (fake) likeness of a divinity; finally, he is exiled from his own self, which has become a copy without an original. A consideration of such a metaphoric exile in simulation raises questions of shape-changing, reduplication and imitation, authenticity and the disappearance of the real, and of the ultimate fluidity of identity.

References

Braidotti, Rosi. Nomadic Subjects: Embodiment and Sexual Difference in Contemporary Feminist Theory. New York: Columbia University Press, 1994.

Miller, Kerby A. Emigrants and Exiles: Ireland and the Irish Exodus to North America. Oxford: Oxford University Press, 1985.

Ward, Patrick. Exile, Emigration and Irish Writing. Dublin: Irish Academic Press, 2002.

Theorising Exile

Michael Böss

Meanings of exile

In his famous essay 'Reflections on Exile' from 1984, Edward Said described 'true exile' as 'a condition of loss', an 'unhealable rift forced between a human being and a native place, between the self and its true home' and a 'crippling sorrow of estrangement' (173). At that time Said reserved the term exile for a person who is literally and legally prevented from returning to his homeland, i.e. the political exile. Because he discussed the state of exile in fundamentally negative terms – 'like death but without death's mercies' – he was sceptical of the way in which its 'mutilations' had been banalised in modern Western culture: from Romantic aesthetics to post-Nietzschean humanist philosophy. Yet, he did concede that there were experiences related to the life of the exile – which is led 'outside the habitual order' and which is characterised as 'nomadic', 'decentred' and 'contrapuntal' (186) – which have certain likenesses to experiences normally associated with modernity. He also did grant that the exile's 'plurality of vision' might offer new perspectives on the human condition in general. In his memoir *Out of Place*, published fifteen years later, he qualified his position. It is clearly marked by recent theories of modernity and is less dismissive of symbolic uses of 'exile'. Once more, Said refers to personal experience, but now as points of departure for general reflections on the nature of personal identity in the modern world.

Indeed, a definition of exile which excludes symbolic uses would be limiting for a full understanding of the complex social, cultural and psychological structures and historical meanings of exile. Most national histories – and Irish history arguably more than others – offer abundant illustrations of the difficulty of

Re-Mapping Exile: Realities and Metaphors in Irish Literature and History, ed. Michael Böss, Irene Gilsenan Nordin and Britta Olinder, *The Dolphin* 34. © 2005 by Aarhus University Press, Denmark. ISBN 87 7934 010 5.

drawing clear lines between voluntary and involuntary exile. They also demonstrate how little sense it makes to discuss exile exclusively in terms of a dichotomy between a territorial 'home' and 'abroad'. Furthermore, the historicity of the concept must be acknowledged in order to understand its changing and local meanings. Both for theoretical and pragmatic reasons, then, a broad approach to the concept of exile ought to be adopted.

As is well known, the etymology of 'exile' goes back to the Latin noun *exsilium*, which had three meanings in Antiquity: (1) enforced removal from one's native land in accordance with an edict or sentence, (2) penal expatriation or banishment; (3) the state or condition of penal banishment to a foreign land. The noun was a derivation from the verb *salire*, to jump, and the prefix *ex-* , a fact which emphasises the character of exile as a crossing of a boundary. That the crossing has disruptive implications is reflected in later uses in Romance languages, for example in Old French where the noun may refer to the ravage, ruin and utter impoverishment of a country.

By this time, i.e. the Middle Ages, the term could also mean expatriation and prolonged absence from one's native land by voluntary decision. This novel use is likely to have been the result of encrustations from Biblical/Jewish tradition, which associated exile with the narratives of Exodus and the Babylonian captivity. Also Christian theology and anthropology had added new, spiritual dimensions derived from the doctrine of man's fall and expulsion from Paradise into his earthly exile in which he lived in a state of despair longing for salvation and a return to the true home of his immortal soul. This perception informed the medieval institution of *perigrinatio* (pilgrimage), which the medievalist Diana Webb defines as 'the abandonment of the security and stability of the setting into which one had been born, and of the social ties which most men took to be a necessity of life [which] might in fact amount to a sentence of exile, passed on oneself and embraced rejoicingly' (*Medieval Pilgrimage* 1, see also 'Pilgrimage').[1] *Perigrinatio* was a characteristic, but not unique feature of Irish monasticism.

It was the historian Kerby Miller's pioneering contribution to the history of exile to show how such – vernacular, local and literary – uses informed the way in which Irish economic emigrants interpreted their experience in the 19th century. Miller demonstrates how their notion of themselves as exiles could be derived from a long process of cultural sedimentation, which (1) began with the monastic and eremitic traditions of 'white martyrdom', (2) continued with the practice of territorial banishment for confessional-political reasons in the Post-Reformation age and its interpretation in Gaelic poetry and popular history, and (3) culminated in the 19th century, an age in which the modernisation of the rural economy led to mass emigration and the rise of Irish nationalism. Other nations, of course, have had their own experiences and traditions of exile, which must be considered in their particular historical contexts and expressions.

This is not to say that there is nothing to be gained from comparative studies of exile. On the contrary, contemporary Irish studies, ironically still marked by the nationalist tradition of cultural particularism, may benefit from placing the discussion of Irish exile in a wider European or global context.

In his extensive survey of the historical examples of exile, however, Paul Tabori describes exile as a universal social, political, indeed even biological phenomenon. He chronicles its various manifestations from the animal world and 'primitive' societies, first recordings in ancient Egyptian papyri, Biblical literature and classical sources over the Middle Ages up to the present age, pointing out evidence of an 'anatomy of exile' in the writings of famous exiles such as Ovid, Dante, and Voltaire. Tabori's Irish examples of exile are scholars 'fleeing from the increasingly severe Viking raids and other Scandinavian depredations', Catholics whose faith and 'national consciousness brought them into double conflict with Protestant and expansionist England', and 'refugees from starvation' (85, 143). For the sake of completeness, he might have added that forced banishment is known to be a common political instrument as far back as the Iron Age in Ireland as well as the rest of Europe.

Tabori is critical of restrictive definitions of exile based on linguistic, legal, and political criteria – i.e. 'purist' definitions (33) – because what is important, he argues, is whether an exile defines himself as such. Exile is seen first of all as a psychological experience, and Tabori's 'compromise' definition reflects this perception: 'An exile is a person who is compelled to leave his homeland – though the forces that send him on his way may be political, economic, or purely psychological. It does not make an essential difference whether he is expelled by physical force or whether he makes the decision to leave without such an immediate pressure.' (37)

Tabori offers a number of points that he finds fundamental to the nature of exile:

1. The status of the exile is dynamic as it may change – 'from exile to emigrant or emigrant to exile' – as a result of altered circumstances and the process of assimilation an exile undergoes in his or her new country.
2. The exile makes a 'contribution' to the reception country, determined by his/her own efforts at assimilation and the spiritual, intellectual and other skills s/he brings with her/himself.
3. The exile's resolve to return is likely to become weaker in direct proportion to the length of her/his absence from her/his homeland.
4. The exile will always retain an interest and affection for her/his homeland, whether conscious or not.
5. The contribution of the exile is likely to be greater in his adopted country than her/his influence in the land of her/his birth. (37-38)

Tabori's psychological portrait of the exile seems slightly reductionist, however. Human beings respond to banishment and life in exile according to the particular circumstances and nature of their exile. Responses are dependent on the personal, spiritual, social and cultural resources of the exile himself/herself, for example the availability of a culture and/or literature of exile through which the exile may interpret his/her lot. Take, for example, the different ways in which Ovid and Seneca endured their exiles in Tomis and Corsica respectively. As Gareth Williams points out, Seneca took comfort in Stoic doctrine, seeing himself as a citizen of the universe and adopting its consoling topos that an exile makes his home in any land. Ovid's lack of such philosophical resources, in contrast, made his exile unbearable, and his poems written in exile offer a study in melancholy, manic rage and utmost alienation.

If used carefully, however, it does make considerable sense to point out a few recurrent psychological features – among involuntary and territorial (henceforth called 'structural') exiles. The key feature, which distinguishes the exile from the voluntary emigrant and the cosmopolitan, is the divided nature of the exilic mentality: the exile's nostalgia, constant hope for return and sense of having been dislocated and estranged and of living outside, not only home but also adopted country. Hallward Dahlie rightly characterises the exile as a 'displaced individual' who 'continues to be at odds with both the world he has rejected and the one he has moved into' (93). Comparing the rebel and the exile, Raymond Williams writes that the 'exile is as absolute as the rebel in rejecting the way of life of his society, but instead of fighting it he goes away. Usually, he will remain an exile, unable to go back to the society he has rejected or that has rejected him, yet equally unable to form important relationships with the society to which he has gone' (qtd in Wagner 105). Williams' distinction between rebel and exile is untenable – in Irish history, for example, there are many rebellious exiles – but his perception of the exilic mentality is quite to the point, namely, as Peter Wagner puts it, that 'there is something unrecoverable, once one leaves one's place of origin. The social bond cannot be recreated in the same way in which it existed before; the same density of social relations and the density of meaning in the world around oneself can no longer be reached' (105).

In the light of the preceding discussion, then, the following definition of exile is suggested: Exile refers to the status or experience of individuals and collectives who, against or with their own will, are subject to exclusion, expulsion, removal, severance, marginality, dislocation, and estrangement for political, religious, cultural, sexual, and economic reasons.[2]

For the sake of analysis, exile as a general category may be broken down into a number of ideal subcategories:

1. Political exile: Individuals/groups forced to leave or who have fled their native land for fear of arrest and/or harassment by ruling authorities, be they local or national. This category includes political deportees, refugees, and political enemies of a state hoping to return one day.

2. Religious exile: Individuals/groups who have left or have been forced to leave because they feared arrest or harassment due to their religious beliefs being in conflict with prevailing ones in their local and political community.

3. Cultural and social exile: Individuals who have left their country voluntarily because they did not wish to live in a country where they felt unduly restricted by hegemonic politics, religious observances or social/and sexual mores. This category of exiles includes expatriates, who consider returning when times have changed for the better.

4. Sexual exile: Individuals who have left their country in order to enjoy greater freedom in sexual expression, after having experienced hostility, repression and marginalisation in their home communities.

5. Economic exile: Individuals/groups who have felt forced to emigrate by economic necessity, but would have preferred to stay at home.

6. Penal exile: Individuals transported to a penal colony for criminal offences.

7. Inner exile: Resident individuals/groups suffering political, social and cultural repression, marginalisation or exclusion but have not been able or willing to leave their community/country.

8. Symbolic exile: individuals who understand their lives – or whose circumstances of life may be understood – with reference to religious, philosophical or aesthetic notions of exile. This subcategory includes medieval monastic pilgrims, modernist artists etc.[3]

Drawing a further distinction between structural (territorial) and non-structural types of exile, we end up with the following model:

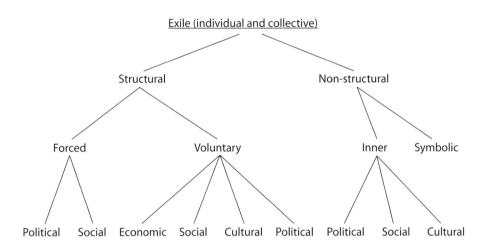

The categories of this model, one should bear in mind, are ideal types used for the sake of analysis only. Hence, in practice, it will often be necessary to combine two or even more for each individual case, as will appear from the elaboration below.

Towards a sociology of exile

In his *Biblical Theology of Exile* (2002), Daniel L. Smith-Christopher discusses how biblical scholarship on the Babylonian exile of the Israelites (597/587-539 BC) in the 1990s has recently been transformed by insights derived from postmodern and postcolonial theory, refugee studies, disaster studies and the sociology of trauma. Conversely, he argues, the study of the Hebrew exile – and the writing which came out of it – may contribute to an understanding of the world we live in today, including the general psychological and cultural implications of living in an age when more individuals than ever before in history

are bound to live as exiles dispersed or banished from their
territorial homelands by political persecution, religious
discrimination, natural disaster or economic necessity. Now, not
only may Ezekiel and Lamentations – i.e. the two books
traditionally considered to be the main sources of the Exile – but
most of the entire biblical narrative be understood in the light of
the exilic experience.

The Babylonian Exile has been broadly reassessed as not only
a political, human, and theological crisis caused by a chain of
imperial strategies, but also, more positively, as a series of
dramatic events which produced a new national – Hebrew/Judaic
– identity based on the biblical narrative that the exiles produced.
Postexilic 'Judaism' was more or less invented, or at least
reconstructed, on the basis of a narrative which stretched back
through the monarchical period and the Exodus to the
Patriarchs.

Apart from reminding us that exile is an ancient phenomenon
and not just a product of modernity and globalisation, this
fascinating new biblical scholarship gives us valuable insight into
some fundamentals about the sociology of exile: firstly, exile is not
just something that happens to individuals, but also to collectives
such as nations. Secondly, representations of exile should be
studied with a view to their broader political, social and cultural
effects and implications (arguably, not only Israelite history, also
Irish historiography has roots in various exilic experiences).
Thirdly, therefore, exile should be seen as significant for the
construction of individual and collective (including national)
identities. Finally: the Biblical example illustrates how exile, as a
dialectical process, affects not only the banished – sitting by the
'Rivers of Babylon' – but also the group left behind in a
devastated 'Jerusalem' deprived of its leadership. The Babylonian
Exile, thus, produced both 'The Book of Ezekiel', written by
structural exiles, and 'The Lamentations', the work of inner,
residential exiles suffering under a foreign hegemony.

Sociologically speaking, exile has always been one of the
means – rituals, practices and institutions – by which differences
and boundaries between self and other have been policed and
maintained (cf. Strange and Bashford). A sociology of exile must

therefore draw on various theories of power. Frank Parkin's theory of 'social exclosure' would be one of a number of approaches one may take.[4] According to Parkin, property, ethnic origin, language or religion are used by hegemonic groups as part of a strategy by which they acquire privileges for themselves by preventing 'outsiders' from getting access to material, social and cultural resources.

A supplementary approach would be Said's discussion of the association of exile and nationalism. Said regarded nationalism as developing from 'a condition of estrangement' and the construction of a 'home created by a community of language, culture, and customs' and thus a way of fending off exile. The reverse side to nationalism, he argued, is that in time nationalism becomes a system which defines insiders and outsiders with reference to the values of the collective *habitus* it has defined. Nationalism, then, ends up producing its own exiles: those who are banished to a territory of non-belonging, whether physically or mentally (*Reflections on Exile* 176-77). Said also has an eye for the proclivity of the nationalist in exile to solve his own mental predicament by seeing himself as part of a prospective, restored nation:

> Exiles are cut off from their roots, their land, their past. They generally do not have armies or states, although they are often in search of them. Exiles feel, therefore, an urgent need to see themselves as part of a triumphant ideology or a restored people. (177)

Whereas such 'defensive nationalism' among exiles may lead to unattractive forms of ethnic self-assertion, exile nationalism also plays a positive role in 'reconstitutive projects', i.e. in the construction of national history, the revival of endangered languages and the founding of national institutions such as universities and libraries (184).

The American Hispanicist, Paul Ilie, suggests that exile should be studied sociologically and culturally as a bilateral phenomenon. In his book on Spanish exilic writers under the Francoist regime 1939-1975, *Literature and Inner Exile* (1980), Ilie notes that studies of exile have usually been too concerned with the political, demographic and economic circumstances of the expulsion of individuals and groups or the way in which they express their experiences in writings or by other means. He raises the question whether this concern has not led to the neglect of something fundamental about exile, namely its character as a reciprocal relationship:

> Separation from one's country means more than a lack of physical contact with land and houses. It is also a set of feelings and beliefs that isolate the expelled group from the majority. Once we acknowledge that exile is a mental condition more than a material one, that it removes people from other people and their way of life, then the nature of this separation remains to be defined not only as a unilateral severance, but as something more profound. Excision is a reciprocal relationship; to cut off one segment of a population from the rest is also to leave the larger segment cut off from the smaller one. (2)

'Rarely has anyone wondered about the hollow left after the exodus, about the repercussions upon those citizens who shared émigré values but who remained in the homeland,' Ilie claims (3), and he stresses the fact that these 'internal structures of exile' are even more important than questions of geographical dislocation, territorial non-communication and physical separation. Exile produces its own mentality, which does not only manifest itself in responses to physical severance and territorial non-communication, but also as conflicts over values:

> I would contend that exile is a state of mind whose emotions and values respond to separation and severance as conditions in themselves. To live apart is to adhere to values that do not partake in the prevailing values; he who perceives this moral difference and who responds to it emotionally lives in exile. (3)

Inner exiles are members of the residential population who stay at home, but who are affected by prevailing conditions in their society as much as those who are expelled by the hegemonic regime or who decide to emigrate for political and social reasons. The experience of inner exile has both psychological and cultural dimensions: It manifests itself as (1) a feeling of isolation (endured by individuals and groups in relation to the dominant group), and (2) a 'partial asphyxiation of an entire culture' (47). Inner exiles may, collectively, represent an exilic culture, which defines itself against the hegemonic – or 'orthodox' – culture. However, surprising as it may sound, the dominant culture may also be regarded as exilic in so far as it is constructed through the banishment of whole segments of the population. A state governed on exilic policies may thus be seen as a nation which is alienated from itself by seeking

> to compensate for the missing segment through self-sufficiency, which it accomplishes by negating the value of what has been lost […]. Beyond those exclusionist centers lies the alienated periphery, where citizens for various reasons decide to maintain their residence even without benefiting from the fruits of the established orthodoxy. The tendencies of both segments, centripetal and centrifugal, interact within the same deprivations. Consequently they constitute and function as a single cultural rootedness […], despite their antagonisms, in distinction from the wandering cultural entity […]. But within the home culture, the further distinction between orthodox and dissenting segments remains, a division that may be described in yet other terms and that always exhibits the incompatibilities of the original, larger rift. (4)

Territorial banishment, political and religious oppression, the introduction of censorship laws, exclusivist definitions of communal and national belonging are the means and strategies by which rulers and ruling groups try to secure privileged access to power and valued resources. In the course of time, however, this situation is likely to lead to cultural, social and economic stagnation and inertia followed by a call for the 'exiles' return', i.e.

for the reintegration of the groups which have suffered under or who have actively resisted hegemonic policies. This process, however, is seldom straightforward and without complications, partly due to the fact that structural exiles in time may become so distant from domestic realities that, even after their return, they find it difficult to communicate with their non-structural allies. The mentality of the structural exile, thus, will first have to be adjusted before a new process of social value formation may take place.

Irish history offers cases which may illustrate this process. For example, the IRB's adoption of the strategy of a 'New Departure' after 1873 may be read as a step towards the gradual integration of exile and emigrant nationalism into the political mainstream.

As referred, the connectives between emigration, exile and nationalism have been studied by the Irish American historian Kerby Miller. Miller argues that exiled Irish nationalists in North America used notions of exile handed down from the past in order to recruit Irish emigrants – not even those fleeing famine but also voluntary emigrants leaving Ireland to improve their lot – for the national cause. This fact alone, however, does not explain the force of the metaphor. It can only be explained by the presence of a common cultural tradition among Irish Catholics:

> Although the undeniable difficulties the Irish encountered in North America might prompt and nurture the piteous content of the exile self-image, the concept itself reflected not the concrete realities of most emigrants' experiences but a distinctive Irish Catholic worldview rooted deeply in Irish history and culture. The origins of both worldview and exile image long preceded the English conquest of Ireland and the mass migrations of modern times. Subsequent historical circumstances of rebellion and defeat, despoliation and impoverishment, served to ratify and magnify aspects of preconquest Irish culture which made the exile motif seem more poignant and appropriate. Armed with a worldview so shaped, the Irish experienced the socioeconomic changes associated with the modern commercial and industrial revolutions with certain psychological, as well as political and

economic disadvantages. Usually lacking capital and political power sufficient to shape the emerging market economy to their own profit, the Irish fell back upon cultural traditions which could be adapted to deal with the strains of modernization. The resultant worldview provided an ideological defense against misfortune, and the basis for a nationalistic assertion of Irish identity. However, it also reformulated and perpetuated the archaic tradition of emigration as exile in the modern context of conflict with England as origin of both political oppression and economic deprivation. (7-8)

It is Miller's thesis, then, that the notion of exile, itself a social construct with deep roots in Irish cultural and political tradition, was reconstructed as an integral part of Irish national identity among Irish Americans at a time when Ireland was undergoing economic, social and political modernisation and moving in the direction of the nation state. In Miller's analysis, nationhood and modernity were associated, and 'exile' formed the link. Notions of a restored Irish nation – as a safe haven where uprooted and dispersed victims of a tragic national history could seek refuge – were projected into the mental universe of people who should rather be seen as victims of modernity.

The geographer Jim Mac Laughlin largely accepts Miller's account of the structural roots of Irish emigration. But whereas Miller insists that there was a cultural and voluntary aspect to emigration, Mac Laughlin's writings represent a re-politicisation of emigration: not in traditional, nationalist terms, however, but from the point of view of world systems and post-colonial theory.

Mac Laughlin explains 19th-century Irish emigration as a result of a colonial land structure and a native rural capitalism linking Ireland to the larger international economy. Capitalist development in the second half of the century generated great labour and commodity surpluses, which compelled Irish young males, especially those from small to medium farms, to seek employment opportunities abroad. Thus, emigration was a 'rational response' to new opportunities offered by developments in the world economy, and as such 'a continuation of trends dating from at least the eighteenth century when Ireland was integrated into an evolving world capitalist order under the hegemony of Great Britain' ('Emigration' 29).

Mac Laughlin connects his structural analysis to a study of the political history of post-Famine Ireland. He argues that the emerging rural middle and lower middle class realised the economic and social benefits of the project of modern British capitalism. In order to establish themselves as the hegemones of a home-ruled Ireland, they first had to rid Ireland of the countryside's poor, who, after the Great Famine, were seen as a hindrance to economic modernisation. The rural poor found little support and sympathy among nation-builders in the Catholic Church and the nationalist movement. Cultural nationalists, who largely came from the same modernising classes, even indirectly contributed to their encrustation by Anglicising the causes of emigration – and its solutions: land reforms, the usurpation of English rule and the 'de-Anglicisation' and re-catholicisation of Irish culture and society. In this way, nationalists contributed to building a nation and a political regime on the basis of exclusionist definitions of Irishness in tacit understanding with the rural bourgeoisie. Through the implementation of this project, a new notion of Ireland came into being predicated on a distinction between insiders and outsiders - the latter numbering not only Anglo-Irish, but also emigrants, labourers, the travelling poor and, in a certain sense, women.

Social and political 'enclosure' was accompanied by cultural enclosure, in so far as the process of de-anglicisation, in its more radical versions, excluded the Anglo-Irish and Protestant tradition from the national project. Anglo-Irish and Protestant writers, for example, found themselves being written out of Irish tradition by critics like Daniel Corkery, who rhetorically asked: 'Can Anglo-Irish literature be a national literature?' (2) To Corkery, the criterion for the Irishness of a literary work was whether it paid tribute and allegiance to Catholic-Gaelic cultural tradition.

The political pursuit of the goals of Catholic-Gaelic notions of Irishness during the first decades of the life of the Irish Free State is reflected not only in the censorship laws that were passed in the

1920s, but also in the institutionalisation of this particular 'identity code' in social, cultural and educational policy as well as the constitutional amendment process which ended with the Constitution of 1937. (O'Mahoney and Delanty 28-29). One of the side-effects of this process was the creation of a new category of Irish exiles: post-colonial, disenchanted and alienated writers, who either endured the oppressive climate of orthodox nationalist culture with other inner exiles, or who chose to leave the country for voluntary exile abroad, like so many other emigrants who voted against 'de Valera's Ireland' with their feet. In this way, Irish exilic writing was to represent more than individual experience, namely the experiences, visions and identities of those who felt excluded – or socially and culturally 'exiled' – from the nationalist project. Given the conservative and anti-modernist tenor of this project, the writings of expatriate Irish writers were bound to be radical, realist or modernist. But it had also many features in common with other types of exilic writing.

Exilic writing

The editor of the comprehensive *Literary Exile in the Twentieth Century*, Martin Tucker, rightly notes that, when it comes to an analysis of expressions of exile in literature, 'it is impossible to label a writer definitively […] simply because a writer's work reflects many moving experiences – that is, the writer's material is transmitted by his or her *being* into a *been* that subsumes differences before they are analyzed' (xvii). Still, like Andrew Gurr, he assumes a complex relationship between the writer's personal experience of exile and the aesthetic work he constructs. His work is, in a sense, part of his 'persona' if 'persona' refers to 'the totality of the writer's content, form, style, personal vision, and intimate baggage of technique by which the gift of personality is made' (xxi).

In the first systematic investigation of the theme of exile in modern literature, *Writers in Exile: The Identity of Home in Modern Literature* (1981), Andrew Gurr sets out from the assumption that '[de]racination, exile and alienation in varying forms are the conditions of existence for the modern writer the world over' - i.e. the late 18th century into the first half of the 19th century – but that exile in this period became particularly associated with colonialism (14).

Writers in structural exile have frequently responded to their situation of voluntary or involuntary severance by writing books that express their search for identity through 'self-discovery and self-realisation', a search which may be summed up metaphorically as a 'quest for home' (14). The homelessness of the exiled writer, however, has often been an enabling factor. The writer felt an urge to recreate his own identity by writing about the 'home'/homeland/colony he fled.

With Mary McCarthy, among others, Gurr distinguishes between expatriates and exiles, seeing the latter as banished victims tortured by their longing for return. He adds that, historically, expatriate writers had a tendency to be poets, who migrated from one metropolis to another, whereas exiles were often short story writers who migrated from provinces or colonies into metropolitan centres. He explains this difference as a result of the exilic writer's need for an audience with whom he could communicate directly about his experiences. Another feature is the exilic writer's tendency to claim the universality of the picture of the world he conveys. Since he is both engaged in reconstructing his own personal identity and in creating a work of art, the world he portrays may seem frozen in time and strangely at odds with present realities, especially if the society he left has undergone great social changes in the meantime:

> All art, whether produced in physical exile, by internal exiles or by determined traditionalists, is static, backward-looking, concerned primarily with a stable image and identity in the individual or in his society at large. [...] The expatriate seeks to identify or create a cultural history and therefore a cultural identity which is necessarily based on the past. [...] And the exile is still more deliberately concerned to identify or even create a stasis, because home is a static concept rooted in the unalterable circumstances of childhood. Insecurity [of homelessness] prompts the writer to construct static worlds, to impose order on the dynamic, to see the dynamic as chaos. (23-24)

Thus, the exilic writer's search for a secure, personal identity – in spite of his feeling of detachment – compels him to a retrospective fabrication of stable images of home from the components of personal memory. It may exactly be the constructed orderliness and universality of exilic narratives of 'home' which make them so attractive to modern readers, who are affected by forces of change within their own time and society and therefore yearn for depictions of a well-ordered world.

Although there may be some valuable insights in Gurr's argument about the artistically enabling aspects of exile, one should be careful not to universalise this claim. For sure, although exile may have been to the artistic benefit of some Irish writers – Edna O'Brien is a name which immediately suggests itself – it has also had traumatic effect for others, who have experienced loss of identity and artistic crisis, even silence, for example James Stephens and Denis Johnston (cf. Ward ; Brown). Paul Ilie is probably more correct when he cautiously points out that writers experience their situation like all other exiles: within the 'polarity of creativity and barrenness' (71).

Ilie himself applies formal analysis to his own study of exilic literature. He finds images of spatiality and temporality particular relevant to the study of exilic writing. As for spatial aspects, he mentions linearity and concavity as figures that reflect the 'dynamics of exile': 'The linearity of a particular journey may denote, in metaphorical language, irrevocability or expulsion, whereas a labyrinth or a hollow may insinuate other displacements' (60). Hence, the circle and the centre are recurrent symbols, and such symbols are not only applicable to individual destinies or private perceptions of existence, but also to entire cultures:

> The cultural entity may perhaps be conceivable in spherical images, but the political disruptions of a national culture also provoke, besides expulsion, maneuvers like mutual exclusion, the building of walls, and amputation. The reader must be alert to the rectangular and cellular forms of enclosure/exclusion […]. Still other strategies in literary texts record the spatial indices of disorientation, irreconcilability,

and ambivalent allegiances. If exile reveals "centripetal"
tendencies nurtured by nationalism, it is a motion at the level
of feeling rather than culture. The cultural implications of
spatiality also include circumstances which generate a
centrifugal force permitting resolution of the exilic vacuum on
both sides of the territorial divide. [...] The imaginative writer
who ceases to share the experiences of the people he left
behind finds himself removed from a solid mass. He is a
fragment chipped away and thrown in one and then another
direction. [... But a writer may also discover] that he possesses
"new eyes" for seeing his condition, a spatial potentiality that
again lends itself to metaphorical recreation. His vision
confers a new freedom to treat or discard formerly censored
material. Such a censorship is not merely political; those
cultural inhibitions which are also harboured subconsciously
in native residence are exposed and discarded in exile. Space
and volume again call attention to their ethical referentiality.
If national residence occupies a center, "centrifugally
enlarging itself", then "exile displaces that center or rather
creates two centers." (60-61)

There is general agreement that structural exile is experienced as
an unexpected and meaningless shock which causes an open and
painful mental wound. This has implications for the
representation of time. However, time tends to heal the wound,
leaving an irremovable scar instead, but without abating the
exile's morally or politically motivated anger. The exile reconciles
himself with his experience of separation, loss and uprootedness
by negating the permanence of his exile, seeing it, instead, as
provisional: 'A sense of "tomorrow I'll return" lingers as a
subliminal coordinate of the emigré's existence' (61). This
'coordinate of hope [of return]' may run in several directions, but
as the passage of time lengthens and the likelihood of a return is
reduced, the feeling of anguish increases. One may thus speak, in
chronometric terms, of a ratio between temporal linearity and
emotional depth. Here memory plays a role. Memories, which
once might have been catalysts of action, begin to stifle and yield
to passive reminiscence, disillusionment and spiritual impotency.

In case of a return to the native land, the act is often futile and becomes a source of bitterness.

Ilie points out another temporal feature characteristic of exilic writing, an observation reminiscent of what Gurr says about the backward-looking proclivity of the exilic writer: Writers in exile have often been fixated on the past and its relation with the personal and political future they hope for. Hypnotized by the past, they tend to convey their country's history in abstract, idealised and stylised terms, reflecting their personal compulsion to live in memory and mythic evocations of the past. In so far as structures and concepts of exilic writings are assimilated by residents in the homeland, however, also inner exiles with access to their writings may assimilate their historical distortions.

There are elements of Ilie's thesis which clearly bear the imprint of the particular subject of his study, Francoist authoritarianism. For obvious reasons his approach will have to be adapted to particular national and historical contexts to be useful to Irish studies. Although Ireland, for example, has had its own experiences of authoritarian rule of various kinds, none of them are immediately comparable to those of Spain 1939-1975. Nevertheless, Ilie's thesis of the bilateral character of exile is highly relevant for both historical and literary studies.

There are indeed certain similarities between Ilie's observations and the way in which literary expressions of non-structural exile is discussed in recent Irish criticism. In his short introduction to a book of essays published in 1991, Neil Sammells discusses exile as a metaphor for anti-colonial subversion which may take various forms: political, cultural and literary. The contributions to the book are multifarious, but the editors seek to link the individual essays with reference to a number of recurrent themes such as 'landscape', 'place' and 'absence' and by what Sammells describes as a common 'conscious desire to subvert literary norms and conventions'. The works dealt with, thus, are seen as responses, 'conscious or otherwise' to 'discourses fashioned for the purposes of their material masters' (xi-xiii). Exile, in other words, has aesthetic dimensions and may be felt and expressed by the inner exile in terms of alienation and a subversion of hegemonic discourses of identity.

This is also one of the messages of Gerry Smyth's book *The Novel and the Nation.* Smyth identifies an exilic tradition in the history of the Irish novel: 'an entire counter-tradition [...] which can be understood as an attempt to escape the limitations of the nation's colonial heritage and the manner in which it was forced to construe the world in terms of rigidly defined, oppositional categories – Irish and English, woman and man, national and alien' (42). Exilic writing represents the beginnings of an enabling post-colonial discourse in which both Irishness and Englishness are seen as contingent and mutually implicated categories. The position of 'exile' thus provides a privileged, 'ironic' position from which the narrowness of the 'Irish-British imagination at home' may be criticised. Hence exile need not involve physical displacement: 'Exile can be an interior process of alienation from the narrow definitions of homeland which characterise post-revolutionary Irishness', Smyth writes, illustrating this with reference to the opening sentence of Flann O'Brien's *At Swim-Two-Birds*, in which the unnamed narrator retires 'into the privacy of his mind with a mouthful of food', and in this way exiles himself 'from the mean spiritual and intellectual fare of post-colonial Ireland' (42-43).

Irish literary tradition almost begs for studies of "exilic cultures" - in Ilie's sense - whether in their inner (marginalised) or orthodox/"victorious" (marginalising) forms. Late 19th-century novels – not only the 'priestly fictions' (cf. Candy), but also the novels of Protestant Irish women novelists – demonstrate, for example, how old traditions of political, social and cultural exclusion came to the surface of literary discourse in a period which saw the rise of a new wave of identity politics, leading to the re-drawing of the boundaries of Irishness and the introduction of new criteria for in- and ex-clusion in and from the nation (leaving new subcategories of exile in its wake). Instead of seeing O'Casey's exile as just a physical and intellectual 'response' to the 'new orthodoxy' of the Free State, for example – as Cairns and Richards appear to do (131) – exile could be rather be read as a theme articulated already in his Abbey plays, i.e. at a time when the writer's vision of Ireland was tainted by his personal experience as a member of Ireland's small community of marginalised and disenchanted socialist republicans.

Patrick Ward suggests a multidisciplinary approach to the study of representations of exile, emigration and internal marginalisation in an international, comparative context. Such studies might not only enable the critic to deal more discriminately with various types of experiences, but may also help 'dispel, demythologise and place into meaningful perspective' the actual, historical and sociological, background of various forms of 'absence' (242). Ward here aligns himself with Seamus Deane (following Said), who is critical of the 'fetish of exile, alienation and dislocation' in writers like Joyce and Beckett (58).

As our discussion has shown so far, however, even aesthetic and symbolic expressions of exile should be taken seriously if we are to develop a full understanding of the historical development of the meanings of exile, whether it be those of Joyce and other expatriate modernists[5] or Yeats's 'mythology of exile' (cf. Harper). Joyce went into voluntary exile abroad in response to the parochialism and national self-obsession of Irish society at the beginning of the century. Joyce's example illustrates the way in which the notion of exile in this period began to acquire a number of new, modern meanings derived from recent philosophy, psychology and sociology.

Exile and modernity

The emergence of modern perceptions of exile was the result of nineteenth-century biographical and socio-historical experiences and the widespread perception in the following century of a loss of tradition and 'home' (cf. Wagner). Large-scale external and internal migration, the emergence of nationalism and, from 1914 and on, the experience of extended warfare combined in altering the way in which people viewed and could view the past. Experiences of physical displacement, the loss of cultural roots and a sense of ontological insecurity gave rise to nostalgia, i.e. a longing for a 'home' and a 'past', i.e. for origins, continuity and coherence.

Intellectually, nostalgia was expressed both in neo-romantic critiques of modernity and in various forms of nationalism. Often, the two would combined, as it did in the case of Ireland. At that time, however, nationalism was also felt as a kind of remedy to modernity. For nationalism held the promise of re-rooting and re-directing social and political life without forfeiting the material benefits of modernisation. In the state envisioned by nationalists, nostalgia would wither away for two reasons: The longing for the past would be dulled by the experience of social, political and material progress, and the sense of continuity with the past would be restored because nationalism re-wrote the past into the present. Nationalism, seen as a response to the fear of 'homelessness', offered a new kind of cultural and spiritual anchoring. However, at the very moment when nationalism appeared to provide a solution for the uprooting and fragmentation of social and cultural life, the break-out of a period of extended warfare, first in Europe and then on a global basis, showed that there was not any solution to such problems, even though a variety of totalitarian and authoritarian regimes acted as if there were.

Admittedly, the First World War was a war fought in the spirit of exalted nationalism. Nevertheless, it inaugurated a counter-narrative, which was to inform twentieth-century philosophy, literature and intellectual life in general: the story of the shattering of 'tradition' and, consequently the loss of certainty and absolute truth in existential, psychological, epistemological, moral and linguistic terms. In modernist thinking, 'exile' became a metaphor for the human condition and became part of a discourse which questioned, among others, notions of cultural roots, the *Dasein* of the world and the unity of individual consciousness.

In modernist philosophy, literature and art, however, the exilic perspective found pessimistic as well as optimistic expressions. Pessimistic versions rejected nostalgia and thus the possibility that metaphysical and cultural notions of origin, presence and authenticity could be restored. Optimistic expressions, in contrast, translated nostalgia into forms of social utopianism and liberal, individualist philosophies predicated on the experience of having escaped from the nightmare of history and the restrictions of traditional beliefs.

Both versions, in various combinations, are represented in twentieth-century Irish writing, criticism as well as literature. The works of Irish writers, most of whom spent extended periods of their lives as expatriates or as inner exiles in Ireland, take much of their colour from the writers' experience of alienation from the infant Irish state and the regime that had created it. Almost all of them were personal victims of literary censorship in their homeland and distanced themselves from the Catholic and socially conservative identity code which had been vindicated after 1922. The nature of their exile, therefore, had personal as well as social and political dimensions. But there was more to it than a rejection of a particular regime. For this regime represented a general European tendency to stem the tide of modernity. Thus, there was a philosophical dimension to their choice to live as expatriate, social and cultural exiles.

As briefly noted earlier, Ward describes these writers' choice as an 'escape' rather than as 'exile' (242). He aligns himself with Seamus Deane and Said in seeing their self-designated exile as merely an aesthetic gesture. However, this seriously limits the possibilities of getting a full understanding of Irish modernism. Even though it does make considerable sense to read the history of Irish literary modernism against colonial and postcolonial experiences and legacies, the broader - international, social and intellectual - context must certainly be considered too. It is in the combination of the Irish and the international perspectives that, what W. J. Mc Cormack calls, the particular 'provenance' of Irish modernism and Irish exile literature should be read (75).

A similarly broad approach is crucial for an appreciation of the way in which new meanings of exile have emerged in the context of late-twentieth-century globalisation and new patterns of migration. Now that the Irish may be said to have become both the 'tourists' and 'vagabonds' of the new world economy (cf. Bauman).

Globalisation and late modern exile
The Irish social and cultural critic Fintan O'Toole has consistently dealt with the changing character of Irish emigration and exile in contemporary Ireland. In an essay on 'Emigration and Irish

Culture', he reflects on how the twin concepts of emigration and exile, once 'at the very heartbeat of Irish culture', have lost their earlier meaning and relevance today (158). In the light of globalisation and the appearance of a multicentred world, the disappearance of the British Empire, the collapse of church authority, and the dissolution of traditional anti-theses – for example, between rural-urban and, British-Irish – there is no longer an Irish 'home' to leave, nor an Irish identity to lose. In such a world, there are neither beginnings nor ends – only movement, only distances to cover. Now that traditional notions of exile have become obsolete and irrelevant, however, a new meaning suggests itself: exile has become 'a prism through which the diverse social forces within Ireland are separated and revealed' (174).

O'Toole argues that the old notion of exile assumed a perception of Ireland as a culturally homogenous, spiritual homeland and saw the emigrant as trading a fixed identity for an anonymous and impermanent one. However, today an Irish person may feel in exile when 'at home' in Ireland and instead take his bearings from a non-territorial Ireland made up of 'songlines', 'road markings' and 'ancient footsteps' left from the journeys of earlier generations of Irish emigrants. However, because globalisation is not simply another term for 'Americanisation', but a two-way process which 'affects different cultures in different ways', the Irish have, as a result of their long history of emigration, succeeded in putting their own mark on the modern world (174).

This, paradoxically, enables them to retain some sense of identity and difference where others are drowned by cultural sameness and forgetfulness, as O'Toole writes in his introduction to a collection of essays with the shrewdly-ironic title *The Ex-isle of Erin*:

> [Ireland] has buried memories, forgotten histories, that offer it some useful precedents for engaging with, rather than being swamped by, the new realities. By remembering and re-imagining them, it can, perhaps, learn how to surf the global

waves without drowning in a flood tide of blandness and amnesia. (22)

The ways in which Irish identity will be articulated today and in the future, O'Toole predicts, is determined by a combination of the 'songlines' from the past and the creative re-imaginings of contemporary writers in Ireland and the Irish diaspora. In this process, 'the Irish abroad will have just as much of a claim on the creation of Irish culture as do the Irish at home' (175).[6]

A similar line of argument is put forward in Richard Kearney's book from 1988, *Across the Frontiers: Ireland in the 1990s*. In his introduction, Kearney discusses how Irishness, far from being a matter of a static national essence, as it was later claimed by nationalists, used to be a 'dynamic cultural identity' which developed in an 'exploratory dialogue' with other cultures (21). Irish cultural history reads like a 'litany of intellectual migrations which have established extensive associations between Ireland and the wider world' (21). However, under the impact of colonialism, famine and emigration, the Irish became obsessed with their enmity with England and therefore developed an insular and monolithic notion of Irish identity. Over recent decades, however, due to political developments and the influence of the communications revolution, the Irish have moved beyond such narrow notions and have begun to recognize the plurality of their cultural heritage.

Kearney invokes Joyce as one of Ireland's many 'migrant minds' who had a keen eye for culture as a 'bringer of plurabilities' rather than as closure and who saw Europe as 'a map without frontiers, a free space of exploration and peregrination, a place where Irish myth and memory could engage in dynamic dialogue with the cultures of other lands' (21-22). The vision of Irish culture as a blending of national and international idioms was forged by Irish writers like Joyce and other artists who have had the opportunity of looking back on Ireland from abroad:

This mixing of the 'foreign with the familiar', to borrow Joyce's phrase, is witnessed in most art forms – in the music of

Irish groups such as the Chieftains, Van Morrison, The Pogues
or U2; in the films of Irish directors such as Jordan, Murphy,
Quinn, Comerford and O'Connor; the writings of Irish
authors such as Heaney, Banville, Durcan, Ní Dhomnaill and
Bolger; and the visual art of an emerging generation which
includes Ballagh, Coleman, Elanna O'Kelly and Dorothy
Cross. (22-23)

In a later chapter, Kearney interviews one of these 'migrant
minds', film director Neil Jordan. Jordan first explains how, in the
early stage of his artistic career, he had been unable to cope with
traditional notions of Irishness, because they meant nothing to his
personal experience of growing up in suburban Dublin in the
1960s.
    Unable to identify with the narratives that provided earlier
generations with a sense of belonging, Jordan explains how he
turned to film making as an 'escape' and a 'liberation' from the
need to deal with 'crippling' issues of national identity. Film
making made him instead free to explore questions of a *personal*
identity because the visual arts were free from the 'constraints
and pressures of our literary tradition' (197).
    Jordan's personal and symbolic 'exile' into a new artistic
medium – and his encounter with the world outside Ireland – had
the ironic and paradoxical effect of bringing him back to the
question of collective identity provided with a new view on
Irishness. As Jordan now sees it, true Irishness combines many of
the aspects of exile discussed so far in this essay: exile as journey,
exile as subversion, exile as exclusion, exile as political and social
alienation, exile as existential homelessness, and, finally, exile as
the necessary position of the artist, whether resident or expatriate:

> The attempt to imagine another state of living, another way of
> being, is I believe very Irish. It's difficult to say what exactly
> underlies this or why it should be so. It's something to do
> with the quest for another place, another manner of thinking.
> It's a dissatisfaction with the accepted and scientifically
> approved explanations of the world. [...] Our mistake was to
> assume that we would be at home in a single nation. We fed

ourselves on ideologies of violence and instant salvation, the illusion that history is a continuum moving forward to its perfect destiny. We thus forgot that we can never be at home anywhere. Perhaps it is one of the functions of writers and artists to remind the nation of this. To expose the old ideologies. To feel in exile abroad and also when one returns home. To remain faithful to the no-place (u-topos) in us all. [...] I think it is only when you accept the condition of being transient, when you realize that home is impossible, that you find a certain peace. (198-99)

What is new and thought-provoking in Jordan's reflection is the way he describes postnational exile by drawing implicitly on all these Irish traditions of exile, ending up affirming the possibility of developing a kind of personal nationhood, which he describes as an existentially and psychologically stabilising factor in a postmodern, globalised world.

Remembering exile: The Irish diaspora and the healing of the nation

In Ireland of the 1990s, political discourse translated the lands of the nation's 'exiles' into the 'Irish diaspora', a trope which both reflects the new postcolonial approach to the study of Irish history and culture and, with its Jewish connotation, suggests cultural unity across political and physical boundaries. Richard Kearney was one of the young Irish intellectuals engaged in this reinterpretation, which translated national tragedy into an alternative national narrative meant to be a remedy against exclusionist identity policies: the Irish diaspora was supposed to be regarded as a resource for a re-defined Irishness characterised by tolerance and pluralism.

Kearney's ideas proved strongly influential on the presidency of Mary Robinson, and, in turn on the general political discourse of the 1990s.[7] In 1995, five years after her election, Robinson used her constitutional privilege to speak to both houses of the Oireachtas (Parliament) on the significance of the Irish diaspora for contemporary Irish identity. Recalling her many visits with

Irish immigrant communities throughout the world during the
first years of her presidency, she said:

> In places as far apart as Calcutta and Toronto, on a number of
> visits to Britain and the United States, in cities in Tanzania and
> Hungary and Australia, I have met young people from
> throughout the island of Ireland who felt they had no choice
> but to emigrate. I have also met men and women who may
> never have seen this island but whose identity with it is part
> of their own self-definition. […] In each country visited I have
> met Irish communities, often far-flung places, and listened to
> stories of men and women whose pride and affection for
> Ireland has neither deserted them nor deterred them from
> dedicating their loyalty and energies to other countries and
> cultures. […] Through this office, I have been a witness to the
> stories these people and places have to tell. The more I know
> of these stories the more it seems to me an added richness of
> our heritage that Irishness is not simply territorial. In fact
> Irishness as a concept seems to me at its strongest when it
> reaches out to everyone on this island and shows itself capable
> of honouring and listening to those whose sense of identity,
> and whose cultural values, may be more British than Irish. It
> can be strengthened again if we turn with open minds and
> hearts to the array of people outside Ireland for whom this
> island is a place of origin. After all, emigration is not just a
> chronicle of sorrow and regret. It is also a powerful story of
> contribution and adaptation. In fact, I have become more
> convinced each year that this great narrative of dispossession
> and belonging, which so often had its origins in sorrow and
> leave-taking, has become – with a certain amount of historic
> irony – one of the treasures of our society. If that is so then our
> relation with the diaspora beyond our shores is one which can
> instruct our society in the values of diversity, tolerance, and
> fair-mindedness.[8]

With her speech, Mary Robinson contributed to the writers' and
critics' construction of a new imaginative Irish nation. People who
had once been dispossessed, lost and forgotten exiles were now

rhetorically – and, in famine commemorations, also ritually – remembered back into national 'belonging': they were translated into membership of a cultural nation existing on a level above politics and territory.

Jim Mac Laughlin is critical of the notion of an Irish diaspora. He sees it as part of an alleged 'revisionist project' aiming at de-politicising Irish emigration by describing it as a product of voluntary decisions, social aspirations and psycho-cultural traditions rather than a result of colonialism and the continued economic dependency of post-colonial Ireland. ('Devaluation' 180ff).[9] On the basis of the analyses of the social, cultural and political dynamics of the cultures of exile offered in this essay, I grant that the diasporic discourse of the 1990s was indeed political. However, it was not political in the sense that Mac Laughlin sees it; it was part of a political process in which the political and cultural elites of Ireland – drawing on the counter-revivalist, modernist and exilic tradition in twentieth-century Irish writing – aspired towards re-imagining Ireland into a pluralistic, outward-looking and modern nation with which structural, inner and symbolic exiles might identify.

Notes

1 According to another medievalist, Stanley B. Greenfield, the notion of "spiritual exile" was common also in the Anglo-Saxon church and reflected in Old English poetry.
2 It should be noted that the definition of exile in terms of international law is not relevant for the definition proposed here.
3 This list is a modified version of the list offered by Martin Tucker xv-xvi.
4 Foucault would be another obvious choice, of course.
5 Cf. Martin Tucker 32-33. See also Terence Brown.
6 The importance of the dialectical relationship between the island of Ireland and the Irish diaspora, the world of 'Irish America' in particular, for the rise of a new sense of cultural Irishness may be exemplified in politics by the amended Article 3 of the Constitution of Ireland, in literature by the acclaim of young, transatlantic writers such as Michael Collins and Colum McCann, and in popular culture by Irish-American bands like Solas and by the Riverdance phenomenon.

[7] Mary Robinson confirmed to the author in 1995 that she had taken a keen personal interest in these debates since they were initiated. Kearney has also confirmed to the author that he wrote the draft of Mary Robinson's inaugural speech, and Fintan O'Toole, likewise, has confirmed that Mary Robinson drew inspiration from some of the notes he provided her with, not least on the subject of paying tribute to the Irish diaspora.

[8] 'Cherishing the Irish Diaspora: Address to the Houses of the Oireachtas by President Mary Robinson on a Matter of Public Importance, 2 February 1995', author's private archive, pp. 2-3.

[9] Mac Laughlin regards Damian Hannan and the National Economic and Social Council as the main exponents of the 'revisionist' reading of Irish emigration, but his article has tacit references also to Lee. For unknown reasons, Kerby Miller's research on the subject is not considered, and Mac Laughlin's article, based as it is on ideological assumptions on the motivations of 'revisionists', fails to take in the full political implications of the 1990s debate on the Irish diaspora.

References

Bauman, Zygmunt. *Globalization: The Human Consequences*. Cambridge: Polity Press, 1998.

Brown, Terence. 'Ireland, Modernism and the 1930s' in Coughlan and Davis 24-74.

Cairns, David and Shaun Richards. *Writing Ireland: Colonialism, Nationalism and Culture*. Manchester: Manchester UP, 1988.

Candy, Catherine. *Priestly Fictions: Popular Irish Novelists of the Early 20th Century*. Dublin: Wolfhound, 1995

Corkery, Daniel. *Synge and Anglo-Irish Literature*. Cork, 1931.

Coughlan, Patricia and Alex Davis (eds.). *Modernism and Ireland: The Poetry of the 1930s*. Cork: Cork UP, 1995.

Dahlie, Hallward. 'Brian Moore and the Meaning of Exile', in Richard Wall (ed.). *Medieval and Modern Ireland*. Gerrads Cross, 1988. 91-107.

Deane, Seamus. 'Heroic Styles: the Tradition of an Idea', in The Field Day Theatre Company, *Ireland's Field Day*. London: Field Day, 1985.

Greenfield, Stanley. *Hero and Exile: The Art of Old English Poetry*. London: Hambledon Press, 1989.

Gurr, Andrew. *Writers in Exile: The Identity of Home in Modern Literature.* Sussex: Harvester Press, 1981.

Harper, George Mills. *'Go Back to Where You Belong': Yeats's Return from Exile.* Dublin, Dolmen Press, 1973.

Ilie, Paul. *Literature and Inner Exile: Authoritarian Spain, 1939-1975.* Baltimore and London: Johns Hopkins UP, 1980.

Kearney, Richard. *Across the Frontiers: Ireland in the 1990s.* Dublin: Wolfhound, 1988.

Lee, Joseph. *Ireland 1912-1985: Politics and Society.* Cambridge: Cambridge UP, 1989.

Mac Laughlin, Jim. 'Emigration and the Construction of Nationalist Hegemony in Ireland', in Jim Mac Laughlin (ed.). *Location and Dislocation in Contemporary Irish Society: Emigration and Irish Identities.* Cork: Cork UP, 1997. 5-35.

— 'The Devaluation of "Nation" as "Home" and the De-Politicisation of Recent Irish Emigration', in Mac Laughlin's *Location* 179-208.

McCarthy, Mary. 'Exiles, Expatriates and Internal Emigrés', *The Listener* 86 (1971): 705-8.

McCormack, J.C.C. 'Austin Clarke: The Poet as Scapegoat pf Modernism, in Couglan and Davis 75-102.

Miller, Kerby A. *Emigrants and Exiles: Ireland and the Irish Exodus to North America.* New York and Oxford: Oxford UP, 1985.

O'Mahony and Gerard Delanty. *Rethinking Irish History: Nationalism, Identity and Ideology.* London: Palgrave, 1998.

O'Toole, Fintan. *The Ex-Isle of Erin.* Dublin: New Island Books, 1996.

Parkin, Frank. *Class Inequality and Political Order* London: McGibbon and Kee, 1971.

Said, Edward. 'Reflections on Exile', in *Reflections on Exile and Other Essays.* Cambridge, Mass.: Harvard UP, 2000. 173-86. First published as 'The Mind of Winter: Reflections on life in exile'. *Harpers Magazine* 260 (161) 1984.

— *Out of Place.* London: Granta, 1999.

Sammells, Neil. 'Introduction', in Paul Hyland and Neil Sammells (eds.), *Irish Writing: Exile and Subversion.* London: Macmillan, 1991.

Smith-Christopher, Daniel L. *A Biblical Theology of Exile*. Minneapolis: Fortress Press, 2002.

Smyth, Gerry. *The Novel and the Nation: Studies in the New Irish Fiction*. London and Chicago: Pluto, 1997.

Strange, Carolyn and Alison Bashford (ed.). *Isolation: Places and Practices of Exclusion*. London: Routledge, 2003.

Tabori, Paul. *The Anatomy of Exile*. London: Harrap, 1972.

Tucker, Martin. *Literary Exile in the Twentieth Century*. New York: Greenwood Press, 1991.

Wagner, Peter. *Theorizing Modernity*. London: Sage, 2001.

Webb, Diana. *Medieval European Pilgrimage*, London: Palgrave, 2002.

— 'Pilgrimage, detachment and exile'. unpubl. paper, 2003.

Ward, Patrick. *Exile, Emigration and Irish Writing*. Dublin, Portland, Or: Irish Academic Press, 2002.

Williams, Gareth D. *The Curse of Exile: A Study of Ovid's* Ibis. Cambridge: Cambridge UP, 1996.

'The lukewarm conviction of temporary lodgers': The Anglo-Irish and Dimensions of Exile in the Work of Hubert Butler

Billy Gray

The common denominator in the experience of metaphorical exile
[…] is the existential sensation of difference, otherness and our
desire […] to retrace the path from the periphery back to the centre.

Johannes F. Evelein, 'Teaching Narratives of Exile'.

It would be well for all outsiders who would understand Ireland
and its tragic history, or indeed any phase of it, to keep before them
the fact that the Ascendancy mind is not the same thing as the
English mind.

Daniel Corkery, The Hidden Ireland.

It is widely accepted that the work of Hubert Butler has not
received the critical attention it deserves. This neglect can partly
be explained by the fact that the original appearance of his
writings was confined almost exclusively to Irish periodicals,
many of them obscure, and also to the avowedly eclectic nature of
his interests; Butler was a literary, political, archaeological,
topographical and historical essayist. Equally, aspects of his work
have been criticised as being 'effortlessly elitist' and 'hopelessly
patrician', qualities seen as anathema to the general trends of our
avowedly egalitarian age. Richard Jones has also claimed that due
to Butler's position as a member of the Irish landed gentry, and an
agnostic, liberal Protestant in an overwhelmingly Roman Catholic
nation, he was, for many years, 'read through a veil of
resentment' (2). However, a small, but nonetheless, growing

Re-Mapping Exile: Realities and Metaphors in Irish Literature and History, ed.
Michael Böss, Irene Gilsenan Nordin and Britta Olinder, *The Dolphin* 34.
© 2005 by Aarhus University Press, Denmark. ISBN 87 7934 010 5.

number of admirers – including eminent scholars such as Roy
Foster and Edna Longley – have recently published laudatory
reviews, and indeed, Chris Agee has referred to Butler as 'one of
the greatest essayists in English, of the twentieth century' (130).
The same writer has defined Butler's sensibility as revealing 'an
ethical imagination', and the latter's work is now viewed as
revealing an elaborate terrain of historical, religious and
philosophical reflections. Indeed, it could be argued that the best
of Butler's essays exemplify those literary qualities so revered by
him in Chekhov: 'The best of [writers] describe life as it is, but in
such a way that every line is penetrated, as it were, with a juice,
with the consciousness of an aim. Apart from life as it is, you feel
that other life as it ought to be, and it bewitches you' (*In the Land*
186).   The aim of this essay is to examine how differing concepts
of exile can be applied to Hubert Butler's perception of the Anglo-
Irish experience after the Act of Union. Butler argues that within
the confines of a comparatively short historical period, the
Protestant Aristocracy, who had been the original progenitors of
Irish nationalism, came to view themselves as exiles within their
own country. My contention will be that, by applying the ideas of
exile theorists such as Joseph Wittlin and Jan Vladeslav –
particularly those concepts which elucidate exilic experiences
pertaining to 'communal trauma' and 'powerlessness' – it is
possible to illuminate Butler's views on what he refers to as 'the
withdrawal of a whole historic class'.

     For the purposes of this essay, the term Anglo-Irish
Ascendancy requires definition. The Anglo-Irish were
descendants of people of English origin who had settled in
Ireland during the fifteenth, sixteenth and seventeenth centuries,
usually after receiving grants of land for military or other services
to the British Crown. In religion, they were not only Protestant
but Anglican, in distinction to the Protestant Dissenting families
of Scottish origins who were planted in Ulster in the early
seventeenth century. They built up a distinctive outlook and
culture which were neither English nor Gaelic, and constituted a
narrow social and political elite, rather than a strictly ethnic
group.

What is beyond dispute is that they felt themselves to be Irish, however they might differ from their Catholic countrymen. Daniel Corkery has written that '[t]he Ascendancy mind is not the same as the English mind' (34), and Robert Kee has noted that, by the end of 1770s, Protestant Irishmen were considering themselves Irish as proudly as an Englishman considered himself to be English (29). Like many other colonialists, they were suspicious of authority claimed by the mother country and, according to J. C. Beckett, were particularly jealous of newly arrived officials who, being English by birth, had a propensity to patronise those who were merely 'English by blood' (24). As Bishop Evans of Meath wrote to Archbishop Wake, '"T is hardly possible for anyone to conceive the generally unaccountable aversion these people [...] have to the English name' (Foster 178). In the view of the Irish aristocracy, the fears and suspicions that divided them from the Roman Catholic majority did not arise from a difference of nationality or represent a continuing struggle between 'Ireland' and 'England'; they were essentially the product of internal rivalry for property and power. Indeed, during the eighteenth century they appeared to find little communality of interest with the metropolitan centre. They felt that Ireland had been subjected legislatively and commercially to the restraints of colonial status, until the American Revolution provided an opportunity for national self-assertion. Emphasising their loyalty to the joint Crown of the two kingdoms, they gradually developed a spirit of independence towards the English government.

The spirit of Irish independence began to manifest itself most noticeably in the early eighteenth century, in the writings of two men: William Molyneux and Jonathan Swift, the latter of whom exhorted Irishmen to burn 'everything English except their coal' (10). In attacking the pervasive injustice of the restrictive commercial measures pertaining between two countries, both Molyneux and Swift claimed that the English Parliament had usurped the Irish Parliament's sovereignty and therefore had no right to legislate for Ireland. By the 1790's, the Anglo-Irish were developing a general unwillingness to recognise the dependence of the Irish Parliament on its British counterpart. They were imbued with the widespread public theory that the Irish Parliament should by right have full legislative sovereignty under the crown and that this had been usurped in times past by the English Parliament.

Through the formation of the Volunteer Movement, the Irish nationalists exerted a strong and well-disciplined pressure which drove Britain from concession to concession, ending with the abolition of Poyning's law in 1782 and the Renunciation Act of the following year. The Irish Parliament passed the Declaration of Independence unanimously and, as G. C. Bolton has stated: 'Every tie between Great Britain and Ireland was specifically removed save that of a common sovereign' (128).

However, despite the fact that the small, oligarchic Irish political world exerted a remarkable and enduring influence on the subsequent course of Irish history, the popular image of the Anglo-Irish Ascendancy in the second half of the eighteenth century is not a flattering one. The poet Louis McNeice has defined them as having nothing 'but an insidious bonhomie, an obsolete bravado and a way with horses' (qtd in Foster 168), and they have been viewed as being guilty of irresponsibility, improvidence and absenteeism. It has been argued that the Anglo-Irish repressed their country with the dead weight of an unassailable proprietary interest, and Wolfe Tone wrote:

> They have disdained to occupy the station they might have held among the people and which the people would have been glad to see them fill. They see Ireland only in their rent-rolls, their patronage, their pensions. They shall perish like their own dung. Those who have seen them will say: 'Where are they?' (Butler, *Escape* 95)

Recently, however, historical revisionists have attempted to present a somewhat more balanced and nuanced depiction of the Anglo-Irish Aristocracy during this period. Foster, for example, has noted that at least some of the income that Ascendancy landlords reaped from their estates was deflected into 'an improving and inquiring approach to Irish life' (193).

The latter opinion is certainly shared by Hubert Butler, who has constantly and repeatedly drawn attention to the valuable contribution that he believes the Anglo-Irish made to their country before the Act of Union. He states that 'the great Protestant nationalists did not consider themselves outsiders', and reiterates their contribution to the concept of Irish nationalism. It is important to recognise that, for Butler, the love of one's country embodies a pronounced spiritual and ethical component. He argues that the nation represents the widest circle in which we can hope to display an active benevolence and that it offers a form of association out of which a true spiritual community can emerge. In an essay entitled 'Fichte and the Rise of Racialism in Germany', he writes:

> In the light of some alleged affinity of spirit or propinquity of person, men look upon each other in the warmth of feeling. However feeble the light may be, it disperses for a moment the darkness of self-seeking. Through the nation, by limitation and focus, this reciprocal regard is made creative. What might be diffused is concentrated and men have the opportunity to discern in each other their deep differentiation and to achieve that fertile contact which is the convergence of opposites. (*In the Land* 73)

To Butler, the Anglo-Irish had a moral and ethical duty to encourage the convergence of seemingly opposing cultural traditions in Ireland. He argues that the century prior to the Act of Union represented an opportunity for the creation of something unique in Irish history; that is, a synthesis of differing concepts of identity resulting in a totally new moral and political landscape. According to Butler, the Anglo-Irish, who had played a part out of all proportion to their numbers in shaping the idea of an Irish nation, viewed themselves during this period primarily as Irishmen and only secondarily as members of a ruling class. He states that they were 'not the dwindling rearguard of English management' (*Grandmother* 123) and believes that only they could give Irishmen a sense of historical continuity. Like Standish

O'Grady, Butler argues that it was only under the guidance of the Anglo-Irish that Ireland could be true to her mixed identity and heritage. It was they who embodied the vision which legitimised the attempt to fuse the differing traditions into an inclusive national identity. 'The imagination and poetry of the Gael' could be assimilated 'with the intellectual vitality and administrative ability of the colonist' (*Escape* 201). He claims that such an ideal was achievable prior to the Act of Union, as during this historical period, the country was almost on a parity with England in regard to the splendour and independence of its leading men. It was essentially an urbane and sociable society, confident in its own values. For Butler, the picture is one of paternalism rather than brute proprietary force and he depicts the Irish Protestant hierarchy as being independent both in their doctrines and behaviour. During the eighteenth century '[t]hey reflected on the vicissitudes of life, its inequalities and injustices, with a freedom that would have seemed to a later generation subversive and disloyal to their class' (*Escape* 18) In their hands, the study of history, 'contrary to her usual habit, seemed, when investigated without prejudice, to heal old grievances rather than to inflame them' (*Escape* 55). Indeed, Butler goes so far as to claim that the absentee landlord was popular in Ireland and writes that 'I have been thinking about them [Irish country houses] as places which once generated light and diffused it' (*Escape* 56).

However, according to Butler, this period in which the Anglo-Irish had, in his own words, 'been able to represent something very precious' disappeared with the signing of the Act of Union, an event of momentous significance and importance and which ultimately forced them to experience a sensation of being exiles in their own country.

The Union of Great Britain and Ireland has been a subject of debate, discussion and argument since it came into being on the 1st of January 1801. Although in the year 2000, the bicentenary of the Act passed singularly unnoticed in comparison to commemorations regarding the United Irishmen or the Great Famine, this does not diminish the significance of the event which was one of the most controversial and contested in modern history, Patrick M'Geoghegan has claimed that 'symbolically, as much as anything else it [the Act of Union] is the defining Act of modern Irish history' (12). It had important and far-reaching legal and constitutional significance and its legislation was the result of the passage of two separate Acts of Parliament, one passed in Westminster and the second by the Irish Parliament in Dublin. It addressed the issue of Parliamentary sovereignty, with the Irish Parliament assenting to be prorogued to a newly constituted sovereign Parliament for the United Kingdom of Great Britain and Ireland. One of the resolutions passed by the British Parliament on 31st January 1799, and which eventually formed the basis of the Union of 1801, started:

> To concur such measures as may best tend to unite the two kingdoms of Great Britain and Ireland into one kingdom, in such manner, and on such terms and conditions as may be established by acts of the respective parliaments of his majesty's said kingdoms. (Batter 27)

The new system abolished the Irish Parliament, while retaining the castle government. The representation of Irish constituencies was to be transferred to Westminster, with the representatives carefully restricted to one hundred. The number of boroughs was diminished and the countries remained as two member constituencies. The idea of a devolved Dublin assembly for purely Irish affairs was dropped at an early stage of the negotiations.

It was the Prime Minister of the time, William Pitt, who had decided to press for a Union for security reasons and to resolve the ambiguities inherent in the Anglo-Irish relationship through the creation of a new political matrix. Equally, the turbulence of 1798, both in Ireland and in France, brought a realisation to the Irish aristocracy and landed gentry that revolutionary action by the lower classes could ultimately overthrow their position of power. The rebellion of 1798 had delivered a profound shock to their whole way of thinking and issues that had caused popular discontent had to be dealt with quickly in order to reduce the threat. Peaceful constitutional change, incorporating the hope of emancipation was therefore deemed to be vital. Such fears were

made clear in a letter from Dean Warburton to Fitzwilliam on July
31ˢᵗ 1798:

> The late events have revived and established religious
> animosity so much that moderate men are of the opinion that
> it will be necessary to remove from this kingdom the object of
> political contention, and they think that if we have no
> parliament, we may have peace and security. (Bolton 62)

It is against this assumption of a continually unresolved
dangerous situation in Ireland that the political manoeuvrings
which led to the Parliamentary Union between Great Britain and
Ireland and the abolition of a separate Irish Parliament must be
understood.

Nevertheless, despite the widespread feelings of fear amongst
the Anglo-Irish, the Act of Union was bitterly contested.
Ascendancy men such as John Foster and Ponsonby, joined forces
with opposition patriots like Grattan in defence of their
parliament. Grattan announced that, under the Union, Ireland
would be 'in a state of slavery' and announced that he would
remain 'faithful to her freedom, faithful to her fall'. Many shared
John Ball's sentiments when he argued in Parliament: 'let us not
deceive ourselves by a name, but consider the projected Union to
be what in fact it is [...] an absolute subjection to the will and
uncontrolled domination of a superior' (Bolton 62). Most of the
anti-Unionists based their appeal to the nation largely on the
performance of the Irish Parliament in giving expression to Irish
nationalism, and emphasised the neglect, apathy and lack of
consideration evinced towards them by Great Britain during the
preceding century. John Foster stated during the Union debate:
'But are you to be improved into British manners and British
customs? Idle talk! Much as I admire Britain, I am not ready to
give up the Irish character or to make a sacrifice for the change'.
(Malcomson 354)

In the face of such opposition, and in order to persuade some
leading anti-Union MP's and peers, the government embarked on
a policy of patronage, granting new peerages, elevating peers and
granting military commissions. It exploited the fact that the anti-

Union factions were naturally separated by temperament and ideology and divided about how far to press their opposition. To ensure success, the Dublin Castle administration was prepared to do whatever was necessary for victory and effectively established a covert secret slush fund to aid their campaign. In the words of the Under Secretary for the Civil Department, the Union should be 'drunk-up, sung-up and bribed up'. This led to a later – overtly simplistic – conviction that the Union could be viewed as a corrupt bargain that had been passed against the wishes of the country after the government had bought the commons. A late nineteenth century Irish poem epitomised the allegations of chicanery and betrayal:

> How did they pass the Union?
> By perjury and fraud;
> By slaves who sold their land for gold,
> As Judas sold his God. (qtd in M'Geoghegan 13)

Irrespective of the methods used to ensure a parliamentary majority, on August 2nd 1800, a total of 161 MP's voted to accept the Union and 115 opposed the Bill; Irish legislative sovereignty had passed into History.

After 1800, therefore, the nature of Ireland's colonial dependency changed. The colonial elite were absorbed into the metropolitan system, and Ireland was excluded from sharing in the nineteenth century constitutional developments of colonies elsewhere. For Hubert Butler, the Act of Union considerably accelerated the political demise of the Ascendancy. Its acceptance could only be interpreted as a form of abdication, a recognition that the Anglo-Irish could no longer manage the affairs of Ireland on their own. In essence, he argues that they transferred their focus of loyalty from their native Ireland to England in the name of both material security and imperial solidarity. Their emotional withdrawal from Ireland led them to experience a profound sense of social and political dislocation, and encouraged communal retreat, loss of power and a form of 'inner emigration'.

All of these experiences can be intimately linked to concepts of exile propounded by certain important theoreticians and writers.

Jan Vladislav, for example, has written that 'exile exists in many forms', and claims that although 'the sense of rupture, loss, fragmentation [and] nostalgia' are generally recognised as commonplace for the exile drama, the manner in which the components of this drama are enacted and articulated differs 'from experience to experience' (Radulescu 3). Equally, Johannes Evelein has stated in 'Teaching Narratives of Exile' that 'it is clear that the concept of exile does not imply physical banishment per se'. Noting that there is such a thing as 'inner emigration', involving a radical mental dissociation, he mentions that 'the common denominator in the experience of metaphorical exile, then, is the existential sensation of difference' (Radulescu 19). In addition, it is common to link representations of exile with the concept of marginality and loss, and Kai Erikson has discussed how the experience of exile does not necessarily have to be restricted to the individual. She asserts that exile and communal trauma can come to dominate a group's spirit, and notes how 'sometimes […] the community can be damaged in much the same way as the tissue of mind and body' (190). It is possible to link the concept of communal trauma with Joanna Zach-Blomska's perception that 'the state of exile is often experienced as a loss of power' (149). In this context, one additional theory of exile is particularly pertinent; that is, Joseph Wittlin's concept of 'destiempo' as outlined in his groundbreaking article entitled 'The Sorrow and Grandeur of Exile':

> In Spanish, there exists for describing an exile, the word "destierro," a man deprived of his land. I take the liberty to forge one more definition: "destiempo," a man who has been deprived of his time. *That means deprived of the time that now passes in his country.* (105) [My italics]

It is my contention that all the aforementioned perceptions and definitions of exile – particularly those linked to the experiences of communal trauma, loss of power, existential sensation of difference, marginality and profound sense of impending political insignificance – can be fruitfully applied to the experiences of the Anglo-Irish after 1800. That these were indeed experiences of the

Protestant Irish gentry after the Act of Union, can be determined when we examine Hubert Butler's depiction of the existential, political and cultural withdrawal from Irish life afflicting the Anglo-Irish during the nineteenth century. His viewpoint essentially corresponds with that of Neal Ascherson who, in his foreword to *In the Land of Nod*, mentions the 'inner emigration' practised by some Ascendant families, who 'shut their doors on the realities of the new Ireland outside and carried on as if nothing had changed until the dining-room ceiling collapsed or the last male heir was killed in Normandy' (*In the Land* xi). In his essay 'The Country House after the Union', Butler writes that they 'began to feel themselves irremediably alien' and states: 'After the union many of the enterprising and intelligent began to speak with the lukewarm conviction of temporary lodgers. They were not prepared to commit themselves as deeply as their ancestors had done' (*Escape* 51).

For Butler, the Anglo-Irish perception of being Irish lost all political content. They were citizens of the United Kingdom and it was to that larger entity that their allegiance was now due. Their former zeal for the national rights of Ireland seemed to have burned itself out. By accepting the Parliamentary Union they had surrendered control of their destiny, and afterwards, Ireland was no longer at the centre of their political life nor the dominating factor in their political conduct. The Union brought about the destruction of the Anglo-Irish and shifted the culture focus of social life from Ireland to London. This was a fate that could have been avoided if the Anglo-Irish interest in Ireland had been more than marginal. In an essay concerned with Robert Fowler, the Bishop of Kilkenny, Butler states:

> In a panic after the 98' rebellion, they passed the Act of Union. A huge price had to be paid. Their country [...] dwindled to an obsequious province. When we meet Irishmen travelling abroad in the days of Thackeray, they are vulgar creatures aping English Manners and ashamed of their provincial origins, fit subjects for the novelist's satire. (*Escape* 44)

Echoing Elizabeth Bowen's view that, after the Union, 'a sense of
dislocation was everywhere; property was still there but power
was going' (*Escape* 53), Butler discusses what he terms 'the
withdrawal of a whole historic class' (*Escape* 87). He argues that 'a
waste period begins' (*Escape* 48) and that those who spent
themselves in the tragedy and intellectual turmoil that preceded
the Union, suddenly became antiquated figures, ignorant of the
country in which they had grown to consequence. For the
Protestant Aristocracy, the constitutional link with England drew
their interests further from Ireland, which began to seem to them
small, unimportant and unwelcoming. As the century advanced a
mood of dislocation crept over the Anglo-Irish, and Irish MP's at
Westminster quickly lost any sense of a corporate national
responsibility:

> They depended too much on wealth and power from across
> the sea. Through not looking to Ireland first [...] they failed to
> man their local defences and were overwhelmed. They did not
> try and play their part in local and national affairs, but
> remained cautiously on the verge of things. (*In the Land* 29)

Equally:

> Sometimes they seemed to live, not in Ireland at all, but in a
> little cocoon, woven of ancient prejudices. They were able to
> live restricted but self-contained lives with only an accidental
> dependence on the organism in which they were encysted.
> They evolved a portable Protestantism which depended for
> nothing on their Irish environment. (*In the Land* 233)

This is why, 'when they erected a pillar in Sackville Street, it was
not Grattan they put on top of it, but Nelson' (*Escape* 50).

Moreover, the transference of loyalty from Ireland in favour of
the Empire, not only led to a sense of being exiles in their own
country, it also encouraged many Anglo-Irish to experience exile
in a literal, physical context. In his essay 'The Cuffs', Butler
criticises 'the everlasting brain drain to England' (*Escape* 95), and
states that 'they were stupid and defenceless simply because,

since the Union, they had exported all their brightest and bravest to England' (*Escape* 87). He believes that the heaviest losses in terms of emigration were endured by the upper-strata, that is 'the favoured breeding ground of the cultivated heretic, liberal and rebel' (*In the Land* 234). Butler, throughout his work, engages with writers such as G. B. Shaw who left Ireland without intending to return. Criticising the magnetism that England held for the Anglo-Irish intellectual, he mentions that 'many had been educated in England and knew nothing of Ireland's problems' (*Escape* 87). In a memorable phrase, he claims: 'Waterloo may or may not have been won on the playing fields of Eton, but Ireland was certainly lost there' (*Escape* .87).

This transference of loyalty led the Anglo-Irish to lose, not only an interest in the concept of national commitment to Ireland, but also inevitably resulted in them experiencing a sense of separation from the small communities in which they had been reared. Butler argues that rather than spread their wings in the wider imperial world which the British laid open to them, the Anglo-Irish should have shifted their energy and focus back towards, not only the national arena but also the local and the regional. Many of his essays converge on the same area of moral choice; that is, the responsibilities of the individual to his community. He believes that we should cultivate our immediate surroundings and that distance and size dilute responsibility. He claims that 'it seems to me to be man's duty to work in and for the community which he acknowledges to be his own' (*Grandmother* 34). Life can only be fully and consciously lived in our own neighbourhood and 'great, far-off' events should only be of marginal concern to us. Arguing that, '[i]n a republic, devotion and loyalty should be used to warm and illuminate the small communities in which they are produced' (*The Children* 37), Butler frequently applauds the plethora of county archaeological societies founded by the Anglo-Irish in their local communities during the eighteenth century. The comments contained in his essay 'I Suppose So: Maria Cross Reconsidered' are particularly relevant in terms of the Anglo-Irish after the Act of Union. 'A […] community is not warmed, like a Rotary Club, by the number and importance of its foreign affiliations. The neighbours whom we are enjoined to love are those nearest to us' (*The Children* 118). That this philosophical view has contemporary relevance in terms of our social and moral relations is made clear by Richard Rorty in his *Contingency, Irony and Solidarity*, in which he argues that 'our sense of solidarity is strongest when those with whom solidarity is expressed are thought of as "one of us" where "us" means something smaller and more local than the human race' (191).

According to Butler, the emotional and physical withdrawal of a whole historic class from Irish political life after 1800 has had a profound affect on the nature of modern Irish society and the fate of Protestantism in the independent Irish state. The Anglo-Irish were unable to challenge the increasingly common view that to be truly Irish meant to be Gaelic, and their reticence enfeebled opposition to the stated aims and preoccupations of the Irish Republic, that is 'to revive the ancient life of Ireland as a Gaelic state, Gaelic in language and Gaelic in ideals' (Foster 518). For Butler, to compel uniformity by restricting the openness of free individuals to each other is to fundamentally destroy the possibility of culture, as it is only by the crystallisation of all cultural elements, both old and new, that modern civilisation can be strengthened and rendered legitimate. Butler saw the decay of nationalism into chauvinism and exclusiveness as a grave and abiding danger. However, the avowedly sectarian ideals of the newly formed Republic consolidated the allegedly indissoluble bond between Catholicism and Ireland and was met only with appeasement by the Anglo-Irish, leading each succeeding generation to find it more difficult to create for Ireland some common culture which embraced all its citizens. Butler frequently draws attention to the sad slow Protestant decline and in his essay 'Grandmother and Wolfe Tone' he suggests that 'a once voluble people now seem to be stricken with aphasia' (*Grandmother* 138). He criticises 'the handful of old country crocks, retired British servicemen, civil servants and suburban car salesmen in whom the spirit of Anglo-Ireland has its contemporary incarnation' (140). He condemns their profound inertia and comments upon their propensity to exercise 'moral cowardice, dressing [itself] up in a diplomatic bemedalled frock-coat' (142). He mentions that 'Protestants in their spinelessness', left the defence of their principles to liberal Catholics, and notes that as a collective body, they were not even particularly active in resisting the invasion of their liberties by the Catholic Church. Equally, in regard to the censorship Bill, it was predominantly left to professional Catholic writers to fight its restrictions.

Moreover, the apathetic attitude of Southern Irish Protestants has led to the Ulster Presbyterians – who are, according to Butler, a more fanatical and bitter champion of the Reformation – assuming the role of leaders of Irish Protestant opinion. He asserts that this development has hindered the possibility of a united Ireland, and has resulted in increasing bigotry and sectarianism. He believes that the Anglo-Irish, with 'their easy-going pragmatic Christianity' (*Escape* 84) could, if they had been more obtrusive, have tempered the religious and political passions of their northern countrymen. However, amiable inertia and refusal to either express grievance, or cherish hopes about Ireland, have led the Anglo-Irish to renounce their rightful position as the main representatives of Irish Protestantism. He states:

> And that leadership really belongs by tradition to the Protestants of the south, the people of Swift and Berkeley, lord Edward Fitzgerald, Smith O'Brien, Parnell, men who often jeopardised their careers and even sacrificed their lives in the cause of an Ireland, free and united. (*Escape* 116)

Interestingly, Butler appears to believe that the withdrawal of the Anglo-Irish has resulted in Ireland being unable to withstand the amorphous presence of what he views as the less edifying aspects of modernism and industrial capitalism. In 'Anglo-Irish Twilight', he writes that, in the nineteenth century, '[a] new and more suffocating ascendancy, that of international commerce was on the way; many of those ruined [Anglo-Irish] houses would have been strongholds of resistance to it' (*Escape* 102). He argues that there has been a real and discernible deterioration in terms of social relationships, and mentions the ubiquitous influence of a 'progressive and appalling vulgarisation' (*In the Land* 55). There has, he claims, been a displacement of Anglo-Irish culture with 'bastard commerce' and 'the dragon of international industrialism' (*Escape* 84). When reading such passages, it becomes clear that Butler was a man whose general sensibility was profoundly at odds with the representative trends of modernism. As Geoffrey Wheatcroft has noted, '[t]here is a perplexed provincial's battlement at the great world, with which he does not always seem quite at home' (13). For example, his analysis of the increasing influence of the United States in world affairs frequently descends into the polemical, a feature he so scrupulously avoids in the vast majority of his writings. Arguing that '[t]o write clearly in America is like trying to take a country walk on an autostrada' (*Escape* 182), he claims that Edmund Wilson's essays 'show how hard it is to think clearly in a land where muddle is mechanised'. In 'A Reply to Silence', he quotes approvingly Bertrand Russell's belief that 'the distinctive feature of American thought and feeling is the determination to have done with the notion of fact. Truth is a mistaken concept' (*The Children* 212). In conclusion, one cannot help feeling that, by the end of his life, Butler himself chose a form of internal exile from the social, cultural and political developments of his time.

References

Agee, Chris. 'Poteen in a Brandy Cask: The Ethical Imagination of Hubert Butler'. *Yale Review* (1998): 129-42.

Batter, Norman S. 'The Law, the Constitution and the Act of Union of 1801' in *The Union: Essays on Ireland and the British Connection*. Ed. Ronnie Hanna, Newtownards: Colourpoint Books, 2001. 20-31.

Beckett, J.C. *The Anglo-Irish Tradition*. London: Faber, 1976.

Bolton, G.C. *The Passing of the Irish Act of Union: A Study of Parliamentary Politics*. Oxford: Oxford UP, 1966.

Butler, Hubert. *Escape from the Anthill*. Mullingar: The Lilliput Press, 1985.

— *Grandmother and Wolfe Tone*. Dublin: The Lilliput Press, 1990.

— *In the Land of Nod*. Dublin: The Lilliput Press, 1996.

— *The Children of Drancy*. Mulingar: The Lilliput Press, 1988.

Corkery, Daniel. *The Hidden Ireland: A Study of Gaelic Munster in the Eighteenth Century*. Dublin: Gill and Macmillan, 1967.

Evelein, Johannes F. 'Teaching Narratives of Exile' in Radulescu 19-26.

Erikson, Kai. 'Notes on Trauma and Community' in *Trauma: Explorations in Memory*. Ed. Cathy Caruth. Baltimore: The John Hopkins UP, 1995. 189-97.

Foster, Roy. *Modern Ireland 1600-1972*. London: Penguin, 1988.

— 'The Salamander and the Slap: Hubert Butler and His Century' in *The Irish Story: Telling Tales and Making It Up in Ireland*. London: Allen Lane, 2001. 176-84.

Jones, Richard. 'Independent Spirit: An Appreciation of Hubert Butler' in *Archipelago* 1-2 (1997): 1-6.

Kee, Robert. *The Green Flag: A History of Irish Nationalism*. Harmondsworth: Penguin, 1972.

Longley, Edna. 'Close-cropped Grass Comes Up Sweet' in *TLS* 1 February 1991: 8.

Malcomson, A.P.W. *John Foster*. Oxford: Oxford UP, 1978.

M'Geoghegan, Patrick. *The Irish Act of Union: A Study in High Politics 1798-1801*. Dublin: Gill and Macmillan, 1999.

Molyneux, William. *The Case of Ireland's Being Bound by Acts of Parliament in England*. Dublin: J. Ray, 1699.

Radulescu, Domaica (ed.). *Nomadism, Diasporas and Eastern European Voices*. Lexington: Lexington Books, 2002.

Rorty, Richard. *Contingency, Irony and Solidarity*. Cambridge: Cambridge UP, 1989.

Swift, Jonathan. *The Prose Works of Jonathan Swift*. Ed. Herbert Davis. Vol. 10. Oxford: Basil Blackwell, 1941.

Wheatcroft, Geoffrey. 'Messages from a Gentle Protestant' in *TLS* 28 June 1996: 13-14.

Wittlin, Joseph. 'Sorrow and Grandeur of Exile' *in The Polish Review* 2-3 (1957): 99-112.

Zach-Blomska, Joanna. 'Memory in Exile: Notes on Milosz, Identity and Writing' in Radulescu 147-54.

Exiles no More:
Ethnic Leadership and the Construction of the Myth of Thomas D'Arcy McGee

Michael Böss

Introduction: Acculturation and ethnic leadership

Ethnic identities are relevant ways of dealing with the challenges and needs of life. But as social, cultural and political circumstances change, so do ethnic identities and the boundaries by which they are defined.

The sociologist Raymond Breton argues that the challenges that a migrant ethnic community deals with under the impact of emigration and settlement invariably have the impact of changing its social identity and structure. The result is a new, negotiated social order. Breton further argues that, in the forging of a new order, the leaders and institutions of the community play a key role in mobilising and re-interpreting its cultural resources in a way that contributes to social and cultural accommodation and to the process of acculturation, which, in contrast to assimilation, means an adaptation to a new social environment without loss of ethnic self-awareness (Breton 3-21).

This theory applies well to the history of Irish Catholic immigration to Canada. In a recent study of how the Irish of Toronto underwent a "waning of the green" (i.e. Irish nationalist) dimension of their collective identity in the period 1887-1922, Mark G. McGowan explains it as the combined result of a number of social, economic and cultural factors and the role of ethnic leadership. By the 1920s, Irish Catholics had bettered their lot by improving their qualifications and adopting the North American gospel of work and success. In this way, they had escaped "Orange" (i.e. anti-Catholic) and English stereotyping of the Irish

Re-Mapping Exile: Realities and Metaphors in Irish Literature and History, ed. Michael Böss, Irene Gilsenan Nordin and Britta Olinder, *The Dolphin* 34. © 2005 by Aarhus University Press, Denmark. ISBN 87 7934 010 5.

as lazy and low-skilled Paddies. They now had better jobs, better living conditions and higher levels of literacy and education. Many owned their homes and were living peaceful, suburban lives. Indeed, they were hardly distinguishable from their Protestant neighbours, not as a result of assimilation, however, but as an outcome of acculturation: by becoming Canadian Irish with the encouragement of their spiritual and ethnic leaders.

The argument of the present article is inspired by Breton's theory and McGowan's empirical study. It suggests that the construction of the myth of Thomas D'Arcy McGee should be read against the background of the process of acculturation: My thesis is that two leading Irish writers and publishers of 19th-century North America, Thomas D'Arcy McGee and Mary Anne Sadlier, contributed significantly to the earliest phase of Irish Catholic acculturation in Canada and the United States. By virtue of their shared sense of mission as leaders of the Irish communities of North America, they helped especially famine immigrants adjust to life in North America. It also suggests that the novelist, editor and publisher Mary Anne Sadlier contributed to constructing a myth of McGee through the portrait she wrote in her introduction to his collected poems, published by her husband's press in 1869, two years after McGee had been assassinated by a frustrated Irish nationalist. Through my reading of this portrait, I demonstrate how Sadlier interpreted McGee's life so as to align it with her own educative and literary project and the interests of the North American Irish Catholic clergy. In doing so, these 'ethnic leaders' helped pave the way for 20th-century non-ethnic (non-sectional) Canadian politics. It will be demonstrated how McGee and Sadlier divested Catholic Irish immigrants of their reasons for maintaining a separatist and exilic identity and teaching them, instead, to see themselves as Catholics of "Celtic" ethnicity.[1]

Young McGee: Romantic revolutionary
Thomas D'Arcy McGee was born 1825 in Carlingford, Co. Louth, in a middle class family. His father, James, an officer of the Coast Guard, descended from a seventeenth-century Scottish Presbyterian family who had later converted to Catholicism. His

mother, Dorcas Catherine Morgan, a devoted Catholic and romantic nationalist, was the daughter of a Dublin bookseller and publisher, who had been ruined after his personal involvement with the cause of the United Irishmen.[2] McGee was particularly influenced by his mother, who appears to have been an artistically gifted and strongly patriotic woman who brought her son up with the songs and melodies of Thomas Moore, which she would play and sing for him at the family's drawing-room piano. Later in life, he would describe her as 'a woman of extraordinary elevation of mind, an enthusiastic lover of her country, its music, its legends, its wealth of ancient lore'[3] (McGee, *Poems* 16).

As a precocious teenager – gifted as a poet and an orator, well versed in Irish and world history, politically aware and socially ambitious – McGee concluded in 1842, at the age of seventeen, that his prospects in Ireland were dismal and that he would do better by emigrating to the United States. With his own background in a family devoted to Daniel O'Connell, it did not take long for him to combine O'Connellism and American republicanism. Indeed, he delivered his first public speech on the quays of Boston on 4 July1842 – on the subject of Irish freedom! The oratorical gifts of the young, enthusiastic patriot caught the attention of a local Irish publisher, who offered him a job as a journalist for the widely circulated *Boston Pilot*.

Enraged by the anti-Catholic agitation of the nativist, militantly Protestant Know-Nothing movement, McGee soon involved himself in American politics as a defender of the rights of Catholics – at a time when the word 'Catholic' was largely synonymous with 'Irish'. At the same time, he sought to restore self-respect among his own by teaching them, in articles and public lectures, about their country's proud past and bright prospects, once the Union had been repealed (cf. McGee's *Historical Sketches*).

The *Pilot* was a weekly newspaper which had developed into the most influential Catholic journal in the United States and Canada, and which now also enjoyed wide circulation in Ireland, Scotland, and England. (Harris 158) It combined news from America politics with news from Ireland and information about life in the Irish American community. In addition, its pages were open to Irish – and to an increasing extent also Irish-American – literature, mainly fiction. This editorial policy made the *Pilot*, like other Irish American periodicals of the time, significant as an instrument of acculturation, alongside institutions and organisations like the Catholic Church and The Ancient Order of Hibernians.[4]

Only two years after his arrival at the *Pilot*, McGee was promoted chief editor. At that time, his pen and oratorical gifts had brought his name to the attention of Daniel O'Connell and the proprietor of the Dublin *Freeman's Journal*, who offered him the post as editor. Deeply flattered McGee returned to Ireland at the age of only twenty to enter the first rank of the Irish press.

However, McGee was soon disappointed with the political moderation and caution of the *Freeman* and began to contribute to the *Nation*, the mouthpiece of the more radical nationalist movement Young Ireland. When Charles Gavan Duffy asked him to assist him in editing this widely circulated newspaper, he immediately accepted his offer, realising how its combination of articles on history, culture and politics fitted his own interests.

McGee believed that it was not only possible to recover the relics of the past but also to restore the traditions and continuities that had been broken. His own contribution to national reconstruction was a series of historical and literary articles published in the *Freeman's Journal* and the *Nation*, some of which were later republished in Duffy's Library of Ireland series in 1846 as *The Irish Writers of the Seventeenth Century*. These portraits, which include a number of Ulster poets, reflect the young author's non-sectarian and cultural pluralist conception of nationality, which, after his move to Canada in 1857, also was to characterise his vision of Canadianness. In the following years, however, his involvement in revolutionary nationalism – and his highly emotional temperament – added strident – racialist and slightly sectarian – undertones to his Ossianic celticism, as it expresses itself in his poetry from this period.

'The Ancient Race', for example, begins with nine stanzas deploring the tragic and sorry state of 'the noble Celtic island race'. In stanza ten, the poem breaks out into a flaming political call for support to the Irish League:[5]

They will not go, the ancient race!
They must not go, the ancient race!
    Come, gallant Celts, and take your stand –
    The League – the League – will save the land –
    The land of faith, the land of grace,
    The land of Erin's ancient race![6]

Thus implicated in the Confederation's failed rising of 1848, McGee escaped arrest and fled back to an America, where he immediately associated his own political exile with that of his poor countrymen fleeing the mortal devastations of the Great Famine. Hence, his poems assumed an even more bitter tone, as in 'Parting from Ireland':

God! It is a maddening prospect thus to see this storied land
Like some wretched culprit writhing in a strong avenger's hand –
Kneeling, foaming, weeping, shrieking, woman weak and woman-loud –
Better, better, Mother Ireland! We had laid you in your shroud! (106)

Thus, in the course of only six years, Thomas D'Arcy McGee, had moved mentally from voluntary emigrant and repealer into exiled, republican revolutionary forced to the shores of a foreign land together with hundreds of thousands of famine victims. The association between political exile and forced emigration made for a strong cocktail which, as Kerby Miller has demonstrated, served to make famine emigrants identify with the cause of a new militant Irish American nationalism, which was given organisational shape with the founding of the Irish Republican Brotherhood in New York in 1858 (Miller 281).

McGee became one of the intellectual leaders of exile nationalism in its initial phase. After his return to the United States, McGee set up a journal in New York, the *New York Nation*, targeting the exiled Irish population in America and trying to win their support for Irish independence. McGee's own articles contributed to enhancing the notion among the new Irish in

America of being exiles, i.e. victims of political oppression and banishment, and in his fiery prose and even more high-strung poetry, he often came close to elevating the achievement of national freedom to the level of religious redemption.

When he also turned against the Catholic Church, blaming the Irish bishops for their lack of support for the rebellion in 1848, McGee not only antagonised the hierarchy, represented by Bishop Hughes of New York – who launched a counter-attack – it also looked as if McGee was distancing himself both from the social and political realities of Ireland and from the more immediate concerns of the Irish communities of North America. McGee thus increasingly found himself speaking to deaf and even hostile ears. For economic reasons he had to give up his New York publishing venture in 1850. He moved back to Boston, where he thought he had more friends and where he founded a new journal, the *American Celt*, in the same year.

From this year, evidently, McGee's editorial messages, lectures and poems began to move towards the position of the Catholic hierarchy in North America. He began to acknowledge the unlikelihood that the Irish in America would ever return to Ireland and instead regained his former enthusiasm for America and its political ideals, as reflected in his poem 'Hail to the Land', for example:

> Hail to the land where Freedom first
> Through all the feudal fetters burst,
> And, planting man upon their feet,
> Cried, Onward! Never more retreat!
>   Be it yours to plant your starry flag
>   On royal roof and castle crag;
>   Be it yours co climb Earth's eastern slope
>   In championship of human hope,
>   Your war-cry, Truth! Immortal word;
>   Your weapon, Justice! Glorious sword;
>   Your fame far-traveled, as the Levin,
>   And lasting as the arch of heaven.
>   Hail to the happy land! (67)

The amateur historian who used to devote his public lectures to the history of Ireland now wrote a *History of Irish Settlers in America*, and in his newspaper articles, he urged Irish famine exiles to make America their home and improve their lot through their own effort, for example by educating themselves. He initiated a campaign to persuade his compatriots to leave their urban ghettos and settle in the rural west. In a poem allegedly written on the shores of Lake Erie in 1852, 'An Invitation Westward', he concludes, although with a degree of resignation, that emigration and settlement in the 'forests of the West' might be the wisest thing to do for a people 'weary [...] of warfare and [...] woes':

> It grieves my soul to say it – to say to you, Arise!
> To follow where the evening star sings vespers down the skies;
> It grieves my soul to call you from the land you love the best –
> But I love Freedom better, and her home is now the West.
>
> Then, children of Milesius, from your house of death arise,
> And follow where the evening star sings vespers to the skies;
> Though it grieve your souls to part from the land you love the best,
> Fair Freedom will console you in the forests of the West. (146-47)

Even though he was greatly disappointed to see his scheme for the establishment of special Irish colonies in the West rebuffed and defeated by Bishop Hughes,[7] he soon after began to assume the view of Hughes and other members of the hierarchy who saw their role as spiritual guardians of Irish Catholics in America as being incompatible with ethnic separatist policies.

This happened in a period when McGee was becoming increasingly sceptical of the American way of giving expression to 'fair freedom': the republican cult of freedom, which implied the separation of state and religion, and which, to him, also implied a rejection of historical continuity. Already in 1852, in a 'Letter to a Friend', published in the *American Celt*, he had addressed the question of 'the recent Conspiracy against Peace and Existence of Christendom'. Here he claims that Christianity provides the 'primary principles that govern, and must govern, the world', but that 'there is, in our own age, one of the most dangerous and general conspiracies against Christendom that the world has yet seen'. It is, he writes, 'the highest duty of "a Catholic man" to go over cheerfully, heartily, and at once, to the side of Christendom – to the Catholic side, and to resist, with all his might, the conspirators who under the stolen name of "Liberty," make war upon all Christian institutions'.[8] (*Poems* 26).

McGee's growing accommodation to ultramontane doctrines – and his distancing from American libertarianism – was reflected in his *Catholic History of North America*, which was published in 1855 by his recent friend, James Sadlier, owner of the biggest Catholic publishing company in North America and husband of the novelist Mary Anne Sadlier. Both of them appreciated McGee's turn to political moderation and religious conservatism, and two years later James Sadlier offered to buy the *American Celt* when members of the Catholic community of Montreal invited McGee to help them start their own newspaper.

Mature McGee: Canadian with a Celtic soul

In 1857 Montreal had a population of about 70,000, 20% of which was Irish. At that time Canada consisted of two colonies loosely united since 1847 as Canada West and Canada East (today's Ontario and Quebec). The mostly French-speaking eastern province had an English speaking minority. This minority, however, was divided in itself between Protestant Anglo-Canadians, people of northern Irish (i.e. Scots-Irish Presbyterian) descent, and recently immigrated Catholic Irish. The relationship between the Irish groups, however, was here characterised by a degree of tolerance which was unheard of in the towns and cities of Canada West, particularly Toronto where the Protestant community had a strong Orange (Order) element.

The Irish Catholics of Montreal had recently become worried at seeing the increasing political influence of the Orange Order in Canada West, where the order had begun to air the idea of banning Catholic schools. Combined with the proposed 'representation by population', i.e. a constitutional measure according to which Canada East and West should be represented in the union parliament according to the size of their populations. Such a ban would mean a threat also to the Irish Catholics of Canada East. Therefore, Montreal's St. Patrick's Society had passed a series of resolutions in 1857 demanding that Catholics in Canada West should enjoy the same minority rights as Protestants did in Canada East. It was in this context that they saw a need for their own newspaper, having come to the conclusion that Irish interests were not fully represented in Montreal's already existing English-language Catholic newspaper, *The True Witness*.

Upon his arrival in Montreal, however, McGee sent out a clear message that he intended to work for continued good intercommunal relations. His first editorials in *The New Era*, confirmed this policy. The first called for unity among the ethnic groups of Montreal, the second discussed the position of the French-Canadians in the colonies, and the third suggested a tighter union among the British colonies in North America, including the Maritime colonies. McGee's editorials caused wide public attention, and, although his line differed from that of the established parties, leading members of the St Patrick society soon persuaded him to represent the Irish of Montreal in the general election of 1857.

If one looks at McGee's political career in Canadian politics, one will see the fruits of the development he had gone through over the years: from militant nationalism through Irish Catholic and ethnic leadership to a kind of cross-sectionalism, which had its roots in the anti-sectarianism of his youthful commitments to the nationalism of Thomas Davis. McGee, who started his career as a candidate for the liberal Reform Party, hoped for the day when the political parties in Canada would no longer draw their support from ethnic and religious factions but would be able to secure support from all ethnic groups and, in this way, settle the linguistic, religious and other cultural differences of the colonies. He thought that they would have to enter into political unity. He envisioned a federalist state where the rights of religious minorities would enjoy full protection. In order to create such a state, all ethnic groups in Canada, including his Irish co-ethnics, would have to get used to the idea of forming alliances with groups outside their own community.

McGee found support for such ideas among the Catholics of Canada West. In Montreal, however, some Irish Catholics – although far from all - were deeply suspicious and considered McGee an opportunist and a traitor to his own people because he now downplayed oppression in Ireland to further his own political career. The first strong reaction to his vision and strategy came after he and the liberal Catholic clergy of Toronto in 1858 suggested that the traditional St. Patrick's Day parade in the city should be banned in order to put a stop to the recurrent sectarian riots between Irish of 'Green' and 'Orange' loyalties. McGee was not deterred by the outrage he caused, however, and in the following years he caused even further provocation among his own. The climax came in 1863 when he decided to leave the Reform Party in order to support the Conservative leader John McDonald's idea of forming a Great Coalition to secure Canadian unity, knowing full well that the party's association with the Orange Order would be seen by many Irish Catholics as treason to his people.

The decisive moment for McGee's transformation from ethnic leader into Canadian politician occurred with the Fenian attacks on British North America in the aftermath of the American Civil War. Between 1866 and 1871 small, private armies of American Fenians (i.e. members of the Irish Republican Brotherhood) launched a series of forays across the border between Upper Canada (present-day Ontario) and the United States. Their ultimate strategy appears somewhat confused: Did they seriously attempt to capture territory or just to provoke an Anglo-American war, something which might lead to a rebellion in Ireland. Regardless of the ultimate goal, the fact remains that the Fenians expected the Catholic Irish of Canada to support their cause, even if it meant a challenge to the colonial government, which was dominated by Anglo-Canadian Tories and descendants of Irish-Scots, i.e. Presbyterian, immigrants (see O'Broin and Senior). However, their attacks, though ultimately amounting to little more than skirmishes, only brought about an even firmer intent in McDonald's Great Coalition to seek Canadian unity against the potential threats from south of the border. Thus, Fenianism was one of the contributing factors of the 1867 Act of Confederation.

Although the Catholic Irish community were reluctant to give Fenianism their full support, the Fenians certainly did cause serious deep splits within the community due to the fact that Fenianism was not only anti-British but also potentially anti-Canadian. Fenians held that the Irish owed their primary loyalty and obligation to Ireland, not to their adopted country.

The Fenian project failed to draw the full support of the Catholic Irish because they were met with strong political resistance from Thomas D'Arcy McGee (1825-67), who had moved from the United States to Montreal in 1857 to take up a leadership position in the Catholic Irish community as a publisher and, shortly after, become a member of the Ottawa Parliament. McGee argued that, even though Canada was still a part of the British Empire, Irish Catholics in Canada should not transpose the old enmity between Ireland and Britain to Canadian soil, for one thing because Canada was only nominally British, for the other because it would only lead to a continuance of the sectarian conflicts which they were only too familiar with from Ireland. Responding to the annual St. Patrick day riots, where Irish Catholics and Protestants fought each other in the streets of Toronto, McGee warned in 1861:

> I know, and you know, that I can never for a moment cease to regard with an affection that amounts almost to idolatry, the land where I spent my best, my first years; where I obtained the partner of my life, and where my first-born saw the light. I cannot but regard that land even with increased love, because she has not been prosperous. Yet I hold we have no right to intrude our Irish patriotism on this soil; for our first duty is to the land where we live and have fixed our homes, and where, while we live, we must find the true sphere of our duties. While always ready, therefore, to say the right word, and to do the right act for the land of my forefathers, I am bound above all to the land where I reside. (Qtd in McGibbon 10)

Inspired by the ideals of his own youthful engagement with the ideologies of the United Irishmen and Young Ireland, McGee rhetorically painted prospects of a Canadian nation in which all traditions and ethnicities had melted into a nation bound together by the sharing of a variety of landscapes and a literature.[9] First of all, however, the new nation would draw its identity from a constitution built on the principle of freedom. In a famous speech given at the Ottawa parliament as early as 1860, he said:

> I see in the not remote distance one great nationality, bound, like the shield of Achilles, by the blue rim of ocean. I see it quartered into many communities, each disposing of its internal affairs, but all bound together by free institutions, free intercourse, free commerce. I see, within the round of that shield, the peaks of the Western mountains and the crest of Eastern waves. The winding Assiniboine, the five-fold lakes, the St. Lawrence, the Ottawa, the Saguenay, the St. John, the Basin of Minas, by all these flowing waters, in all the valleys they fertilize, in all the cities they visit in their courses, I see a generation of industrious, contended moral men, free in name and in fact – men capable of maintaining, in peace and in war, a Constitution worthy of such a country. (Qtd in Davis 461)

In preaching the virtues of a Canadian national identity to the Catholic Irish of Canada, McGee was clearly ahead of his own time and many Catholic Irish saw involvement in cross-party politics as a treachery towards his own ethnic community. This explains why McGee was assassinated in Ottawa on 7 April 1868, shortly after taking his seat in the first Parliament of the new dominion of Canada.

The Myth of McGee
In his doctoral dissertation from 1974, Peter M. Toner argues that there was not widespread support among Canadian Irish in his own lifetime, and that it therefore important to distinguish the historical McGee from the myth that was later constructed about him. Toner demonstrates, for example, that, in the 1860s, many members of the Canadian communities of Canada, who up till

then had followed his leadership in his verbal attacks on Fenianism, nevertheless failed to endorse his political tactics, which they regarded as ethnic treason.

The myth of McGee has many sources: the Canada First Movement, Liberal-Conservative politicians, historians such as D. C. Harvey, Isabel Skelton and Josephine Phelan. Instead of considering them all, I will here, more narrowly – in order to demonstrate my argument - focus on the particular contribution of elements of the Catholic Church and, especially, the Catholic novelist Mary Anne Sadlier, to constructing a myth of McGee which served the institutional interests of the church as a guardian of the spiritual and material welfare of Irish Catholics in Canada.

The Catholic Church in Canada did not have an "official" view on Mcgee, and some bishops – Horan (of Kingston), Lynch (of Toronto) and Bourget (of Montreal) did not regard him favourably. Many did, however, and one of the clerics who contributed to sanctifying the memory of McGee and his vision for national unity was Archbishop Thomas L. Connolly of Halifax.

Connolly shared McGee's dream of a Canadian nation and his resentment of American republicanism. In his funeral oration in honour of McGee in the Metropolitan Church of St. Mary's in Halifax in 1868, Connolly expressed his personal admiration for McGee, whom he described as a man who 'without compromise of a single principle, religious or political' had sought to bring 'rich and poor, Protestant and Catholic, English, French, Irish and Scotch and Canadian, into the bond of amity and the social compact, and unified a whole mass of heterogeneous people, far more than the most ardent lover of this new and interesting country could ever have anticipated' (18-19). Towards the end of his oration, he declared that McGee's vision not only served Canada, but also the 'interests of the Catholic Church' and the 'material as well as spiritual welfare' of his own 'people', the Irish. McGee himself was described as a martyr lying dead at Canada's 'altar':

There is one more crime for which McGee suffered, to which I must again allude before concluding, and that is, that for the last ten years he laboured to amalgamate Protestant and Catholic, French and Irish, into one body politic and social, in this happy land. I, too, in my own way, have been guilty of the same crime, and I confess it not with remorse, but with honest pride. For the true interests of the Catholic Church, and still more for the material as well as spiritual welfare of the people committed to my care, I feel that it as much my duty to conciliate Protestants, and to preserve heavenly peace and happiness in this land, as to preach a sermon or to perform any other portion of my Episcopal functions. I believe that my humble efforts in this particular have brought more real blessings of every kind on the Catholic community over which I preside, than all my other labours together. I found my people nine years ago in the turmoil of religious strife; and, if I die to-day, thanks to God and to the co-operation of clergy and laity, I leave them without any polemical heartburnings – in peace, happiness and union with their fellow citizens of every creed and class. – It was for the attainment of this glorious position for the Irish in this country, that the mighty dead whom we honour to-day lived in the last years, and *like a martyr laid down his life in the Holy Week of 1868, at the foot of his country's altar.* (23)

Church leaders such as Connolly were not alone in constructing the myth of McGee, however. Another important, but hitherto neglected, voice in this period was that of the novelist Mary Anne Sadlier.

The project of Mary Anne Sadlier
Sadlier and McGee developed a friendship after McGee decided to publish her novel *The Blakes and the Flanagans* in serial form in his newspaper the *American Celt* in 1855. McGee must have felt an affinity with the message of Sadlier's novel at a time when he had begun to see his own role *vis-à-vis* the Irish immigrant communities of North America in a new light: as leader of Irish Catholic communities in North America.

Mary Anne Sadlier was born in 1820 at Cootehill, Co. Cavan, as the daughter of Francis Madden, a wealthy merchant, who encouraged his daughter's poetic ambitions. After her father's death, following serious financial setbacks, she emigrated to Montreal in 1844, where, in 1846, she met and married another émigré, the successful publisher James Sadlier.

James Sadlier and his brother, Denis, had left Co. Tipperary in 1830 with their widowed mother and in 1837 established a Catholic publishing company in New York, specialising in devotional literature, such as Butler's *Lives of the Saints*, for the growing number of Irish Catholic pre-famine immigrants. After buying the company of another Irish-American publisher, John Doyle, the Sadliers were in possession of the largest Catholic publishing house in the United States. A branch was established in Montreal with James as manager. Later the company also set up a branch in London and expanded into newspapers.

Far from putting a stop to her literary ambitions, Mary Anne Sadlier's marriage gave it a boost. Even though she was a mother of six children, she produced, from 1849 on, numerous novels, essays and translations. Ten of her novels take their plots from Irish history because Sadlier shared McGee's belief in the edifying value of national history. She saw it as her purpose as a novelist to present the 'great and noble deeds' of the Irish past in order to restore the pride of her countrymen in America, 'ennoble our country and give her that place amongst the nations to which the glory of her sons entitles her' (*Confederate Chieftains* 3).

However, because she invariably identified Ireland with its Catholic tradition, not only her historical but also her eight 'American' novels ultimately served a more elevated purpose: 'It is needless to say that all my writings are dedicated to the one grand object: the illustration of our holy faith, by means of tales and stories,' as she wrote in her preface to *The Blakes and the Flanagans* (v), and she added:

> I do not profess to write novels – I cannot afford to waste time pandering merely to the imagination, or fostering that maudlin sentimentality, which is the ruin of our youth both male and female. [...] One who has Eternity ever in view,

cannot write mere love-tales; but simple, practical stories embodying grave truths, will be read by many, who would not read *pious books*. Such, then is *The Blakes and the Flanagans*. (vi)

Thus, Sadlier's main concern as a writer was to be a spiritual and moral educator for Irish Catholic immigrants. She was worried about the threat that the materialism of the New World posed to the moral values and faith of Irish immigrants, and she regarded their Catholicism as a shield against their assimilation of 'American' values such as materialism, individualism and secularism.

The Blakes and the Flanagans follows the lives of three generations of two immigrant families in New York. The families react in different ways to their experiences in the New World: the Flanagans are 'good, old-fashioned Catholics', who successfully raise their off-spring to become 'cheerful, docile, and obedient children well liked by God and man' (11-12). The Blakes, in contrast, after having 'shipwrecked' their faith, enter 'the front ranks of the Know-Nothings, urging on the godless fanaticism of the age, in a crusade against the religion of their fathers and the children of their own race', as the author puts it (378). Whereas the Flanagans desist from social climbing and remain true to expressions of Irishness in customs, culture and faith – thereby literally saving their family from disaster – the Blakes, having shed themselves of their Irish identity, destroy themselves. The critic Charles Fanning has rightly pointed out that what Sadlier advocated was 'taking the pious, unambitious peasant out of Ireland, and making him a pious, unambitious working-class American' (126). Sadlier demonstrated that the Irish famine immigrants would only be able to survive socially if they kept to the values and rituals of the rural Irish family. What the social anthropologists Arensberg and Kimball, in their study of rural Ireland, described as a Catholic 'familist' ideology, is here seen as crucial for the social survival of Irish immigrants.

As for a possible conflict between 'Irishness' and 'Americanness', Sadlier saw no real dilemma because, to her, Irishness was a spiritual and cultural category that was compatible with American citizenship and loyalty to the Republic. In a scene in which Miles Blake warns his nephew, Ned Flanagan, that 'men can't be Irishmen and Americans at the same time', Ned answers:

> I myself am a living proof that your position is a false one. I was brought up, as you well know, under Catholic – nay, more, under Irish training; I am Irish at heart – Catholic in faith and practice, and yet I am fully prepared to stand by this great Republic, the land of my birth, even to shedding the last drop of my blood, were that necessary. I love America; it is, as it were, the land of my adoption, as well as of my birth, but I cannot, or will not, forget Ireland. (164)

Sadlier's reading of McGee's life

Only a year after McGee had been assassinated by a frustrated Fenian radical, McGee's collected poems were published by Sadlier, edited by the publisher's wife, who also added a 'Biographical Sketch of the Author'. The purpose of Mary Sadlier's reading of his life and political career was to explain how McGee's rejection of Fenianism was in the material, spiritual and political interests of the Irish of North America.

Sadlier argues that McGee's showdown with revolutionary nationalism occurred at a time in his life when he had learned to accept and respect the role of the Catholic Church for the communities of Irish immigrants to North America. However, she also explains it as a result of his personal experiences in Canada:

> He regarded it from the first as an off-shoot of the great universal scheme of revolution which, like a network, overspreads, or rather underlies, every state and kingdom of the Old World – that very 'conspiracy' against religion, law, and order, in relation to which he had warned, as already seen, one of his early associates in the 'Young Ireland' movement on his landing in America, after escaping from penal servitude in Australia. But it was in regard to Canada, and their avowed intention of invading that country, his home and the home of his family, where he had been kindly

welcomed and raised by his own countrymen and others, to honor and eminence, that Mr. McGee most severely denounced the Fenians. He rightly considered that it was a grievous wrong to invade a peaceful country like Canada, only nominantly dependent on Great Britain, and where so many thousands of Irishmen were living happily and contentedly under just and equitable laws. And it is quite certain that the great body of the Irish in every part of Canada reprobated these projects of 'Fenian' invasion as strongly as did Mr. McGee. (*Poems* 34)

Those who had regarded McGee as a traitor to his own people are described as 'artful and unprincipled persons' who had set the 'vilest calumnies' afloat concerning him. Influenced by the 'mean and dastardly underhand proceedings of his enemies', a minority of his countrymen in Montreal – chiefly, if not completely, 'of the lowest classes' – had been induced by Fenian elements to challenge McGee's long-held seat in the Ottawa parliament with their own candidate. But although he defeated his opponent, his

victory, however, cost him dear, for the vile means that had been used to turn the Irish of Montreal against him for electioneering purposes were the immediate causes for his assassination a few months later. The evil passions of the basest and most degraded of his countrymen had been excited against him, and he was thenceforth a doomed man, although he probably knew it not. (35)

Sadlier represents McGee as a man who had never chosen to pursue a career in politics, but who had drifted into the 'troubled waters' of public life by the 'forces of circumstances' (35). McGee would have preferred to have spent his time in the 'calm pursuit' of literature, Irish history and antiquarian lore, besides 'the cultivation of that poetic genius which had so early developed itself in his wonderfully-gifted mind' (35-36). Indeed, even those who had heard him deliver one of his many public speeches on literary and historical subjects knew that his convictions – his hopes and his wishes – sprang from 'the dim retreats of quiet life, with his books and his pen, and that harp whose chords were his own heart-strings' (36). Sadlier, in other words, sketches the life of a man who, with the guidance of religious faith, sacrificed his own personal happiness and interests in order to serve his people and as a man who learned, through personal hardship and experience, to spurn the 'emptiness of fame, the nothingness of earthly things' and instead to turn towards 'the grandeur and solidity of the imperishable goods of eternity':

> In the deep silence of his soul, shut in from the great tumult of the outer world, he pondered on the eternal truths and on the religious traditions of his race, and the strong faith that his Christian mother had implanted in his heart grew and flourished until it brought forth flowers of piety that would have shed a glory and a beauty on the altar of religion, had he been permitted to live to carry out his exalted and purified ideas. (35)

Although Sadlier does not refrain from pointing out the political errors McGee made in his rebellious youth, she, nevertheless, glosses over them because he later regretted his past and pursued a project of ethnic leadership similar to her own.

In accounting for McGee's conflict with the Catholic Church in the United States after his return from Ireland in 1848, Sadlier sides completely with Bishop Hughes and the hierarchy. However, she underlines that, although the first issues of the *American Celt* show that McGee's conflict with the Catholic Church was not yet over, there are signs that showed that his convictions were undergoing a gradual change towards her own convictions. She makes it a cardinal point to tell her readers that, years later, he would deeply regret his attacks on Hughes and regain a 'truly Irish respect' for the Catholic clergy. What McGee obviously had begun to acknowledge, she maintains, was that the bishop's stance was in accordance with the social and personal interests of Irish Catholics, whether in Ireland or North America:

> Mr. McGee stoutly maintained his own opinion, and many took sides with him; but all the religious sympathies of the

Irish people, and their profound reverence for their clergy, were arrayed against him, and he found, when too late, that he had lost ground considerably in the favour of the best portion of his countrymen in America. To do him justice, his own truly Irish respect for the clerical order speedily regained its paramount place in his mind and heart, and he not only desisted very soon from writing against the Bishop, but ever after deplored this controversy with him as one of the false steps in his life. (22)

Sadlier warmly endorses McGee's rejection of revolutionary republicanism after his arrival in Boston:

During the first two years of the Celt's existence, it was characterized by the same, or nearly the same, revolutionary ardour; but there came a time when the great strong mind and far-seeing intellect of its editor began to soar above the clouds of passion and prejudice into the regions of eternal truth. The cant of faction, the fiery denunciations that, after all, amounted to nothing, he began to see in their true colors; and with his whole heart he then and ever after aspired to elevate the Irish people, not by impracticable Utopian schemes of revolution, but by teaching them to make the best of the hard fate that made them the subjects of a foreign power differing from them in race and religion; to cultivate among them the arts of peace, and to raise themselves, by the ways of peaceful industry and increasing enlightenment, to the level even of the more prosperous sisterland. (23)

Sadlier ascribes McGee's turn of mind and principles – which strongly alienated his former revolutionary friends – to the effects of greater maturity nourished by 'the sage counsels of such profound Christian thinkers as the late most eminent Bishop Fitzpatrick of Boston' (23). Seeing how he had now developed into a 'conservative statesman' who held 'a high place amongst the eminent literary men of the day', Sadlier fully appreciates the success that befell the *American Celt* over the next five years after

it, first, had been transferred to Buffalo, at 'the urgent request of
the late Bishop Timon', and, later, to New York, where it was to
hold 'the first position in the Irish-American press'. In this period,
she records, McGee became a true leader of his people, tirelessly
writing and lecturing on historical, literary and religious subjects,
besides instituting and inaugurating 'various associations and
movements having the social and moral elevation of the Irish race
for their object'. Sadlier underscores the now non-political and
spiritual character of McGee's efforts. It was his aim to make the
Irish into good and self-respecting 'citizens' of their 'adopted
country', yet united by a shared faith and 'memories of their
common past' (27-28). Seeing how McGee now fully shared her
own validation of spiritual values over politics, she, therefore,
now saw McGee as an ally and became instrumental in the
decision of the Catholics of Montreal to send an invitation to
McGee.

Whereas McGee's enemies saw his later political manoeuvres
as treason motivated by personal opportunism, his friends and
supporters, such as the Sadliers, were convinced that he was
motivated by higher ideals than those of political power and
office. Accordingly, the last pages of her biographical sketch
develop into a hagiography celebrating a national martyr. It is a
portrait of a man who had constantly been preaching peace and
unity but, nevertheless, ended his life with an assassin's bullet in
his heart. Even on the eve of his violent death, we read,

> he delivered one of the noblest speeches ever heard within the
> walls of a Canadian Parliament, and fully equal to the best of
> his own. The subject was the cementing of the lately-formed
> Union of the Provinces by bonds of mutual kindness and
> good-will; but, alas! alas! the echoes of that all-potent voice
> had scarcely died on the air, when the great orator, the
> preacher of peace, the sagacious statesman, the gifted son of
> song, the loved of many hearts, had ceased to live! (36)

After having accounted for his death, Sadlier relates how the sad
news violated the sacred unit of an ordinary Catholic family

preparing to celebrate Easter with their husband and father. The news arrived

> flying on the telegraph's wings to the quiet home in Montreal where the wife of his youth and their two fair daughters were wrapped in sleep, dreaming, it might be, of the calm delights of the coming days which the husband and father was to spend with his family; for it was the Tuesday morning in Holy Week, and the next evening he was to have reached home for the Easter recess. Over the sorrow of that household we cast a veil; it was too sacred for the public eye. (37)

Sadlier weaves the private tragedy of the McGees into the fate of a new-born Canadian nation when accounting for the funeral rites and 'lofty honors' that had greeted the infant nation's martyr:

> His obsequies were solemnized first in the Cathedral of Ottawa; then in St. Patrick's Church and in the Church of Notre Dame, in Montreal; and again in the beautiful Cathedral of Halifax, N.S., on which latter occasion a noble funeral oration was delivered by his true and most appreciative friend, Archbishop Connolly. And the people of Canada mourned him many days, and still do mourn the great loss they sustained in his premature death. In their social *reunions*, in their national festivals, they speak of him, whose voice was wont to delight all hearts, whose subtle and bright, yet gentle humour shed light all around, whose genial nature diffused a spirit of brotherly love and the best of good-fellowship wherever its influence reached. (37)

Sadlier emphasises, however, that McGee's status as Canadian hero and martyr does not contradict his Irishness. She points out how McGee, only three weeks before his death (on St. Patrick's Day) had spoken at a public banquet in Ottawa on the 'general interests of the Irish race, with the present condition and future prospects of Irish literature – shadowing forth, in no indistinct lines, his own abiding and all-enduring love of his race and country, and the work he had marked out for himself in the after years for the service of one of the other' (38). She also mentions that, at the time of his death, he had been writing an essay for the *Catholic World* on 'Oliver Plunket [sic], Archbishop and Martyr'.

Noting, thus, that '[h]is last writings were for Ireland – his last words for the peace and unity of his adopted country, the New Dominion of Canada', Sadlier is able to conclude that McGee died as he had lived, 'loving and serving his mistress, Ireland, as a true knight' (39). This implication was in accordance with her own belief: that it was no betrayal of Ireland for the Irish of North America to become Canadian or American.

Conclusion

This was in fact what Sadlier's narrative of the life of Thomas D'Arcy McGee was all about. And this was what the Catholic hierarchy found so worthy of being retold and remembered: The myth constructed over McGee's life carried the message that the Catholic Irish in Canada should no longer see themselves as exiles in a foreign country. McGee had shown them the way forward by teaching them to regard Canada as their new national home and to understand themselves as Catholic Canadians of Celtic origin. In this way, his myth contributed to making ethnic politics a thing of the past and to negotiating a new social order among Catholic Irish immigrants and their later descendants thus acculturated through ethnic leadership.

Notes

[1] For the distinction between 'exile' and 'immigration', I refer to Kerby Miller's definitions in his introduction to *Emigrants and Exiles*.

[2] Biographical details, other than those given by Sadlier, may be found in Skelton and a number of essays in O'Driscoll and Reynolds, i.e. Burns 'From Freedom to Tolerance: D'Arcy McGee, the First Martyr'; William G. Davis, 'Thomas D'Arcy McGee: Irish Founder of the Canadian Nation', in *The Untold Story*; William G. Davis, 'Thomas D'Arcy McGee: Irish Founder of the Canadian Nation'; William M. Baker, 'Turning the Spit: Timothy Anglin and the Roasting of D'Arcy McGee; Ann Dooley, 'D'Arcy McGee, Fenianism and the Separate School System in Ontario by Ann Dooley; William Kiwin, 'Thomas D'Arcy McGee: Turning Points in the Life of a Nationalist', and Peter

Berresford Ellis, 'Ridgeway, the Fenian Raids and the Making of Canada'.

3 Mary Anne Sadlier, 'Biographical Sketch, in Thomas D'Arcy McGee', in McGee, Thomas D'Arcy, *The Poems of Thomas D'Arcy McGee*, 16. All references in the text to this edition.

4 For a full list and history of the many organisations that contributed to this process, see Michael F. Funchion (ed.), *Irish American Voluntary Organizations* .

5 The Irish League was a short-lived alliance in 1848 between O'Connell's repeal movement and the Irish Confederation, which was the militant off-shoot of Young Ireland. At the time when McGee wrote the poem, he was secretary of the Irish Confederation, having now departed conclusively with the political legacy of O'Connell, i.e. constitutional nationalism.

6 All poems quoted from *The Collected Poems of Thomas D'Arcy McGee*. These lines from 'The Ancient Race', 132.

7 McGee pursued this goal on behalf of the Irish Emigrant Aid Convention which as late as 1856, but was defeated by the opposition of Bishop Hughes. See Kevin Kenny, *The American Irish,* 106.

8 Quoted by Sadlier, in *Poems of Thomas D'Arcy McGee*, 26.

9 *Canadian Ballads* (1858) was McGee's early attempt to forge a Canadian identity with reference to the literary heritage of British North America.

References

Arensberg Conrad M. and Solon T. Kimball. *Family and Community in Ireland*. Cambridge, Mass.: Harvard UP, 1940.

Bielenberg, Andy, ed. *The Irish Diaspora*. Harlow, Essex: Longman/Pearson, 2000.

Breton, R. 'Collective Dimensions of the Cultural Transformation of Ethnic Communities and the Larger Society', in Burnet, J. et al., eds. *Migration and the Transformation of Cultures*. Toronto: Multicultural History Society of Ontario, 1992. 3-21.

Connolly, Thomas L. *Funeral Oration on the Late Hon. Thos. D'Arcy McGee*. Halifax: Compton and Co., 1868.

Davis, William G. 'Thomas McGee: Irish Founder of the Canadian Nation', in O'Driscoll and Reynolds 453-63.

Fanning, Charles. *The Irish Voice in America: Irish American Fiction from the 1760s to the 1980s*. Lexington: UP of Kentucky, 1990.

Funchion, Michael, ed. *Irish American Voluntary Organizations*. Westeport, Conn.: Greenwood Press, 1993.

Harris, Ruth-Ann M. 'Searching for Missing Friends in the *Boston Pilot* Newspaper, 1831-1863' in **Bielenberg pp?**

Kenny, Kevin. *The American Irish*. Harlow, Essex: Longman/Pearson, 2000.

McGee, Thomas D'Arcy. *Canadian Ballads*. Montreal: Sadlier, 1858. *Catholic History of North America*. Boston: P. Donahoe, 1854.

— *Collection of Speeches and Addresses*. Ed. Charles Murphy. Toronto, 1937.

— *Historical Sketches of O'Connell and His Friends*. Boston, 1844.

— *Irish Writers of the Seventeenth Century*. Dublin: Duffy, 1846.

— *Poems of Thomas D'Arcy McGee*. London, Montreal and Boston: Sadlier, 1869.

McGibbon, R. D. *Thomas D'Arcy McGee: An Address Delivered before the St. Patrick's Society of Sherbrooke, P.Q.* Montreal: Dawson Brothers, 1884.

McGowan, M. G. *The Waning of the Green: Catholics, the Irish, and Identity in Toronto, 1887-1922*. Montreal and Kingston: McGill-Queen's UP, 1999.

Miller, Kerby A. *Emigrants and Exiles: Ireland and the Irish Exodus to North America*. New York and Oxford: Oxford UP, 1985.

O'Broin, Leon. *Fenian Fever: An Anglo-American Dilemma*. New York, 1978.

O'Driscoll, Robert and Lorna Reynolds. *The Untold Story: The Irish in Canada*. 2 vols. Toronto: Celtic Arts of Canada, 1988.

Sadlier, Mary Anne. *The Blakes and the Flanagans*. New York: Sadlier, 1855.

— *The Confederate Chieftains*. New York: Sadlier, 1860.

Senior, Hereward. *The Fenians and Canada*. Toronto, 1978.

— *The Last Invasion of Canada: The Fenian Raids, 1866-1870*. Toronto, 1991.

Skelton, Isabel. *The Life of Thomas D'Arcy McGee*. Gardenvale: Garden City Press, 1925.

Toner, P. *The Rise of Irish Nationalism in Canada 1858-1884*. Galway: National University of Ireland (unpublished), 1974.

From Reformer to Sufferer: The Returning Exile in Rosa Mulholland's Fiction

Heidi Hansson

In literature, the figure of the stranger and the figure of the returning exile can both be used to convey social critique, as they are characters who are able to look with fresh eyes at stale conventions and narrow-minded attitudes. In Irish literature, however, there is a significant difference between the two. The stranger is a central character in the national tale, as exemplified by Lady Morgan's *The Wild Irish Girl* and Maria Edgeworth's *The Absentee* (see e.g. Ferris). In these novels, and others belonging to the same tradition, the stranger is introduced to Ireland and Irish culture and in the course of the tale is made to shed his (more seldom her) preconceptions. The stranger is normally portrayed as only ignorant regarding Ireland, and once he has been educated in the Irish way of life he comes to realise Ireland's superior qualities. The story commonly ends with the stranger's marriage to an Irish girl, and when the stranger is an Englishman, this marital union may frequently be understood as a symbolic parallel to the Union between England and Ireland.

The exile who returns, in contrast, is well acquainted with Irish ways but less willing to accept Ireland's superiority. While the stranger's negative expectations are founded on prejudice, the returning exile's criticism is based on his or her experiences of other countries and other kinds of social organisation. He or she is often described as an instigator of reform, as the character Kerrigan in Jane Barlow's *Kerrigan's Quality* (1892) and *The Founding of Fortunes* (1902) or as the voice of caution, as Colonel O'Driscoll in Emily Lawless's *A Colonel of the Empire* (1895). The

Re-Mapping Exile: Realities and Metaphors in Irish Literature and History, ed. Michael Böss, Irene Gilsenan Nordin and Britta Olinder, *The Dolphin* 34. © 2005 by Aarhus University Press, Denmark. ISBN 87 7934 010 5.

Colonel's words neatly summarise the most common position of
this figure in late nineteenth- and early twentieth-century Irish
fiction:

> [...] to a man like myself, coming back with fresh eyes to the
> country, a stranger, and yet at home, living in the midst of the
> people and neither richer nor of more importance than they,
> though treated – Heaven bless them for it – as if able to make
> them all kings and queens. To such a man – meaning myself –
> it does seem little sort of madness, the foolish talk he has to
> listen to, and the foolish topsy-turvey ideas that get taken up
> by everybody – English or Irish alike – that have anything to
> say to the governing of the country. (75)

The returning exile combines an outsider's view with an insider's
authority and is therefore often used to express critical ideas. The
stranger, on the other hand, is generally shown to finally shed his
or her critical opinions and embrace the initially foreign culture.

The returning exile's special position is a result of his or her
belonging to two (or possibly more) separate places, and since my
discussion is chiefly concerned with the return, I define the places
of both exile and home as fairly stable, geographical locations.
Exile, then, is a three-tiered concept that involves the experience
of dwelling in a place perceived as alien in some respect; the idea
that home is located elsewhere, and the prospect or futile hope of
a return to this lost home-place. My definition proceeds from the
dichotomy between home and exile established in pre-modern
texts such as the Old Testament stories of the Babylonian and
Egyptian exile where the lost home-place is regarded as an
integral part of the subject's identity and the possibility of a return
home – the dream of the Promised Land – is constantly present.
Nevertheless, while I see both home and the place of exile as
geographically permanent, this does not make them ontologically
stable, and since I will focus on the exile's completed return to
home, and not as in the Bible the dream of such a return, the
concepts exile, home and return will all have to be problematized.

In psychoanalytic terms, the original home is the womb and the
original experience of exile is consequently the child's banishment

from the mother's body. This view has a number of ramifications and clearly reveals the gendered nature of the home-exile opposition. The idea of the exile as a coherent subject is mainly a masculine construction, strengthened as such in the Irish context through its connections with High Modernism and famous exiles like James Joyce. Home, on the other hand, is frequently regarded as feminine, and is connected with stability, but also with immobility and stagnation. Exile is going out, home is staying in. The traditional exilic narrative is thus an instance of the hero-myth, as described by Joseph Campbell, and the idea of a woman exile cannot be easily accommodated in this paradigm. Edward Said's terms 'filiation' and 'affiliation' underline how the subject's relationship to place is perceived to have a gendered basis (16-17). Filiation, in Said's definition, is a matter of continuity, as in childbirth and family ties and because of this connected with femininity, whereas affiliation is a matter of choice and entails the kind of activity traditionally seen as masculine. Filiation is a matter of automatic belonging in contrast to the constant negotiations affiliation involves. Though affiliation is perhaps more obviously used about foreign experiences, Said also sees it as the kind of attitude distance creates to the native culture, that is, since the experience of exile severs any automatic link with a place of origin the subject is forced to establish a new, more conscious relationship with home. The picture is blurred when gender is introduced into the equation, however.

The dream of a return is a central element in most stories of exile (as opposed to stories of immigration, for instance) and descriptions of a completed return frequently focus on a triumphant homecoming that commonly involves retribution or the righting of past wrongs. The exile has grown in strength, perhaps in wealth, and is able to come home and be reinstated in his – since this is a predominantly masculine story – rightful place. These ideas are all present in the *Odyssey*, perhaps the most famous of all exile narratives. In his travels, Odysseus is exposed to various adventures where he is forced to use cunning, intelligence and rational thought to escape magical dangers. In the process he frees himself from the grip of myth and tradition as well as from irrational desires, and in Horkheimer's and Adorno's interpretation of the story, this means that he manages to become a modern individual. The classic story of exile thus becomes a tale of modernity. But the return in triumph presupposes that although the exile has changed, home – represented by Penelope in the *Odyssey* – has remained more or less the same. Since a woman is less likely to be the protagonist of the return-in-triumph story, the inclusion of gender again complicates matters and it may be that when women are concerned it would be better to use terms like 'emigrant', 'displacement' or 'diaspora' to describe an existence away from home, since 'exile' seems to imply 'a coherent subject or author and a more circumscribed, limited conception of place and home' (Israel 3). 'Expatriate' is a particularly resonant term in connection with women since it involves the idea of leaving a fatherland, a *patria* that curtails women's opportunities (St. Peter 42).[1] These other terms are less romantic, but they are also less charged with ideas of masculine heroism. In the association between exile and martyrdom, the male subject is more likely to emerge as the hero-martyr while the woman is more often seen as a victim.

Gender theory, then, destabilises the concept of exile in several ways. Mainly, it discloses the highly gendered underpinnings of traditional, romantic ideas surrounding the subject and reveals how the story of exile – as opposed to the experience of exile – has been resolutely masculine. The woman exile, whether fictional or actual, is in limbo, because there are no narrative models to attach to. As Carolyn Heilbrun points out, 'lives do not serve as models, only stories do that. And it is a hard thing to make up stories to live by. We can only retell and live by the stories we have read or heard' (37). The persistent association between masculinity and exile means that women's experiences of exile risk being minimised or even suppressed. Yet the other side of this coin is that the figure of the woman exile has the potential to subvert common perceptions of womanhood precisely because the romantic view of exile is so connected with masculinity. Another effect is that the woman exile foregrounds the exile's status as a hybrid, both in the place of exile and in the event of a return home. From this follows that the woman exile in literature can profitably be used as a vehicle for social critique.

She is both inside and outside her culture, both inside and outside the limitations placed on her gender. It is the hybrid position of the returning woman exile that Rosa Mulholland utilises in some late nineteenth-century and early twentieth-century novels about women who come to Ireland after having lived part of their lives abroad. This enables her to introduce social problems and feminist ideas into to the conventional format of the romantic novel.

Rosa Mulholland (1841-1921) was the daughter of a Belfast physician, and in 1891 she married the historian John Gilbert and moved to Blackrock, Dublin. Her first novel *Dunmara* was published under the pseudonym Ruth Murray in 1864 and some of her early stories and poems appeared in Charles Dickens's *Household Words* and *All the Year Round*. Mainly, however, she was what could be termed a Catholic novelist, associated with Fr. Matthew Russell's journal the *Irish Monthly* which was the primary outlet for Catholic fiction from the last decades of the nineteenth century. Mulholland consequently belonged to the upper middle class and to an intellectual set anxious to create 'a positive image of Ireland within the parameters of Anglo-Saxon culture', as James H. Murphy expresses it (17). The returning exile can apply lessons learned in England or America to Irish culture and habits, and is thus a particularly suitable vehicle for conveying favourable images of Ireland while still remaining within the Anglo-Saxon cultural sphere.

The exile who comes back to Ireland after a period abroad is consequently a prominent character in Mulholland's late nineteenth-century and early twentieth-century novels, though there is a clear development in how this figure is treated in her works. In the early novel *A Fair Emigrant* (1886) the returning exile is a reformer, engaged in philanthropic projects to improve the situation of the poor who are regarded as more or less unable to help themselves. The protagonist belongs to Mulholland's own class and the solution to Ireland's social and economic problems is, in true Victorian manner, seen as charity and reform. As a philanthropist the returning exile remains within the boundaries of acceptable femininity, though the fact that she – as a well-educated middle-class woman – takes active part in organising and running a small industrial project makes her challenge the gender and class rules of the rural environment where she settles. As Margaret Kelleher notes in relation to a Mulholland story about famine, the personal engagement of the philanthropist serves to 'displace political analysis' (925), and this is true also of *A Fair Emigrant*. The novel inspires belief in improvement and progress. Any awareness of structural or political reasons for Ireland's poverty is absent from the work and the remedy Mulholland appears to recommend is to replace the corrupt English landlords with a new paternalistic order of benign, enlightened Catholic landholders. The former exile in *A Fair Emigrant* returns to a country where nothing has changed, and her task is to modernise an old-fashioned society according to principles learnt abroad.

The situation is radically different in the later Mulholland novel *The Return of Mary O'Murrough* (1908). First of all, the protagonist is no longer a middle-class woman, but a peasant, and though she returns after a period as a servant girl in America expecting to find everything unchanged, she has to realise that nothing remains the same. There is no place waiting for her in her old community. An important theme in the novel is the agrarian outrages and although Mulholland apportions blame both to Land League activists and the authorities, the police in particular are described as utterly corrupt. Ireland's problems are shown to have political causes and therefore Mary's experience of life in America does not make her better equipped to deal with the situation, as was the case in the earlier work where good intentions and a modern approach were enough. Mary also returns to a place she has left herself, whereas the protagonist of *A Fair Emigrant* returns to the land of her father, and is a free agent to a greater extent than Mary can be said to be. The main differences between *The Return of Mary O'Murrough* and the earlier novel, however, are the opposite views of the results of exile they impart and the way the hybrid gender roles caused by the exilic experience are presented.

A Fair Emigrant (1886) is the story of how Bawn Desmond goes back to Ireland to clear her father's name from suspicion. Her father Arthur Desmond was a true exile in the romantic manner, and was forced to leave Ireland after being wrongly accused of having murdered a friend. Bawn's experience of exile is thus that although she was born and brought up in America, she has learnt to think of Ireland as the lost homeland that will be available to her only if she can prove her father's innocence. Her attitude to Ireland is the mixture of bitterness and wistfulness characteristic of the exilic narrative, though originally her intention is not to settle in her father's country after her mission is completed, but to go back to America. Through Bawn's circumstances Mulholland shows that the borders between what constitutes 'home' and 'exile' are weakening in the modern world, while she at the same time reinstalls the notion of an original home. Ireland is not Bawn's birthplace, but it is a location that carries the same significance for her as the Promised Land did for the exiled Jews – a place to be reclaimed as 'home' because it is her birthright.

In her outward appearance Bawn is the quintessential romantic heroine, and Mulholland describes her as 'a goddess of the woods', with a 'May-blossom face' and 'shining hair' (12) who moves 'noiselessly' and speaks 'softly' (20). But because of her American background she also represents vitality and independence, and throughout the novel her vigour is contrasted with the degeneration that is slowly destroying both the old Irish families and the country itself. On the boat from America she meets a representative of these old families, the MP Somerled who is later revealed to be Rory Fingall, nephew and namesake of the man Bawn's father allegedly murdered. Like Bawn, Somerled is an advocate of reform and has journeyed to America on an emigrant ship to be able to state in parliament what the conditions are really like. His belief in progress does not extend to women's liberation, however, and when he first contemplates marrying Bawn he pictures her knitting at the fireside, living only for him, safe in his protection. But insisting on autonomy and self-sufficiency Bawn shows that a feminine body does not necessarily produce feminine behaviour and contradicts the ideal her physical self seems to embody:

'Do you not know,' she said, 'that American women go where
they please and do what they have a mind to?'
'I have heard a great deal that I do not like about certain
females of your nation. But I did not expect to see them
looking like you.' (90)

As a consequence of what he regards as Bawn's unsuitable
feminine behaviour, Somerled changes his mind about possibly
marrying her:

> No, he was not going to fall in love with a nameless, secretive,
> obstinate-tempered, wilful woman. His wife must be open as
> the day, transparent in thought, and with all her antecedents
> well known to the world. She must be of a particularly
> yielding and gentle disposition, and have exceedingly little
> will of her own. (86)

His reaction is obviously ironically described, but serves to
underline Bawn's difference from traditional conceptions of
womanhood. For Somerled, this difference can be explained by
her American background, with the implication that his female
ideal is an Irish home-girl. But since Mulholland presents Ireland
as old-fashioned and hidebound in other respects, the Irish model
of femininity is questioned too. Through her hybrid status as a
returning exile, Bawn challenges both gender norms and societal
organisation, and gradually Somerled's initial dislike changes into
grudging admiration: 'What might not such a girl undertake if she
could only get hold of a motive sufficiently lofty and unselfish!'
(100).

   Assuming the name Ingram, Bawn rents a farm in County
Antrim, close to her father's birthplace, and before meeting her,
the people of the area picture her as a monster since she is doing
something so thoroughly unfeminine: 'American females from the
backwoods hardly count as women, major, do they?' (166-67). Her
interest in new farming methods certainly sets her apart from the
middle-class women of the area, but the fact that her concern is
with milk in all its forms – butter-making, creameries, how to get
a good yield of milk – reinforces her femininity by linking her to

products so clearly connected with reproduction. Bawn's femininity is frequently compromised in the eyes of her neighbours, but Mulholland is careful to show that in spite of her self-reliance, she is not an androgynous being, but thoroughly feminine. She is a hybrid in Irish culture, but she does not have a hybrid nature. When Somerled reappears, now under his real name Rory Fingall, he nevertheless comes to the conclusion that Bawn is not woman enough: 'With your practical head and cool heart you are exactly suited to be a man's friend' (244). The independent habits she displays mean that he does no longer regard her as wife material.

Lady Flora Fingall, wife of Rory's cousin Alister, is Bawn's main contrast in the novel and the primary representative of old attitudes, both when social order and gender issues are concerned. She attempts to persuade her young relatives to marry for money to help the family who is in trouble because of the Land War – there have been 'sad doings on Lady Flora's property in the West' (137) – and she thoroughly despises her sister-in-law Shana's fiancé because he has no fortune. She regards women as merchandise, and encourages the visit of a Paris heiress with the intention of getting her to marry Rory. Lady Flora is utterly unable to see beyond her own wishes, and when her sisters-in-law tell her that they do not wish to spend money on ball-dresses for a season in Dublin when 'the country is in such a miserable state' (137) she completely fails to understand why the plight of the cottagers should interfere with the family's enjoyment. She is Mulholland's example of conventional femininity as well as of a bad landlord, absent from her estates in the west and too arrogant to get close to her tenants in Antrim. Unlike Bawn, she does not 'believe in philanthropy and political economy and that sort of thing' but holds with 'people minding their own affairs' (220).

Bawn, on the other hand, regards the dozen girls she employs on her farm as 'part servants and part her pupils' (255). She engages in reform projects, and manages to revolutionise the butter-making industry by building a new dairy on her farm 'upon improved principles never heard of in the glens' (249). It is primarily Bawn's forward-looking attitude Mulholland focuses on, and she continually emphasises the stagnant ways of the

Antrim community by juxtaposing them with Bawn's
modernising zeal. Bawn also seeks out her father's former
sweetheart, Mave Adare, who lives under inhuman conditions in
her dilapidated house. During their first meeting the old woman
tells her: 'You come from America, where everyone is free, and
there are no old families; and you are better without them' (271).
America is presented as 'a very levelling place' (194) where the
hierarchical order of the dying Irish society is absent, and just like
Lady Flora is the representative of the old views, Bawn is the
representative of the new. In a conversation with Rory she voices
the contrast between Irish and American ways:

> 'You are a strange girl.'
> 'Am I? So strange that I do not like waiting calmly to see a
> broken roof drop down upon a fellow creature. I ought to
> have been born in a place like Ireland, in order to take such
> things philosophically. In America we have no such roofs and
> no suffering humanity mouldering away under them
> unheeded. My 'American audacity' – I think that's what I
> heard a lady call it – has prompted me to make a raid upon
> this ruin while it is still accessible; to snatch a poor woman
> from a horrible death.' (316-17)

She decides to break the deadlock of old quarrels, and brings the
destitute old woman to her home to care for her. 'What was
impossible to us may have been made easy to her, being a
stranger' (331) is Rory's grandmother's comment. Bawn's reaction
is humane and rational, whereas tradition has crippled the old
Irish families to the point where they are unable to help a
suffering fellow-being, and once more Mulholland accentuates
the returning exile's freedom from narrow-minded conventions.

Bawn functions as a catalyst for the younger generation, and
her example gives Rory's cousin Shana the confidence to break
away from Lady Flora's demands, marry the man she loves and
leave for New Zealand. For Shana, as for Bawn, mobility is what
leads to change, and it is symptomatic that the new life she
envisions cannot be found in Ireland. Shana becomes an
expatriate, because in Ireland, she would be locked into a

patriarchal system that would deny her the opportunity to make her own choices in life. There is a tension between Bawn's and Shana's stories since Bawn is able to introduce change, whereas Shana is forced to leave. The implication is that mobility is necessary to break deep-rooted patterns, and Shana, as born and bred in Ireland, has to go abroad to escape the burden of past conventions. The old generation is certainly regarded as lost, and the clearest emblem of the devastating effects of pride and inability to change is the ruined Adare house with its 'jagged rents in the boards' and 'gaps bridged over by loose planks or pieces of slate' (266) and its passages 'dripping with damp and choked with rubbish' (267) where Mave Adare and her brother live in squalor, too proud to ask for help. The half-measured attempts at making the house habitable – bridging gaps with loose planks instead of properly repairing them – become further symbols of the difference between old Ireland and new America, indicating that Ireland needs a complete renovation to survive in the modern world.

Nevertheless, Bawn is caught up in the past as long as the shadow on her father's name remains, and therefore her final union with Rory, promised by the romance script from their first meeting on the boat, has to be postponed until the very end when it is revealed by an eyewitness that the alleged murder was an accident. Rather disappointingly from a feminist point of view, Mulholland chooses to let Bawn react to this news by fainting into Rory's arms like a true romantic heroine. In the end, she reverts to the conventional romance formula despite the fact that most of the novel has been concerned with testing its limits through the freedom from convention embodied in the returning exile. Feminist theory has highlighted the interrelations of gender and genre, and as a writer of romance Mulholland was caught up in both genre and gender conventions. Her works frequently exemplify the strategies of negotiation employed by women writers who wished to convey social critique and the idea of female autonomy, yet could not afford to unambiguously defy the rules of the society they belonged to. Her reputation as a wholesome writer whose novels could be safely chosen as school prizes and given to young girls is probably an important reason why she seems to accept a traditional gender order at the end of the novel. A subplot in the novel where she describes how Shana sets out to write a historical tale about her ancestors, but comes to the conclusion that stories 'that get published are generally chiefly about marriages' and 'the publishers won't allow us to strike out a new line' (131) suggests that Mulholland was well aware of what was expected from a woman writer. The exilic narrative that she flirts with in *A Fair Emigrant* may be the basis for a male coming-of-age story, but the female Bildungsroman is the romance. Despite the conventional ending, however, the figure of the returning exile is clearly used to expose the prejudice and stagnant life of the Irish upper class and to interrogate gender imbalance and social hierarchy.

A Fair Emigrant is organised through the dualities mobility – immobility, progress – stagnation, vitality – death and old – new. America as the place of exile and Ireland as 'home' represent either end of the spectrum and their meanings are quite fixed. The ability to move between places is presented as unconditionally positive and though Ireland is severely criticised as backward and stagnant, the novel primarily paints a utopian picture where the country only needs the clear-sightedness of the returning exile to prosper. Bawn is a representative of progress and modernity, and Rory's position as an MP indicates that Mulholland believes in reform through parliamentary work, within Unionist principles. To some extent, the continuous emphasis on Ireland as old and America as new can be understood as a reaction against the antiquarian spirit permeating nationalist thought at the time (see e.g. Eagleton). There is no sentimentality in Bawn's emotional repertoire, and no sense in the novel that something is about to be lost in the modernisation process. *The Return of Mary O'Murrough* (1908) conveys a much bleaker image. Mobility is no longer unquestionably beneficial, America and Ireland are both depicted as places where changes occur and the returning exile is displaced and initially incapacitated in her old culture.

The Return of Mary O'Murrough opens with a beautiful description of the green district of Killelagh, 'a place of pastures, blue mountainy distances, swift-sailing clouds dropping rain in the very face of the sun' (1) and continues with the information

that 'some years ago' there used to be dancing at the cross-roads
(2). The first pages conjure up a happy, moderately prosperous
village characterised by a strong sense of community, but also
locates this place in the past. This is the place that Mary left for
America. According to Janet Nolan, emigration patterns from
Ireland in the period 1885-1920 are unique in that more women
than men left Ireland for a life elsewhere and that more women
emigrated on their own than was the case of any other European
country (2). One reason, Nolan suggests, was that agricultural
prosperity after the Famine depended on depopulation rather
than modernisation and change, which meant that fewer women
could hope to marry. Since there was no expansion of other
opportunities for women, their only choice was emigration
(Nolan 9). Those who wished to remain in Ireland or return had
to adapt to a situation where romantic attachment was no longer
enough as the basis for marriage but where the size of her dowry
determined the prospective bride's eligibility (33). Some
Irishwomen consequently left for a period to make enough money
to be able to come home and marry. Though the 'dowry theory' of
women's emigration has been severely criticised since it
presupposes marriage as women's sole aspiration and denies the
possibility that women might have left Ireland to escape the
confines of a patriarchal society (St. Peter 47).[2] Mulholland's
Mary O'Murrough is described as a woman whose reason for
going to America is to earn money for her dowry.

Mary consequently leaves with the express purpose of
returning. For her, Ireland remains 'home' and when she finally
returns every feature of the landscape is familiar and looks right
(120). But 'home' is also a matter of security, intimacy and
belonging, and Mary's American experience has changed her so
that nobody recognises her. She spends the first night in an inn
run by an old school-friend who believes her to be an older
relative of the long-gone Mary since this now half-mythical
person 'wasn't a bit like you, any way, except that you have
somethin' of the blue in the eyes' (118-19). Paradoxically, Mary's
exile begins when she comes home, because it is only then that
she realises that she has lost her home. Through the story of
Mary's homecoming, Mulholland destabilises the idea of 'home'

and robs it of its nostalgic connotations, forcing a reconsideration of its overtones of primordial identity.

The sense that exile truly begins at the moment of coming home is strengthened when Mary first meets her fiancé Shan Sullivan again. Shan has been sent to prison, wrongly accused of maiming a neighbour's cattle and is bitter and resentful. When Mary comes to see him he fails to recognize her:

> Shan was staring over her head, and away beyond her at the distance, across the years, looking at the vivid picture never obliterated, never faded by a line or a tint, of a face that had been the companion of his fidelity, a countenance rounded in loveliness, blue eyes running over with laughter, dimpled cheeks the colour of the wild hedge-roses. That was Mary O'Murrough who went from him, and he had been told she had come back to him. Who was this woman weeping before him, who had taken her name and was claiming her identity? (157)

Shan's love has been kept alive by the memory of Mary's beauty, and when she returns from America, plain and worn, he cannot accept her as the same woman. For him, Mary's identity is defined by a beautiful face – she is nothing but surface. Through the theme of Mary's lost beauty Mulholland challenges the view that women should be decorative, at the same time as she problematizes the common connections in nineteenth-century literature between beauty and goodness, ugliness and evil, body and character. She also presents a much more negative view of emigration than the one found in *A Fair Emigrant*, where mobility is connected to freedom and self-definition. In *The Return of Mary O'Murrough* emigration is seen as an economic necessity that deprives Ireland as well as the individual emigrant of youth and beauty. When Shan finally accepts that it is indeed Mary who has come back to him he exclaims: 'But oh, Mary, Mary, what did they do to y' over there' (159). Exile is no longer linked with opportunity and a necessary modernisation, but with abuse and the destruction of the old world and its values: 'the big emigration is puttin' sentence o' death on the ould Irish race. Where's the childher to come from, I wondher? When was here a young woman's weddin' in Killelagh?' (206).

The idea that emigration deprives Ireland of its future is reinforced through the story of Bess Dermody and Miles Donohoe, the only young people to marry in the novel. But Bess's mother withholds her consent because Miles does not have any land, and the young couple leave for America. Bess's letters to Mary are happy and full of descriptions of her children, but the narrator comments:

> But they are American boys and girls, and there is little hope of the longed-for return of the father and mother to Killelagh. Work is constant and exacting, and old age comes on quickly in a land that pays freely, but will have youth and unimpaired energy in ample return for its generous wage! (281)

Mary, on the other hand, has been left barren after a stillbirth and at the end of the novel there are no children at all around the village. Through her sterility, Mary becomes a radically different symbol of Mother Ireland, an image of the country that is being bled by emigration. In contrast to the belief in parliamentary reform expressed in *A Fair Emigrant*, the authorities, as represented by the police, are described as utterly corrupt and Home Rule is seen as a futile dream – 'in the distance still' (114). There is no outlet for people's frustration, only disillusion and lack of hope. As one character expresses it: 'I was in the Fenians myself. I was always in wan thing or another. But there's nothin' to be in now' (203).

Mulholland's treatment of the figure of the returning exile can be linked to both Irish political developments of the period and a changing attitude towards modernity. 'Home' in *A Fair Emigrant* is firmly located within the British Union and the characteristics of English industrialised society where Ireland is constructed as 'behind', whereas in *The Return of Mary O'Murrough*, 'home' is the hope of Home Rule where Ireland is separate and need not be seen within an English paradigm, though this is also presented as only a distant hope. The concepts 'home' and 'exile' in the works can be compared with nostalgia and modernity, and when the prevailing attitude is that modernisation is a positive development, exile is connected to the escape from a claustrophobic home, as illustrated by Shana's story in *A Fair Emigrant*, but when the overall sense is that modernisation leads to the loss of important values, exile becomes yet another factor contributing to the destruction, as in *The Return of Mary O'Murrough*. As the Swedish historian Karin Johannisson points out, nostalgia is a symptom of a collapse of the belief in the future (9) and therefore the feeling has no currency during periods when progress is perceived as beneficial but becomes very important when the future seems uncertain. It seems obvious that Mulholland is much more pessimistic about Ireland's future in 1908, when *The Return of Mary O'Murrough* was published than she was at the time of the publication of *A Fair Emigrant* in 1886.

An important difference between the novels is their attitude to women's place in national life. As returning exiles, both Bawn in *A Fair Emigrant* and Mary in *The Return of Mary O'Murrough* are bearers of cultural critique, but in directly opposite ways. Through Bawn, Mulholland boldly introduces women into the grand narrative of modernity by making a woman the protagonist of a traditionally masculine story. This is a powerful feminist gesture and a strong support of female autonomy, despite the conventionally romantic ending. The novel exudes optimism since social ills are described in individual terms and can be remedied by charitable acts, which means that women are perceived to have a real opportunity to influence the future of the country. The novel's critique centres on Ireland's social and cultural backwardness, and because of her hybrid position as a woman occupying the centre of a male story and her ability to effect change, Bawn becomes a hero of modernity. Mary O'Murrough, in contrast, is modernity's victim. In *The Return of Mary O'Murrough*, Ireland's problems are shown to have structural causes, and as a result, the solution is seen as much farther away, and the power of a woman to effect real change is seen as virtually non-existent. The belief in gender equality present in the early novel is replaced by a scathing criticism of the tendency to define women through their bodies in the latter work, and Mary's lost beauty and sterility become symbols not only of the price women have to pay in the modern world, but also of failed feminist hopes. While Bawn is a hybrid because she encroaches on traditionally male territory, Mary is a hybrid because she cannot fulfil her society's expectations of becoming a mother. The function of the returning exile in these novels is thus tied up with the view of modernity and gender expressed in the works. In both novels the returning exile to some extent stands for redemption, but the buoyant atmosphere of the early work is replaced by a representation of redemption as vicarious suffering in the later novel.

Acknowledgement

The research for this article was made possible by a grant from the Helge Ax:son Johnson Foundation, for which I wish to express my sincere gratitude.

Notes

[1] Christine St. Peter suggests that many present-day women writers focus on the necessity of going into exile to escape a patriarchal society or describe the experience of exile within Ireland as an effect of the country's patriarchal heritage.

[2] St. Peter bases her discussion on a study of oral histories of emigration by Grace Neville.

References

Barlow, Jane. *Kerrigan's Quality.* 1892.

— *The Founding of Fortunes.* 1902.

Campbell, Joseph. *The Hero With a Thousand Faces.* 1949. London: Paladin, 1988.

Eagleton, Terry. *Scholars and Rebels in Nineteenth-Century Ireland.* Oxford: Blackwell, 1999.

Ferris, Ina. 'Narrating Cultural Encounter: Lady Morgan and the Irish National Tale'. *Nineteenth-Century Literature* 51.3 (1996): 287-303.

Heilbrun, Carolyn G. *Writing a Woman's Life.* 1988. London: Women's P, 1989.

Horkheimer, Max and Theodor W. Adorno. *Dialectic of Enlightenment*. 1944. Trans. John Cumming. New York: Continuum, 1994.

Israel, Nico. *Outlandish: Writing between Exile and Diaspora*. Stanford: Stanford UP, 2000.

Johannisson, Karin. *Nostalgia. En känslas historia*. [Nostalgia: the History of an Emotion]. Stockholm: Bonnier, 2001.

Kelleher, Margaret. 'Women's Fiction, 1845-1900'. *The Field Day Anthology of Irish Writing: Women's Writing and Traditions*. Vol. 5. Cork: Cork UP, 2002. 924-29.

Lawless, Emily. *A Colonel of the Empire: From the Private Papers of Mangan O'Driscoll, Late of the Imperial Service of Austria, and a Knight of the Military Order of Maria Theresa*. New York: Appleton, 1895.

Mulholland, Rosa. *A Fair Emigrant*. Dublin: M. H. Gill and Son, 1886.

— *Dunmara*. 1864. (Published under the pen name of Ruth Murray.)

— *The Return of Mary O'Murrough*. Dublin: Phoenix, 1908.

Murphy, James H. *Catholic Fiction and Social Reality in Ireland, 1873-1922*. Westport, Conn.: Greenwood P, 1997.

Nolan, Janet. *Ourselves Alone: Women's Emigration from Ireland 1885-1920*. Lexington KY: UP of Kentucky, 1989.

Said, Edward W. *The World, the Text, and the Critic*. 1984. London: Vintage, 1991.

St. Peter, Christine. *Changing Ireland: Strategies in Contemporary Women's Fiction*. Houndmills: Macmillan, 2000.

(Dis)Location and Its (Dis)Contents: Translation as Exile in James Joyce's *A Portrait of the Artist as a Young Man* and *Finnegans Wake*

Ida Klitgård

Now the whole earth had one language and few words. And as men migrated from the east, they found a plain in the land of Shinar and settled there. And they said to one another, 'Come, let us make bricks, and burn them thoroughly'. And they had brick for stone, and bitumen for mortar. Then they said, 'Come, let us build ourselves a city, and a tower with its top in the heavens, and let us make a name for ourselves, lest we be scattered abroad upon the face of the whole earth'. And the Lord came down to see the city and the tower, which the sons of men had built. And the Lord said, 'Behold, they are one people, and they have all one language; and this is only the beginning of what they will do; and nothing that they propose to do will now be impossible for them. Come, let us go down, and there confuse their language, that they may not understand one another's speech'. So the Lord scattered them abroad from there over the face of all the earth, and they left off building the city. Therefore its name was called Babel, because there the Lord confused the language of all the earth; and from there the Lord scattered them abroad over the face of all the earth.

Genesis 11:1-9 (Revised Standard Edition)

Translatentic norjankeltian
James Joyce, *Finnegans Wake* (311.21-22)

Re-Mapping Exile: Realities and Metaphors in Irish Literature and History, ed. Michael Böss, Irene Gilsenan Nordin and Britta Olinder, *The Dolphin* 34. © 2005 by Aarhus University Press, Denmark. ISBN 87 7934 010 5.

Introduction

In Brian Friel's play *Translations* (1981), the myth of the falling of
the Tower of Babel is evoked through the English demolition of
the Irish language and identity in 1833. In the first act, the hedge-
school in an Irish-speaking community in County Donegal is
presented as a prelapsarian Babel of harmony between language
and identity. With the recently arrived Royal Engineers' First
Ordnance Survey, every single local Gaelic place name suddenly
has to be recorded and renamed into English. The fall of Babel is
inevitable. The Anglicized expatriate Owen, the hedge-school
master Hugh's 'lost' son, returns to Ireland as cartographer and
mediator between the locals and the English intruders. With a
gigantic map spread out before him on the floor he says fervently:
'We are trying to denominate and at the same time describe that
tiny area of soggy, rocky, sandy ground where the little stream
enters the sea, an area known locally as Bun na hAbhann...
Burnfoot! What about Burnfoot?' (35) This feeble and absurd
translation is symptomatic of the growing English disrespect,
however romantic it becomes during the play, for Ireland's
original cultural autonomy. The play examines the devastating
effects of this culturally postlapsarian 'exile' on the lives of the
local inhabitants. One effect is the confusion of having to find a
new voice in the translation between two tongues: 'English', says
Hugh, 'couldn't really express us' (25). This problem is everwhere
imperative in the works of James Joyce, too. Especially in his
representations of the Irish artist-hero. In the present essay I have
chosen to analyse the establishment of Joyce's early rebellious
ideas about this cultural dilemma in his first novel, *A Portrait of
the Artist as a Young Man* (1916) and the ultimate stylistic
expression of these ideas in his last novel, *Finnegans Wake* (1939),
thus covering the span of artistic development in Joyce's *oeuvre*.

Since the translation theorist George Steiner's seminal work
After Babel: Aspects of Language and Translation (1975), the myth of
the Tower of Babel has almost become a travesty in modern
translation studies. According to the Old Testament, man's
overweening plan of building a tower that could reach into God's
Kingdom was overthrown as God deprived human beings of their
common, universal tongue by condemning them to the confusion

of multiple languages and by sending them into exile in all corners of the world. The myth raises a number of linguistic and philosophical questions: Was there, originally, only one language? And is our present-day linguistic multiplicity, then, a state of perpetual exile from the homeland of Edenic linguistic oneness? The myth has inspired several modern philosophers and writers, such as Derrida and Walter Benjamin, Franz Kafka in his story 'Das Stadtwappen', Jorge Luis Borges in his postmodern philosophical fabulations, and James Joyce throughout his works, reaching its multilingual peak in *Finnegans Wake*. In the present study, I am going to argue that translation to Joyce is a kind of cultural and linguistic exile, not only between Irish and English, but across all languages. But first, let me explain the premises on which this argument is based.

Exile is defined as a physically long stay away from one's country or home – from choice or from force. The reason behind exile is often a non-acceptance of the administration or moral habitus in the home country, and thus the notion of exile is often linked with the hope of returning when things have changed for the better. During the exile, the person may feel either divided between two cultures, two languages, or feel as a hybrid, as an 'Exilian'. As Salman Rushdie puts it about the imam in *The Satanic Verses*, echoing Stephen Dedalus' 'silence, exile and cunning' in James Joyce's *A Portrait of the Artist as a Young Man:*

> Who is he? An exile. Which must not be confused with, allowed to run into, all the other words that people throw around: émigré, expatriate, refugee, immigrant, silence, cunning. Exile is a dream of glorious return. Exile is a vision of revolutions. Elba, not St Helena. It is an endless paradox: looking forward by always looking back. The exile is a ball hurled high into the air. He hangs there, frozen in time, translated into a photograph; denied motion, suspended impossibly above his native earth, he awaits the inevitable moment at which the photograph must begin to move, and the earth reclaim its own. (Rushdie 211-12)

When translating a work of literature, i.e. transferring its body and soul from one language community to another, we may say, metaphorically that that literary work is also sent into exile. The work travels to foreign parts of the world, is either welcomed or rejected by their inhabitants, and settles there in different robes in order to transcend into strange cultures, whether it be well received or not. In this essay I argue that, culturally, translation is not a *substitution* of the target language (TL) meanings for the source language (SL) meanings, as the translation theorist J. C. Catford proposed in the seminal work *A Linguistic Theory of Translation* (1965), but a *transference* of the source language *into* the target language.[1] And, on a textual level, the translation process is not *only* a metaphorical praxis of selection and substitution, which has been the predominant mode of optics in traditional translation studies, breeding narrow binarisms such as *literal/free* translation and *formal/dynamic* translation. The translation process is most certainly also a fabric of metonymical contiguities, connections and contextures. With a view to the understanding we have of intertextuality, both the source work and the translated work must be perceived as rewritings in which the SL text and the TL text interact. [2] It is my contention that literary translation is a metonymically intercultural hybrid – just as hybrid words formed from a stem or word in one language plus a suffix or prefix in another. For instance *television* (Greek and Latin) and *gullible* (English and Latin).

   The idea that any work of art is an instance of exile goes as far back as Monroe C. Beardsley and W. K. Wimsatt's New Critical point of view that for instance a poem 'is not the critic's own and not the author's (it is detached from the author at birth and goes about the world beyond his power to intend about it and control it). The poem belongs to the public. It is embodied in language, the peculiar possession of the public, and it is about the human being, an object of public knowledge' (5). If we, tongue in cheek, interpret 'about the world' literally, the theory of the intentional fallacy may be regarded (however unintentionally) as an instance of the idea that when a writer has finished his work, he must part with it and watch it embark on multicultural adventures, out of his reach. The very translation of this work in remote parts of the world, then, is the ultimate 'defamiliarisation' between writer and work – the ultimate cutting of the umbilical cord.

In extension to New Criticism, this notion is also supported by the American deconstructionist critic J. Hillis Miller who proposes that 'Translation is the wandering existence of a text in perpetual exile'.[3] In his essay 'Translation and literary history - an Indian view', the postcolonial critic Ganesh Devy regards this statement as a typical Western expression of the Christian myth of the Fall, exile and wandering, 'a post-Babel crisis' (182). Thus, in the Western tradition a translation will always be regarded as having a secondary status in the shadow of the *original work*.

This essay suggests that one great Irish modernist writer, i.e. James Joyce, an exile himself, possessed a similar conception about the ability of language and art to travel, and about the ability of national literature to be adopted in an international context. Both through his fiction and through his own work with translation, James Joyce expresses a pronounced trust in language to roam and mingle with foreign influences. Joyce's 'theory' of translation, as it is expressed in the thematics of *A Portrait* and in the poetics of *Finnegans Wake*, does not delimit translation to be a matter of linguistic and cultural substitution only, but cultivates the metonymic, intertextual nature of translation *par excellence*. To Joyce, the original work is not a Holy Grail, to use another Christian metaphor, which will bestow on us the glorious light of bygone days before the Fall, as it were, but is always already (to use familiar jargon) suffused with foreign influences. In extension, translation proper is a cultural *transference* of one kind of multilingualism into another: an 'Exilian' hybridity, or *crossover*, of influences.

J. Hillis Miller's comparison of the Christian myth of the Fall, exile and wandering with translation's eternal search for the essence of the original word is not up James Joyce's alley. In contrast, his contention of translation as exile is as a resurrection of the Tower of Babel exactly *through* the very chaotic and protean polyglot hybridity of the modern urban environment, such as Dublin, which, in the end, becomes a literary representation of the entire world itself.

Exile in Literature

To James Joyce, Dublin represented narrow-minded provincialism and *bourgeois* moral paralysis. The Dubliners' refusal to remove their Victorian blinkers and their inability either to move or to *be* moved, physically as well as emotionally, which is most painfully expressed in the story 'Eveline' in *Dubliners*, drove Joyce into self-exile as he left for studies in Paris in 1902. After having briefly returned, he left Ireland for good, applauded by the citizens in Dublin, and moved like a wandering exile between various cultural centres of Europe, such as Trieste, Zürich and Paris. In exile he wrote three of his four masterpieces, *Dubliners, Ulysses* and *Finnegans Wake*. All of them dealt with Dublin. The (dis)location of exile gave him a stronger, though hardly more distanced, sense of home. In spite of the artistic freedom exercised in the alien Continental locations, Joyce's scrupulous fingernail-paring project became increasingly immersed in highly subjective memories, fantasies and yarns of home. In other words, the foreign dislocations never became a substitute for his home location, but an existential extension to and creative re-writing of it to the degree that it became an allegorical emblem of 'the world' across time and space. *Ulysses*, we may suggest, is the first modern 'book of the world' since the ancient Sanskrit literature. It is a gathering of knowledge of the global village like none other.

Even though modern man generally no longer thinks of the kingdom of God as our home, in the way that a return to God is a return to a spiritual, essentialist state of identity before the Fall, the sense of home as a source of identity or cultural heritage, indeed as 'a goal of all voyages of self-discovery', has not diminished in 20th century literature according to Andrew Gurr in his book on *Writers in Exile: The Identity of Home in Modern Literature* (13). The modern creative writer is *per se* a writer in exile: 'He is a lone traveller in the countries of the mind, always threatened by hostile natives' (13). Thus, T. S. Eliot returned to ancient mythos, D. H. Lawrence cried for a resurrection of Pan and Joseph Conrad went on a voyage to the heart of darkness in order to find a base for identity.

However, taken together, separation and alienation also foster a new being. In *Speak, Memory,* Vladimir Nabokov acknowledges the tantalising enchantment of the defamiliarisation of exile. The 'break in my own destiny affords me in retrospect a syncopal kick that I would not have missed for worlds' (250). As with Joyce, Nabokov's perception of exile as that of a musical syncope makes him in the long run extracognizant of home and national identity enabling him to write narratives of Russia.

In his study, *Exile and the Narrative Imagination,* Michael Seidel perceives exile not only as a state of creative defamiliarization, but as a symptomatic metaphor for the general state of the narrative imagination and as a material resource for legend, literature and history in the West:

> The exilic projection is originary, whether the Tartarian and Luciferian expulsions, the trek east from Eden, the sagas of Io and Europa, the flight of Daedalus, the exposure of Oedipus, the voyage of the Argonauts, the Exodus, Captivity, and Diaspora of the Jews, the wanderings of Odysseus, the displacement of Aeneas, the trials of the prodigal son, the medieval and gothic myths of the Wandering Jew, the journey of Dante the pilgrim, the outlawry of El Cid, the 'fugitive' fable of the castaway Robinison Crusoe, the river odyssey of Huck Finn, even the intercontinental trauma of Tarzan and the intergalactic adventure of Superman. In the exilic plot the extraneous becomes foundational, the blighted and ill-fated from one sphere become instigators and originators in another. The powers of exilic imagining represent desired territory, lost or found, as narrative fate. (8)

Seidel's sweeping list of examples, to which could be added the myth of the Tower of Babel, leads him to conclude that exile serves narrative as an initiating and supplementing action, and thus it also serves as a figure for allegory itself (13). The record of exile in narrative is an 'alien voicing', which is what the word allegory in fact means etymologically (*al*, 'other'; *goria*, 'voicing'). Allegory, and by implication exile, then, are both representations of an alien voicing of something familiar.

If we take this theoretical argumentation a step further, to stay on the route of this essay's thesis, it may make more sense to us as to how exile can serve as a figure for translation, too. As translation is also an alien voicing of something familiar, at least to the SL users, the concepts of exile, allegory and translation all denote, metaphorically, the particular imaginary and verbal activity of the mind to carry out a *transference* of the familiar into the unfamiliar 'desired territory' – *without* losing sight of the familiar. 'Are we translators, psychologically speaking, all in-betweens, all exiles?' asks Walter Redfern in his essay 'Traduction, Puns, Clichés, Plagiat', in which he switches between English and French to prove this point (262). And he adds: 'When we straddle two languages, we develop an alien eye, a binary perspective (or strabismus), a foreign ear' (262). Like Rushdie's exiled imam, translators are 'looking forwards by always looking back'.

A Poetics of Translation

In his essay on 'Ireland and Switzerland: The Cases of James Joyce and Fritz Senn' (1987), the critic John Paul Riquelme argues that Joyce's life-long project in creating a new artistic language takes its starting-point in the recognition that English was a foreign language, to him and to the Irish in general. Having studied while in Ireland Latin, French, Italian, Dano-Norwegian and German, at school, at the university as well as on his own (including taking Danish lessons in Rome!), Joyce's linguistic awareness gradually reveals to him that there is a major difference between the King's English and English as the Irish speak it, and yet another difference between these uses of English and Irish, i.e. Gaelic. English is in principle not his own language. It has, as in Brian Friel's play *Translations*, been imposed on him and his fellow Irishmen through a long history of colonization.

This recognition participated in forcing Joyce to go into exile, a most unusual expatriation all over the Continent. Here Joyce became increasingly influenced by the polyglot milieus in Pola, Trieste, Zürich and eventually Paris where he was confronted with a variety of languages and accents such as Serbian, Greek, Austrian, Swiss-German, Hungarian and the Triestine dialect.

One way of learning new languages was for instance by exchanging language lessons with his colleagues at the Berlitz School in Zürich where Joyce taught English.

In his work on the language of travel writing entitled *Across the Lines: Travel, Language, Translation,* Michael Cronin narrates an anecdotal, but in this case relevant, story about Joyce's fascination with languages in Zürich:

> Joyce never missed his rendez-vous at half-seven each evening in the railway station in Zürich. His appointment was with the Orient Express. When the train came to a halt, Joyce rushed to inspect signs in French, German and Serbo-Croat on the side of the train. His sight an uncertain ally, he often traced the outlines of the letters with his long, sensitive fingers. Joyce asked Eugène Jolas questions about people getting on and off the train and scanned the languages he overheard for dialectical differences. For Joyce, travel was language in motion. The train brought its freight of languages and cultures to the Zürich station and, for ten minutes, he remained absorbed in the manifold possibilities of 'transluding from the Otherman'. (98)

'In this unusual, and transient, atmosphere, Joyce's transformation of English prose style became possible', says Riquelme. And further, 'it should be no surprise that a writer with his cultural and educational background could develop a sense of language usage and a practice of style that are comparable to those of the translator, even when he is writing in what is ostensibly his native language' (111). In other words, Joyce's prose style is that of a polyglot translator. In *Nomadic Subjects: Embodiment and Sexual Difference in Contemporary Feminist Theory,* Rosa Braidotti's characterisation of a nomadic polyglot artist may very well fit James Joyce:

> The nomadic polyglot practices an aesthetic style based on compassion for the incongruitites, the repetitions, the arbitrariness of the language s/he deals with. Writing is, for the polyglot, a process of undoing the illusory stability of

fixed identities, bursting open the bubble of ontological
security that comes from familiarity with one linguistic site.
The polyglot exposes this false security. (15)

The nomadic polyglot's linguistic and cultural identity is situated
in a hybrid border zone between languages giving him/her
insight into the heterogeneity of any one culture.

After having thus been exposed to multiple languages, and
having tried translating a number of texts himself, Joyce became
utterly dissatisfied with the inadequacy of his ostensibly native
language.[4] When Vela and Olga Bliznakoff, two of Joyce's
language students, asked him 'Aren't there enough words for you
in English?' (in *Ulysses*), he replied, 'Yes, there are enough, but
they aren't the right ones' (Ellmann 397). Joyce had to make
neologisms: 'For example, take the word *battlefield*. A battlefield is
a field where the battle is raging. When the battle is over and the
field is covered with blood, it is no longer a *battlefield*, but a
bloodfield' (Ellmann 397). And to a friend, Joyce said: 'I'd like a
language which is above all languages, a language to which all
will do service. I cannot express myself in English without
enclosing myself in a tradition' (Ellmann 397).

At first, this notion may smack of an ethnocentric
debabelization of artistic discourse. It expresses the demand for a
superior language, perhaps a universal language that will restore
the project of the Tower of Babel. As quoted at the beginning of
this essay, God said unto the builders of the Tower of Babel: 'they
have all one language; and this is only the beginning of what they
will do; and nothing that they propose to do will now be
impossible for them'. Likewise, there would be no limits to what
Joyce proposed to do had he but one sublime language that
would transcend all others. This would enable him with a
transpositon of new detached thought. However, what Joyce had
in mind was not a wiping out of other languages, as with the
English extinction of the native Irish, or indeed as with God's
extinction of the Babelians' native language, but, as we shall see in
the literary analyses below, a transformational absorption of a
plurality of languages in an intercultural, synthetic language of
historical-universal significance.

As Joyce felt nowhere at home in any *one* language, such a hybrid language would provide him with a transcendent simultaneous travel in space, through geographical scattering, and in time, through the various overlapping uses of languages in history. This ideal artistic language would provide him with a new outlandish land, as it were, of multilingual translation, allowing his readers to join him in his exilic wanderings. 'You have to be in exile to understand me,' he once said knowingly to the Danish writer Tom Kristensen (Ellmann 693).[5]

Silence, exile, cunning: *A Portrait of the Artist as a Young Man*

In *A Portrait of the Artist as a Young Man*, the programmatic apothegm of the young artist Stephen Dedalus' desire to express himself as freely and wholly as possible is 'silence, exile, and cunning' (269). He will no longer serve - *non serviam* - that in which he no longer believes, whether it be his home, fatherland or church. As both a fictional *Künstlerroman* and personal *roman à clef* the novel lays bare the modernist artist's revolt against the trammels of Irish society.

Besides the well-known themes of the clashes between Stephen and his family, church and friends, one recurrent theme is Stephen's growing awareness of the meanings and functions of language. Throughout the novel, Stephen exiles himself increasingly from the oppression of Englishness and sublimates himself, as a genuine romantic artist-hero, to be the creator of the true expressiveness of the Irish: 'Welcome, O life! I go to encounter for the millionth time the reality of experience and to forge in the smithy of my soul the uncreated conscience of my race' (276). This ambition is also reflected in the narrative technique of the novel, moving from the impersonal third-person narrator to a highly fragmentary and free indirect first-person narrative style, replacing the language of others with Stephen's own. The novel ends with a new beginning, or rebirth, that serves both as a concrete and a symbolic embarkation on a life-long voyage of artistic creativity.

Stephen's experiences of language and culture manifest themselves mainly on three levels: in the revelation of English as a language of oppression, in the revelation of language as flexible, sensuous and otherwise capable of assuming ever new forms, for example in story-telling, and the revelation of the fact that the world has more languages to offer his talent than English and that he must strive to release in his own language the essence of all such languages. Thus he will grasp the living 'uncreated conscience' of his race.

This series of revelations is intertwined with classical myths of falling, exile and wandering as metaphors of both creative defamiliarization and a general narrative imagination. Stephen for instance enacts, figuratively speaking, the Cretan father-son conflict between Daedalus and Icaros in the labyrinthine Dublin, as Stephen will no longer listen to his father(land) and flies high on his wings of inspiration. His fall becomes a flight of freedom and is yet more intertwined with the Latin myth of the cunning rebel angel Lucifer who would not serve God and consequently fell from grace and was exiled from heaven. Analogously, Stephen's revelations serve as a fall from traditional Irish grace (the hypocritically religious meanings of which Joyce hilariously mocked in the story 'Grace' in *Dubliners*), his new path of a free, 'Soulfree and fancyfree' (270) and defamiliarized narrative imagination is his exile, and the wanderings are yet to be fully explored in the succeeding novel *Ulysses*.

To borrow a phrase from Brian Friel's *Translations*, 'English doesn't really express' the budding artist Stephen. At university, Stephen stumbles on the Dean, an English convert to Catholicism, as the Dean is lighting a fire. The Dean explains to Stephen that he must be careful when he pours oil on a lamp through its 'funnel'. Stephen does not recognize this word: 'Is that called a funnel? Is it not a tundish?' 'What is a tundish', asks the Dean. 'Is that called a tundish in Ireland? [...] I never heard that word in my life'. Stephen replies that that is the word they use in the Dublin suburb of Lower Drumcondra – 'where they speak the best English', he adds laughingly. But the whole incident embitters and enrages Stephen in this much-quoted passage:

> The language in which we are speaking is his before it is mine. How different are the words *home, Christ, ale, master*, on his lips and on mine! I cannot speak or write these words

without unrest of spirit. His language, so familiar and so foreign, will always be for me an acquired speech. I have not made or accepted its words. My voice holds them at bay. My soul frets in the shadow of his language. (205)

Later, in his diary, Stephen expresses an acute confusion as to what is English and what is Irish: 'That tundish had been on my mind for a long time. I looked it up and find it English and good old blunt English too. Damn the dean of studies and his funnel! What did he come here for to teach us his own language or to learn it from us?' (274).

Consequently, Stephen no longer acknowledges the borrowed robes of his oppressors' language. In a discussion with his friend Davin, Stephen refuses to sell his Irish soul to the English: 'My ancestors threw off their language and took another [...] They allowed a handful of foreigners to subject them. Do you fancy I am going to pay in my own life and person debts they made? What for?' (220). Stephen chooses to listen to the voice of his own soul which of course has not yet matured at this stage of cunning youth: 'It [the soul] has a slow and dark birth, more mysterious than the birth of the body. When the soul of a man is born in this country there are nets flung at it to hold it back from flight. You talk to me of nationality, language, religion. I shall try to fly by those nets [...] Ireland is the old sow that eats her farrow' (220).

To Stephen, true Irish conscience is only waiting to take off and be steered away from the enclosing traps of English tradition. And *he* is going to be the ultimate redeemer. But, paradoxically, not by cleansing his language of English influence in order to get to the roots of his race. As Michael Seidel has noted in his chapter on *A Portrait* in *Exile and the Narrative Imagination*, the little word *by* in 'fly by those nets' means both 'with' and 'past', implying that Stephen will in fact use the language at hand as a tool to perform his revenge on English colonization and Irish cowardice (87). Stephen aims to shatter ordinary, straightforward English. This is, as earlier mentioned, for instance done in the narrative style that, towards the end of the novel, changes into a disruptive first-person voicing. His outlook on the identity of his language as disjointed becomes increasingly global, too, as he dreams of transcending the barriers of his language by both transferring it to a new world far away from Ireland (analogous with *fly with*) and substituting it with a new language (analogous with *fly past*). This strategy echoes the fabric of the metaphorical and metonymical interaction of SL and TL in the process of translation, as explained at the beginning of this essay.

Such drastic measures are in the novel heralded through the maturing Stephen's growing fascination with the flexible sounds and rhythms of words and voices. The boy Stephen is inclined to almost inhale the rhythmical sounds of langauge. In his quiet mind, he often ponders on the meaning of 'big' words: 'God was God's name just as his name was Stephen. *Dieu* was the French for God and that was God's name too; and when anyone prayed to God and said *Dieu* then God knew at once that it was a French person that was praying. But though there were different names for God in all the different languages in the world and God understood what all the people who prayed said in their different languages still God remained always the same God and God's real name was God. It made him very tired to think that way. It made him feel his head very big' (13).

Stephen is generally fascinated by names and often repeats them in order to get a feel for their rhythmical combinations: 'I am Stephen Dedalus. I am walking beside my father whose name is Simon Dedalus. We are in Cork, in Ireland. Cork is a city. Our room is in the Victoria Hotel. Victoria and Stephen and Simon. Simon and Stephen and Victoria. Names' (98). The fascination stays with him as he, when much older, continues this self-indulgent play with the lyrical plasticity of words, as exemplified in this passage of chiasmus: 'He would fall. He had not yet fallen but he would fall silently, in an instant. Not to fall was too hard, too hard: and he felt the silent lapse of his soul, as it would be at some instant to come, falling, falling, but not yet fallen, still unfallen but about to fall' (175). Repeating words and names creates a chanting quality of strangeness, that of poetry.

The older, budding poet and aesthete Stephen propounds to his friend Lynch that when it comes to 'the phenomena of artistic conception, artistic gestation and artistic reproduction I require a new terminology and a new personal experience' (227). This search is reflected in his revelatory experience of the intensifying cadences of the opening lines in Yeats' play *The Countess Cathleen*. The sounds make his soul flow freely: 'A soft liquid joy flowed through the words where the soft long vowels hurtled noiselessly and fell away, lapping and flowing back and ever shaking the white bells of their waves in mute chime and mute peal and soft low swooning cry; and he felt that the augury he had sought in the wheeling darting birds and in the pale space of sky above him had come forth from his heart like a bird from a turret quietly and swiftly' (245). The incantatory effects of new constellations of words in poetry make every such word lose its everyday meaning and transform into a new language altogether – an alien voicing. Working with language in a work of art translates the language of common use and conversation into a new sphere of communication. But to Stephen, this revelation is not sufficient to satisfy the pursuits of the dark avenger. The English language must be genuinely transformed into a cultural conglomeration of the foreign and the familiar.

Just before the famous epiphany of the bird-girl on the beach, Stephen's soul flies towards Europe:

> [...] he raised his eyes towards the slowdrifting clouds, dappled and seaborne. They were voyaging across the deserts of the sky, a host of nomads on the march, voyaging high over Ireland, westward bound. The Europe they had come from lay out there beyond the Irish Sea. Europe of strange tongues and valleyed and woodbegirt and citadelled and of entrenched and marshalled races. He heard a confused music within him as of memories and names which he was almost conscious of but could not capture even for an instant; the music seemed to recede, to recede, to recede: and from each receding trail of nebulous music there fell always one longdrawn calling note, piercing like a star the dusk of silence. Again! Again! Again! (181-2)

This imaginary exilic fall towards a new world inhabited by multiple languages transforms his thoughts into a musical confusion of words and memories. His imagination takes him to a new world - not by discarding the old world, but by taking Ireland *with* him.

The Babbelers with their Thangas: *Finnegans Wake*

With a view to the above, Joyce's last novel, *Finnegans Wake* represents the ultimate exploration of an expression of a pure, sublime, suprahistorical language in constant flux. And while *A Portrait* is mostly bent on probing the hybrid relations between English and Irish identities, *Finnegans Wake* expands this horizon by travelling to the 'Europe of strange tongues' (at least 50 languages can be deciphered) that the poet Stephen Dedalus could vaguely hear in the musical 'fall' from grace and 'call' to action that drove him into Continental exile towards the end of the novel (182-83).

The central characters in the *Wake* are Humphrey Chimpden Earwicker, his wife Anna Livia Plurabelle, their twin sons Shem and Shaun and one daughter Issy. The story is conventionally explained as a translation of a dream vision from the point of view of an unidentified dreamer. The text is, however, not one big symbol-loaded Freudian or Jungian dreamscape, but a weaving of a dream-like language that enables Joyce to transcend historical and cultural borders of language. The text includes seventeen chapters divided into four books forming the Italian philosopher Giambattista Vico's (1668-1744) cyclical theory of history, arguing for three ages of the world: the Divine, the Heroic and the Human age followed by chaos leading to renewal. Such stages of rebirth in *Finnegans Wake* are represented through 100-letter words such as on the very first page of the novel:

The   fall (bababadalgharaghtakamminarronnkonnbronntonnerronntuo nnthunntrovarrhounawnskawntoohoohoordenenthurnuk!) of at once wallsstrait oldparr is retaled early in bed and later on life down through all christian minstrelsy. The great fall of the offwall entailed at such short notice the pftjschute of Finnegan, erse solid man, that the humptyhillhead of humself prumptly sends an unquiring one well to the west in quest of his tumptytumtoes: and their upturnpikepointandplaces at the knock out in the park where oranges have been laid to rust upon the green since devlinsfirst loved livvy. (3.15-24)

This passage in chapter one declares the fall of Finnegan and foresees his resurrection. But who is this Finnegan? The title of the book refers to the Irish ballad 'Finnegan's Wake' about the fall and resurrection of often drunk hod-carrier Tim Finnegan. He dies when falling from a ladder and is resurrected when one of the guests at the festive wake spills a drop of whiskey on his corpse. Whiskey, from the Gaelic *uisce beatha*, means 'water of life'.

By omitting the apostrophe in *Finnegans Wake*, Joyce playfully suggests both the double meaning of the noun 'wake' as in being dead and as in waking up, and the verb to wake as in 'all Finnegans wake' (Fargnoli and Gillespie 77). Linking this with the general assumption that Joyce's Finnegan also refers to the archetypal myth of the Irish tribal warrior hero Finn MacCool, who lies sleeping beneath Dublin, we get a mixed character to say the least. According to legend, Finn MacCool's head is the stone cairn on top of the towering hill of Howth – 'that the humptyhillhead of humself prumptly sends an unquiring one well to the west in quest of his tumptytumtoes' (3.21) - and his feet or 'tumptytumtoes' are two hills near Phoenix Park – ' their upturnpikepointandplaces at the knock out in the park where oranges have been laid to rust upon the green since devlinsfirst loved livvy' (3.22-24).

In a letter to his Belgian poet friend Fritz Vanderpyl, Joyce says: 'the title of [*Finnegans Wake*] signifies at once the wake and the awakening of Finn, that is, of our legendary Celtic-Nordic hero' (Fargnoli and Gillespie 74). But Tim Finnegan and Finn MacCool are also associated with HCE to such an extent that Eearwicker assumes mythological proportions – as a wa(l)king and dreaming allegory of the cyclical nature of human life – beneath the city of Dublin: 'Hohohoho, Mister Finn, you're going to be Mister Finnagain!' (3.10). It is telling that Humphrey Chimpden Earwicker's nickname in the story is 'Here Comes Everybody'.

Two aspects of this first presentation are pivotal in my investigation of translation as exile in *A Portrait* and the *Wake*. First, the theme of falling and rising is closely connected with the myth of the Tower of Babel. Second, the play on words bears witness to this very fall of the oneness of language. We are in a borderland between total linguistic confusion and a translation into a pure form that begs for universal comprehension.

In his essay 'Adamology', Bruce Stewart makes the now widely accepted claim that the myth of Babel is the central myth of *Finnegans Wake*:

> In writing the *Wake* Joyce told his confidant, Frank Budgen, that he had come to understand the story of the Tower of Babel […] The *Wake*-fall is primarily that of the Tower, and the resultant confounding of language, "that they may not understand one another's speech" is both the fundamental topic and the determining modality of the book: Joyce's obsessive use of many languages ("Polygutteral"), and the continual presentation of "intermisunderstanding minds" refer to the discontinuities of human speech whereby falsehood, deception, hypocrisy all arise. (201-2)

After the Fall, 'The babblers [the Babelians] with their thangas [tongues] vain have been (confusium hold them,) they were and they went; thigging thongs were and houhnhymn songtoms were and comely norgels were and pollyfool [polyphonic] fiansees' (15.12-15). In Joyce's cycle, a state of linguistic exile follows the apocalyptic Fall of the Tower, a thunderclap, but towards the end of a cycle, comprehension, that is the pentecostal-like gift of tongues, becomes possible before everything is shattered anew in a great thunderclap, a new fall: 'abide Zeit's summonserving, rise afterfall' (78.7).

In the *Wake* passages I have chosen for my reading, the central point of interest is the father's role in the procreation of language. Language is nothing but an empty shell without meaning ('In the beginning is the woid', 378.29), a signifier without a signified, and such meaning is provided by the father. The fall of Finn MacCool, the giant father-figure of Irish mythology and protector of Dublin (described as an 'overgrown babeling' (6.31), i.e. a Tower of Babel), and Tim Finnegan, the father-figure of Irish drinking and bawdiness (who fell from a high ladder/tower), are coupled with motifs of the fallen Tower, the fallen God, and the fallen artist. I will try to clarify this in the following.

In her work on *The Decentred Universe of* Finnegans Wake, Margot Norris argues that the role of the figurative father of language is represented in Joyce's understanding of the close connection between form and content:

> The stylistic incorporation of the novel's themes depends on the most fundamental correspondence between social and linguistic structures. The law of man and the law of language are homologous systems because they share an identical unconscious structure. The father's symbolic function as figure of the law is therefore analogous to the semantic function of language, which assigns to lexical items their meanings and their grammatical functions. (124)

It is the law of language personified in the law of the father that Joyce wants to overthrow in the *Wake*.

As already explicated, *Finnegans Wake* is not made out of easily graspable meanings, but multi-layered ambiguities. Joyce's deconstruction, as it were, of conventional English suggests a fundamental violation of or revenge, even, on the ruling laws of Ireland's *English* father, the King. Joyce simply blows the language into smithereens: 'wipe alley English spooker multaphoniaksically spuking off the face of the erse' (178.6-7). The linguistic strategies of such payback terror typically consist of punning, neologisms (as in the previous *bloodfield*), portmanteaus and cultural hybrids. 'Puns and exile go hand in hand and not only because puns often involve translingual play', says Suzanne Jill Levine in a chapter on the translation of puns in her book *The Subversive Scribe: Translating Latin American Fiction* (17). 'The exile acquires an objective, "binary" view of his adopted language and culture, the second language making her aware of the mechanisms of language, both one's own and the other', she continues (17). As quoted from Redfern earlier on, exile enables an extracognizant perspective of multiple cultures which in Joyce's case became handy in the creation of a fallen, splintered and alienated English in his last opus.

The pun, the play on words that are either identical or very similar in sound, but with different meanings, receives but little esteem in traditional English literary criticism, according to Derek Attridge in his chapter on 'The Pleasures of the Pun' in *Peculiar Language: Literature as Difference from the Renaissance to James Joyce* (1988). Ben Jonson, crusading knight of proper English, looks down upon the 'malignant power' of the 'poor and barren' quibble in Shakespeaere's works. To Ben Jonson the pun:

> remains an embarrasment to be excluded from "serious" discourse, a linguistic anomaly to be controlled by relegation to the realms of the infantile, the jocular, the literary. It survives, tenaciously, as freak or accident, hindering what is taken to be the primary function of language: the clean transmission of a pre-existing, self-sufficient, unequivocal meaning. It is a characteristic mode of the dream, the witticism, the slip of the tongue: those irruptions of the disorderly world of childhood pleasures and unconscious desires into the clear, linear processes of practical and rational thought, those challenges to what Johnson precisely articulates as the domain of "reason, propriety and truth". (Attridge 189)

It is precisely the typically English 'reason, propriety and truth' that Joyce exiles in his jocular puns. It is precisely the very imperfect communication of the pun that Joyce celebrates in the face of the English stiff upper-lip.

The portmanteau word is coined by Humpty Dumpty in Lewis Carroll's *Through the Looking Glass* (1871) and explained as the blending of two or more words with separate meanings such as 'slithy' in 'Jabberwocky' meaning both 'lithe' and 'slimy' (270). It is an experimental fabrication of what linuigistics recognize as hybrid words (cf. my introduction). To Attridge, this linguistic trick is a 'monster': 'a word that is not a word, that is not authorized by any dictionary, that holds out the worrying prospect of books which, instead of comfortingly recycling the words we know, possess the freedom endlessly to invent new ones' (196). Thus the portmanteau challenges the myth of the law of the *Ursprache* of the Tower of Babel. Joyce fabricates his own bi- or multilingual dictionary in the confusing hybrids between distinct national languages, such as, to stay within the Scandinavian context of this volume, 'Miss Forstowelsy' (444.11) which is a hybrid of a title in English and the Danish noun *misforståelse* (misunderstanding); 'funkleblue' (171.17) pairing the Danish verb *funkle* (sparkle) with the Enligh 'blue'; and 'a stinksome inkenstink' (183.6) coupling the Danish phrase *en stank som ingen stank* (a stink like no other stink) with the English 'stink', 'some' and 'ink'.[6]

In the passage on the blasting of English quoted above, 'wipe alley English spooker multaphoniaksically spuking off the face of the erse' (178.6-7), we also detect several portmanteaus, such as 'spooker' blending 'speaker' and 'spooky' to give an indication of the haunting presence of English in Ireland. The pun in 'erse' is playing on the word 'earth' and the word 'erse' which is both a Middle English term for 'arse' and an early Scottish word for 'Irish' (Attridge 205). To suggest the role of the Irish as the arse of the earth is indeed rather daunting and provocative and provides at the same time a suprahistorical dimension. The word is the construction of a double movement between synchrony and diachrony. The same pun was used in describing 'Finnegan, erse solid man' on the first page of the *Wake*, stressing the universality of the fall of man in the particular case of the fall of the Irish.

But what about the Redeemer-Artist? How is the Stephen/Joyce poet coping in this defamiliarised universe? Well, he is in fact represented as the Irish poet, as shameful arse of the earth mocking the law of the father of the English language. Chapter seven of Book one is a portrait of the exiled artist Shem the Penman, or 'Pain the Shamman', unsympathetically narrated by his twin brother Shaun:

> Shem is as short for Shemus as Jem is joky for Jacob. A few roughnecks are still getatable who pretend that aboriginally he was of respectable stemming (he was an outlex between

the lines of Ragonar Blaubarb and Horrild Hairwire and an inlaw to Capt. the Hon. and Rev. Mr Bbyrdwood de Trop Blogg was among his most distant connections) but every honest to goodness man in the land of the space of today knows that his back life will not stand being written about in black and white. Putting truth and untruth together a shot may be mad at what this hybrid was actually like to look at. (169.1-10)

He is physically described as a monster and a morally crude creature, 'Shem was a sham and a low sham' (170.25), whose Continental exile is heavily scorned: 'He even ran away with hunself and became a farsoonerite, saying he would far sooner muddle through the hash of lentils in Europe than meddle with Ireland's split little pea' (171.4-6). He is 'Tumult, son of Thunder, self exiled in upon his ego', that is alienated from his country in a preoccupation with himself (184.6-7). Fargnoli and Gillespie explain Shem as a self-parody of Joyce (Fargnoli and Gillespie 81). He is the combined marginalised Irish Artist-Outlaw on the Continent and heroic Artist-Redeemer of all artists. Margot Norris sees Shem as 'Joyce's recalibanisation of the artist' casting out the English Ariel from the island of Ireland (71).

Shem virtually transforms his role as expatriate Irish trash (or shit) by transsubstantiating his own urine and feces into ink. The passage describing this is written in Latin, but an English translation printed in Fargnoli and Gillespie is given below:

First the artisan, the profound progenitor, approaching the fruitful and all-powerful earth, without shame or pardon, put on a raincoat and ungirdled his pants, and with buttocks naked as they were on the day of birth, while weeping and groaning defecated into his hand. Next, having relieved himself of the black living excrement, he – while striking the trumpet – placed his own excrement, which he called his scatterings (purgation), into a once honourable vessel (chalice) of sadness, and into the same place, under the invocation of the twin brothers Medardus and Godardus, he pissed joyfully and melodiously, continuously singing with a loud voice the psalm that begins: "My tongue is a scribe's quill writing swiftly." Finally, he mingled the odious excrement with the pleasantness of the divine Orion, and, from this mixture, which had been cooked and exposed to the cold, he made for himself indelible ink. (254)[7]

As in much contemporary performance art, Shem the Penman uses his ecological ink, as it were, to write 'over every square inch of the only foolcap available, his own body, till by its corrosive sublimation one continuous present tense integument slowly unfolded' (185.35-186.1).

From a metafictional point of view I suggest that this act represents a spiteful mockery of the law of the father of English in 'black and white'. The English language in Ireland is here neither perceived as embryo, foetus or flesh, but as ultimately a fusion of bodily wastes, and the Irish poet seems doomed to work with such a 'new Irish stew' (190.9). The sublimated imperfection of hybrid language is at the same time mocked and celebrated in the 'split' identity of the fallen uprooted Irish artist. Shem is at once 'poetic Celt' and 'urban brute' (Norris, *Joyce's Web* 71).

By way of conclusion, the close correspondence between themes and stylistic strategies of *Finnegans Wake* form an exercise in translating the King's English into a language beyond everyday time and space. Joyce's punning and coining new words in the portmanteau, in the 'new Irish stew', is the ultimate dynamic recycling of an ever-expanding relativist language which goes to the edge of comprehension. However, as there will always have to be traces of established meaning if we are to understand anything in *Finnegans Wake,* the ideal language to Joyce proves to be always far away in the idealised world of metaphysics. This is as far as literary language can go in exiling English before it turns into meaningless, wasted syllables. The *Wake* is close to a dead end of translation as exile and point of no return. At the very end of 'Shem the Penman' this condition is reflected in the repetition of the French 'quoi' causing the word to lose its meaning and turn into a deadening sound of silence: 'He lifts the lifewand and the dumb speak:

– 'Quoiquoiquoiquoiquoiquoiquoi!' (195.6)

Conclusion

The two texts by James Joyce demonstrate a complex preoccupation with the conflicting identities of the Irish and the English. In his revolt against English-imposed language, culture and history, Joyce gradually builds his writing practice on a poetics of translation as exile in order to subvert the law-making role of the English colonisers. It is a poetics that challenges the traditional apprehension of translation as substitution rather than transference, i.e. translation as inferior to the Father of the Original.

Joyce wants to 'invent' a foreignized language that defies national borders by reaching a nucluous of expressiveness, the intentionality of language. In Finnegans Wake, the Babel mythos assumes a prominent place, as Joyce's image of the ethnocentric English grows increasingly associated with the linguistic oneness of the Tower of Babel. The marked polyphony of voices may indeed be interpreted as a celebration of heteroglossia in the Bachtinian terminology. The multiple variants of languages are rendered to the reader through a poetics of translation which the reader comes to know by engaging in a dialogical reading process similar to that of a translator's close reading of the continuous variants of every word. The pursuit of a language in motion is, however, not an absurdist cul de sac, as may be thought when reaching the ultimate expansion of English in the Wake. The book is only close to the edge of nonsense by remaining an overall joyous, life-affirming practice of contingent translation. As R. B. Kershner says in his book on Joyce, Bakhtin, and Popular Literature:

> Discourse is a sort of palimpsest in which languages arise and falter through time, generate their own opposition, triumph or fall, but are never wholly lost. Bakhtin's vision of the human world, like Joyce's, is filled with conflict and opposition, but there is a joy and affirmation in its energy, dynamism, and continuity in the heart of change. As he [Bakhtin] wrote in a fragment soon before his death, 'There is neither a first nor a

last word and there are no limits to the dialogic context [...]
Nothing is absolutely dead: every meaning will have its
homecoming festival'. (21)

Translation as exile in Joyce is associated with the nostalgic exile's
dream of resurrecting the Tower - not as restrictive law, but as
pentecostal universality in diversity. Joyce's nomadic (dis)location
in self-willed exile becomes a borderland between utmost *content*
represented in the freedom of language to travel, and utter
discontent in the recognition that the yearning for a pure
suprahistorical language inevitably leads to an artistic Fall
followed by new exile and wandering. Hence language in
perpetual motion provides Joyce's works with an allegorical
dimension of cyclical universalism.

Notes

[1] Catford says: 'In *translation*, there is substitution of TL meanings for
SL meanings: not transference of TL meanings into the SL. In
transference there is an implantation of SL meanings into the TL text.
These two processes must be clearly differentiated in any theory of
translation' (48)

[2] Perhaps one of the most famous passages on the intertextual nature of
translation is Octavio Paz's proposition of texts as translations of
translations, etc.: 'Every text is unique and, at the same time, it is the
translation of another text. No text is entirely original because
language itself, in its essence, is already a translation: firstly, of the
non-verbal world and secondly, since every sign and every phrase is
the translation of another sign and another phrase. However, this
argument can be turned around without losing any of its validity; all
texts are original because every translation is distinctive. Every
translation, up to a certain point, is an invention and as such it
constitutes a unique text' (Bassnett 38).

[3] Quoted from a lecture by J. Hillis Miller at the IX Centenary
Celebration Symposium of the University of Bologna, Italy, in
October 1988 (Devy 182).

[4] For further details on all translations, see Fargnoli and Gillespie 245.

[5] Joyce asked Tom Kristensen, writer of *Hærværk (Havoc)*, which is
greatly inspired by Joyce, would he translate *Ulysses*. 'Yes, but give
me ten years,' Kristensen said (Ellmann 692-93). The project,

however, fell through, and *Ulysses* was not translated into Danish until 1949 when Mogens Boisen undertook the task which led to a total of five translations of *Ulysses*. Three of which were published in 1949, 1970 and 1980.

6 For more details on Scandinavian elements of *Finnegans Wake*, see Bunis.

7 The original reads: 'Primum opifex, altus prosator, ad terram viviparam et cunctipotentem sine ullo pudore nec venia, suscepto pluviali atque discinctis perizomatis, natibus nudis uti nati fuissens, sese adpropinquans, flens et gemens, in manum suam evacuavit (highly prosy, crap in his hand, sorry!) , postea, animale nigro exoneratus, classicum pulsans, stercus proprium, quod appellavit deiectiones suas, in vas olim honorabile tristitiae posuit, eodem sub invocatione fratrorum geminorum Medadi et Godardi laete ac melliflue minxit, psalmum qui incipt: Lingua mea calamus scribae velociter scribentis: magna voce cantitans (did a piss, said he was dejected, asks to be exonerated), demum ex stercore turpi cum divi Orionis iucunditate mixto, cocto, frigorique exposito, encaustum sibi fecit indelibile (faked O'Ryan's, the indelible ink)' (185.14-26).

References

Attridge, Derek. *Peculiar Language: Literature as Difference from the Renaissance to James Joyce*. London: Methuen, 1988.

Bassnett, Susan. *Translation Studies*. London: Routledge, 2000.

Beardsley, Monroe C. and W. K. Wimsatt. *The Verbal Icon: Studies in the Meaning of Poetry*. New York: The Noonday Press, 1954.

Braidotti, Rosa. *Nomadic Subjects: Embodiment and Sexual Difference in Contemporary Feminist Theory*. New York: Columbia UP, 1994.

Bunis, Christiani Dounia. *Scandinavian Elements of* Finnegans Wake. Evanston: Northwestern UP, 1965.

Carroll, Lewis. *The Annotated Alice: Alice's Adventures in Wonderland and Through the Looking-Glass*. 1871. Harmondsworth: Penguin, 1970.

Catford, J. C. *A Linguistic Theory of Translation*. London: Oxford UP, 1965.

Cronin, Michael. *Across the Lines: Travel, Language, Translation*. Cork: Cork UP, 2000.

Devy, Ganesh.'Translation and literary history - an Indian view'. *Post-Colonial Translation: Theory and Practice.* Eds. Susan Bassnett and Harish Trivedi. London: Routledge, 1999. 182-89.

Ellmann, Richard. *James Joyce.* 1959. Oxford: Oxford UP, 1982.

Fargnoli, A. Nicholas and Michael Patrick Gillespie. *James Joyce A to Z: An Encyclopedic Guide to his Life and Work.* London: Bloomsbury, 1995.

Friel, Brian. *Translations.* London: Faber and Faber, 1981.

Gurr, Andrew. *Writers in Exile: The Identity of Home in Modern Literature.* Sussex: The Harvester Press, 1981.

Joyce, James. *A Portrait of the Artist as a Young Man.* 1916. Harmondsworth: Penguin Classics, 1992.

— *Finnegans Wake.* 1939. London: Faber, 1950.

Kershner, R. B. *Joyce, Bakhtin, and Popular Literature: Chronicles of Disorder.* Chapel Hill and London: U of California Press, 1989.

Levine, Suzanne Jill. *The Subversive Scribe: Translating Latin American Fiction.* Saint Paul, Minnesota: Graywolf Press, 1991.

Nabokov, Vladimir. *Speak, Memory: An Autobiography Revisited.* New York: Penguin, 1966.

Norris, Margot. *The Decentred Universe of* Finnegans Wake: *A Structuralist Analysis.* Baltimore: The Johns Hopkins UP, 1974.

— *Joyce's Web: The Social Unravelling of Modernism.* Austin: U of Texas Press, 1992.

Perkins, Jill. *Joyce and Hauptman, Before Sunrise: James Joyce's Translation and Notes.* San Marino: E. Huntington Library and Art Gallery, 1978.

Redfern, Walter. 'Traduction, Puns, Clichés, Plagiat'. *Traductio: Essays on Punning and Translation.* Ed. Dirk Delabastita. Manchester: St. Jerome Publishing, 1997. 260-69.

Riquelme, John Paul. 'Ireland and Switzerland: The Cases of James Joyce and Fritz Senn'. *Literary Interrelations: Ireland, England and the World.* Vol. I: *Reception and Translation.* Eds. Wolfgang Zach and Heinz Kosok. Tübingen: Gunter Narr Verlag, 1987. 109-16.

Rushdie, Salman. *The Satanic Verses.* New York: Henry Holt and Company, 1988.

Seidel, Michael. *Exile and the Narrative Imagination*. New Haven: Yale UP, 1986.

Stewart, Bruce. 'Adamology'. *The Crane Bag Book of Irish Studies: Mythology*. Eds. Hederman and Kearney. 2: 1 & 2. (1978): 193-204.

John Hewitt at Home and in Exile

Britta Olinder

Considering the meaning of exile in connection with John Hewitt as poet, critic, museum man or as 'honest Ulsterman' I refer to the different categories discussed above in Michael Böss's theorizing essay. In the first place it is clear that in Hewitt's case the original meaning of exile as penal banishment does not apply. The question is if his fifteen years in Coventry could be taken as his being separated from his home country by force of circumstances or just as a voluntary choice. In any case he has himself written about it as exile. Figuratively or symbolically it can be used about the inner exile in his own province, his alienation and dissent seen in his protest against social injustice and his quandary about national identity. As always, however, there are two poles in any exile: home, the point of departure, geographically or symbolically, on the one hand and, on the other, the place or state of banishment, of being away from home.

The general relevance of exile in the Irish context has, of course, to do with the country's history of colonization, oppression, poverty and famine, exemplified by Saint Patrick and Colmcille, the Flight of the Earls in the seventeenth century and large-scale emigration, particularly in the mid-nineteenth century. It is interesting to see the extent to which Hewitt relies on Irish history in his reflections on dislocation. Intellectual oppression has also played a part in it, not least in the last century, witness Joyce, O'Casey and Beckett among many others. Can this be compared with Hewitt's situation? In the case of Northern Ireland the threat of violence during the Troubles forms an added reason for leaving the country. How does Hewitt deal with this?

Edward Said asserts from his own bitter knowledge that exile is 'terrible to experience', 'its essential sadness can never be

Re-Mapping Exile: Realities and Metaphors in Irish Literature and History, ed. Michael Böss, Irene Gilsenan Nordin and Britta Olinder, *The Dolphin* 34. © 2005 by Aarhus University Press, Denmark. ISBN 87 7934 010 5.

surmounted' (173). Even so he concedes that 'while it perhaps seems peculiar to speak of the pleasures of exile, there are some positive things to be said for a few of its conditions' (186). Thus Joyce sees exile as a weapon when he declares that he will employ 'for my defence the only arms I allow myself to use – silence, exile, and cunning' (229). When Andrew Gurr and Salman Rushdie consider 'the enabling aspects of exile [...] they see it as liberating and empowering' (qtd in Ward 240). This seems to some extent to be the case of Hewitt, notably during his years in Coventry.

I will here try to examine some ways in which John Hewitt deals with this dichotomy, this tension between home and exile, at times feeling at home in his exile and in other situations alienated in his native country. Protesting explicitly against a definition of him as alien or rootless he actually indicates the interior exile in his own society, the marginalization and alienation he does feel. Yet what is of particular interest is Hewitt's firm sense of home and rootedness in Belfast and in the landscape of the Glens of Antrim. Looking into these paradoxes we are reminded of what Robert Johnstone claimed in a review of Hewitt's poems: 'Anyone who feels the need to take account of Ulster Protestants [...] should try to understand why Hewitt matters.'

Exile and immigration

As a trained historian Hewitt imagines the waves of migrants moving across the continents throughout the millennia of human existence. In some poems he evokes pictures of the coming of the earliest inhabitants to Irish soil, making them forerunners of the later waves of people forced westwards away from continental Europe and then on from one island to the other. 'The Mainland' is one of these poems, indicating the threatening force that makes people flee into the unknown. It shows their gradual establishment and yet their lingering memories, their nostalgia and the final loss even of the dream of the old home:

The island people first were mainland people
shouldered from crowded valley to the beach;

some even afloat before the outsiders came
with emblem and ultimatum of invaders
heavily armoured in rumour, invincible.

Always they were the young, the loose of foot,
could grab the few tools handy, bundle up
the little earthen gods, the lamps, the flints,
the pots of seed laid by for the next spring.

Occasionally awe might clear a space
for a grandfather who knew every star
and all the rimes for luck and love and labour,
but this was seldom. Children, goats and women
left little room enough for the rowers' knees.

And so departed while the drift of smoke
from the torched thatches hung a day's march off.
The only choice then was from the known landmarks
into the sunset out of the fierce noon.

When seven generations had been buried
in island earth and all was planted well,
the hill tribes broken and the hill names kept,
a long while since, the story should have ended,
the island now a nation, its people one;
but legends of the mainland still persist
in hearthside talk and rags of balladry:
and now and then a man will test their truth
by sailing back across the ancient track
to find it rich in all but what he sought. (*Coll. Poems* 96-97)

Personally Hewitt is very conscious of belonging to the Ulster
Scots. His family actually came twice as immigrants to Ireland;
first far back in time, so far that he does not know exactly when
his forefathers first arrived – four hundred years ago is mentioned
in one poem – but assuming they were colonizers and more
efficient in cultivating the land than the earlier inhabitants.

Later, in the 1880s, his paternal grandparents, who had left
Ireland for Scotland, returned with all their children after more
than twenty years of exile. Hewitt retells the story of a small baby,
dead during the crossing, in its mother's arms. The first worry for
his grandfather was to get a burial place for the little one. Then:
'Back so to Ireland, working in Belfast/ for better wages at his
well-loved trade' ('The Return'; *Coll. Poems* 274). This means,
surprisingly for the late nineteenth century, immigration to
Ireland for economic reasons.

Exile and emigration

The Hewitt family history contains quite a few stories of exile and
emigration from Ireland as appears from both his childhood
autobiography, *Planter's Gothic*, and in poems, notably among the
sonnets of *Kites in Spring*. There are thus several versions of the
story of his paternal grandparents, mentioned above, who 'fled to
Glasgow' for family reasons. Of the many children who came
back to Belfast with them one uncle went to London: '[...] after
adventures, Edinburgh, he/ settled in Finchbury with his family'
('The Volunteer'; *Coll. Poems* 267). Others emigrated to the United
States seeking 'a fatter life beyond the sea, / and scrawled their
spider's letters once a year / from the raw fenceposts of a new
frontier' ('Freehold'; *Coll. Poems* 377). 'My Brooklyn Uncle' seems
a typical example of many Irish emigrants:

> Thomas, the eldest brother, shipped across
> the broad Atlantic where he found his bride,
> a daughter of the firm, this proved no loss;
> a Wall Street office was no crazy stride.
> From her surname they took their first son's name,
> and sent us stacks of photographs each year;
> with office, house, rooms, cars there would appear
> that family face, the same and not the same.
>
> After depression, his Havana trip,
> the sagging jowls subdued by surgeon's knife,
> the blond son smiling in the partnership;
> it seemed the sort of transatlantic life

which satirists make sport of; yet there were
those Christmas dollars for my grandfather.

(*Coll. Poems* 268)

In addition, as appears from a short chapter in Hewitt's
professional autobiography, his future wife Roberta had actually
emigrated to Canada as a girl with her family ('Chance Encounter'
in the manuscript of 'A North Light').

'This is my home and country ...'
Turning from stories of his family to Hewitt's own perceptions
and experience the poem 'Ireland' from 1932 (*Coll. Poems* 58)
makes a good starting point for his expressions of belonging. It is
again about history and early waves of immigrants but what is
now of specific interest is his perspective. 'We Irish' is repeated
and intensified into 'We were the Keltic wave', including himself
among the patriots telling 'the beadroll of the valiant ones' and of
'mighty fighters and victorious'. At the same time this is a context
where he rejects the very idea of roots in any native soil, since 'we
are not native here or anywhere', only taking part in 'great tidal
movements round the earth'. He seems to say that it was pure
chance that they were stranded 'in this lonely place' and that the
patriotic affection for an unrewarding piece of land is, instead,
'forgotten longing' for something else, some hazy home,
something of almost existential dimensions.

The unquestioning attitude in 'Ireland' turns into something to
work for and assert in 'Rite, Lubitavish, Glenaan' (1952). Here the
Kelt is somebody else and the poem's persona has to defend
himself against patriots:

Above my door the rushy cross,
the turf upon my hearth,
for I am of the Irishry
by nurture and by birth.

So let no patriot decry
or Kelt dispute my claim,[...]

(*Coll. Poems* 83)

It is also worth while comparing the early 'Ireland' with 'The Scar' (1971) written almost forty years later. After telling the story of how his great-grandmother's helpfulness to a poor beggar made her a victim of the famine fever he emphasizes the heavy price to be paid to be 'conscried [...] of the Irishry for ever' and concludes:

> Though much I cherish lies outside their vision,
> and much they prize I have no claim to share,
> yet in that woman's death I found my nation;
> the old wound aches and shews its fellow scar.
> (Coll. Poems 177)

About ten years after 'Ireland' he writes the long poem 'Conacre' (1943), later explaining the title – and thereby the uncertainty of his claim to the soil – as having to do with the renting land under certain conditions, not with its ownership. I could be no more definite than:

> This is my home and country. Later on
> perhaps I'll find this nation is my own.
> ('No Rootless' 93 b)

The poem continues:

> but here and now it is enough to love
> this faulted ledge, this map of cloud above,
> and the great sea that beats against the west
> to swamp the sun.   (Coll. Poems 10)

We can thus see that whether he writes about Ireland as a whole or just the plot of land where he lives he does so in terms of identity – 'we Irish' or 'my home' – and in relation to his nationality. Even so he will speak about 'this mad island crammed with bloody ghosts / and moaning memories of forgotten coasts' (*Coll. Poems* 9). We must keep in mind that nation is a word loaded with Irish meanings. However that may be Hewitt is very far from a sentimental or romantic view of his home, rather turning towards a definition by negation as in the following lines:

> It is not that like Goldsmith I recall
> some shabby Auburn with a crumbling wall
> seen through the sparkling lens of exile grief
> that gilds the lily of a child's belief; (*Coll. Poems* 10-11)

Planter – native and exile

Affirmation by way of a negation of sorts meets us also in 'Once alien here' (1942); 'once' in the sense of not any longer. There are several contrasts in this poem: the past and the present, English and Irish, Planter and Gael and, not least, the difference between the colonist leaving his country while others remain on the mainland where the language is naturally developing and the central, metropolitan literature is being written. Now Hewitt no longer writes in terms of 'we Irish' but 'the sullen Irish'– he definitely sees the Kelts as the others. He feels exiled in Ireland as well as from England, 'lacking skill in either scale of song, / the grave English, lyric Irish tongue' (*Coll. Poems* 20). This is due to his difficulties in suiting language and literature to his marginalized situation in between two cultures. Curiously enough, when he later comments on the poem he, instead, emphasizes other parts of the poem expressing his 'identification with the earth, with the climate […] locating my place on the map, mine by a respectably long tenure' ('No Rootless' 94). It certainly seems as if he does not always recognize the ambivalence expressed in his poems. Similar but less ambiguous thoughts are voiced in 'Ulster Winter' (1942):

> For I am native, though my fathers came
> From fatter acres over the grey sea:
> The clay that hugs the row of exile bones
> Has shaped my phantom nationality. (*Coll. Poems* 485)

The division in society makes him very conscious of where he belongs and makes him speak in 'Sunset over Glenaan' (1950) about 'my chosen ground'– a central concept with Hewitt – and beyond that, 'the fat valleys' of 'another folk', the 'inland Planter folk', who had earlier supplanted a third group, the clansmen who 'limped defeated to the woody glens'. His breed is, however, also Planter:

> [...] I can shew [sic!]
> the grey and crooked headstones row on row
> in a rich country mastered long ago
> by stubborn farmers from across the sea,
> [...]
> Inheritor of these, I also share
> the nature of this legendary air. (*Coll. Poems* 113)

In 'The Colony' (1949-50) Hewitt claims to have 'allegorised the regional circumstance as that of a Roman colony at the Empire's waning, and in what terms the colonists viewed the situation and the future' ('No Rootless' 94). 'They' are first the invaders, the legions who surveyed the land distributing it among 'the great captains down to men-at-arms'. 'We' are the planters who worked the soil. 'They' are later also the Irish, the natives, 'barbarian tribesmen', 'the dispossessed'. Hewitt expresses sympathy with the suffering Irish, he admits 'our load of guilt' and pleads for co-habitation:

> for we have rights drawn from the soil and sky;
> the use, the pace, the patient years of labour,
> the rain against the lips, the changing light,
> the heavy clay-sucked stride, have altered us;
> we would be strangers in the Capitol;
> this is our country also, nowhere else;
> and we shall not be outcast on the world. (*Coll. Poems* 79)

As John Wilson Foster aptly comments: 'The insistent last lines [...] perfectly capture the planter's brittle certainty with its soft centre of despair' (*Imagination* 141). This is only one of many places where we become conscious of Hewitt's being torn between the conflicting claims of colonizer and colonized. Later, in 'No Rootless Colonist' Hewitt will claim that 'this is the definitive statement of my realisation that I am an Ulsterman' ('No Rootless' 94).

By the late forties, however, Hewitt sees himself more clearly as an outsider, as 'the other', marginalized, 'a strange bird', in exile in the province he claims as his home. There was, however, one more step in the exile process, when his family left their farming life,

> [...]when their slow blood was running thin,
> crowded in towns for warmth, and bred me in
> the clay-red city with the white horse on the wall,
> the jangling steeples, and the green-doomed hall
> (Coll. Poems 113)

While claiming Belfast as his home, not least as the site of his childhood memories, Hewitt always distances himself from the ruling set's demonstrative protestantism as hinted at in references to the 'white horse on the wall', the churches and the power concentrated to the City Hall. As a city-dweller in a poem like 'O Country People' (1949-50) it is, thus, not only about the Planter in relation to the Gael that he writes, but even more about the urban citizen in relation to farmers and farmworkers:

> O country people, you of the hill farms,
> huddled so in darkness I cannot tell
> whether the light across the glen is a star,
> or the bright lamp spilling over the sill,
> I would be neighbourly, would come to terms
> with your existence, but you are so far;
> there is a wide bog between us, a high wall. (*Coll. Poems* 72)

It is not least the language that keeps them apart:

> I've tried to learn the smaller parts of speech
> in your slow language, but my thoughts need more
> flexible shapes to move in, if I am to reach
> into the hearths red heart across the half-door. (*Coll. Poems* 72)

Exile in Coventry

So far, then, these are mainly expressions of home and exile from
his first Irish period. An obvious aspect of the concept is, of
course, Hewitt's very real exile due to a painful experience of
rejection by the autorities of his home province. It is also in that
context his feelings about his Ulster background develop.

Hewitt was a poet with an impressive poetic output. By
profession he was a museum man and in that capacity he wrote
numerous books, articles and exhibition notes; as a literary
historian he edited William Allingham's poems and dug up,
published and wrote a scholarly introduction to *The Rhyming
Weavers and other poets of Antrim and Down;* as a critic he published
an untold number of literary reviews. He also began several
autobiographies of which only a few sections have been
published, mainly of his childhood but also some parts of his
professional autobiography, 'A North Light', about his twenty-
five years at the Belfast Museum. In a chapter of the latter entitled
'From Chairmen & Committee Men, Good Lord Deliver Us',
published in *The Honest Ulsterman* in 1968, some fifteen years after
the event, he gives us a sense of the intrigues and plotting going
on when a new director is to be appointed. With his long
experience of museum work, his extensive practice as lecturer on
art, his contribution as broadcaster, his service on cultural
committees, he was still rejected in favour of a man without a
university degree and clearly much inferior in every respect
except his nationality – he was from England. What was held
against Hewitt – unofficially, of course, – was that he was
branded as a communist (this was the MacCarthy era in the US!),
a pro-Catholic, somebody mixing with actors and bohemians.
Being by-passed so unfairly was a hard blow and in the following
weeks, he says,

> my wife and I felt utterly alone [...] generally, there was a
> feeling of remoteness and isolation. The subject was dead.
> And, perhaps most cutting of all, when business took me into
> the City Hall, men in the public service whom I had known
> for years, dodged down corridors or dived round corners to
> avoid me, to avoid being seen near me by any of their

employers. One fellow of supposedly progressive views, stumbled and nearly broke his neck on the marble staircase in his flushed stampede. (*Ancestral Voices* 55)

This description of a frighteningly narrow-minded society provides evidence of a clearly more palpable exile within his own province than he had felt before, an inner exile leading to his real exile in Coventry.

The last, unpublished, chapter of his professional autobiography is entitled 'Exeat', the stage direction for somebody leaving. The stage he left was Belfast and its museum where he had served for more than twenty-five years. After waiting for some time, demonstrating that he 'could stand up unabashed' and being, as he puts it, 'a walking reproach to, a thorn in the conscience of my enemies', he took the opportunity and challenge to apply for a post as director of a new gallery in Coventry. It was, however, not an easy step to take. 'It would, if I were successful, mean uprooting us from a context in which Roberta and I had our own places and interests' and he speaks of 'the strong self-identification' with the past and the future of his province. We get an impression of his deep reluctance to leaving. In the end, however, he sent in his application 'as a gesture of my feeling of independence from the restrictive climate'.

Making his first acquaintance with the new city he happened to stroll into a church. He took notice of a memorial tablet from 1827 with his own name on and had 'an odd friendly feeling, as if, in some way, part of me had come home, that I stood in that place with some sort of right'. So going into exile he can still feel at home, something that is strengthened by the social and political environment in his new city. This is the background of his often anthologized 'An Irishman in Coventry' (1958):

A full year since, I took this eager city,
the tolerance that laced its blatant roar,
its famous steeples and its web of girders,
as image of the state hope argued for,
and scarcely flung a bitter thought behind me
on all that flaws the glory and the grace

which ribbons through the sick, guilt-clotted legend
of my creed-haunted, godforsaken race.
[...]
Then, sudden, by occasion's chance concerted,
in enclave of my nation, but apart,
the jigging dances and the lilting fiddle
stirred the old rage and pity in my heart.
The faces and the voices blurring round me,
the strong hands long familiar with the spade,
the whiskey-tinctured breath, the pious buttons,
called up a people endlessly betrayed
by our own weakness, by the wrongs we suffered
in that long twilight over bog and glen,
by force, by famine and by glittering fables
which gave us martyrs when we needed men,
[...]
This is our fate: eight hundred years' disaster,
crazily tangled as the Book of Kells;
the dream's distortion and the land's division,
the midnight raiders and the prison cells.
Yet like Lir's children banished to the waters
our hearts still listen to the landward bells.
                                        (*Coll. Poems* 97-98)

We may note the emphasis on tolerance, the image of the state
that is only a utopian hope as far as his own province is
concerned, the bitterness in his qualifications of it, 'flaws', 'sick,
guilt-clotted', 'creed-haunted, godforsaken'. When, however, he
suddenly finds himself among fellow-countrymen, sees their
dancing, hears their music, perceives their rural origins, their
comforts in whiskey and their Catholic religion he is
overwhelmed by the conflicting emotions of rage and pity
underlined by the alliteration of wrongs and weakness, of force,
famine and fables, of martyrs and men and of dream's distortion
and division. Even for somebody as well-adjusted and integrated
in his new position as Hewitt, there is the pain of being separated
from his original home at the same time as the pain and bitterness
of having been in another kind of exile there. There is also the not

fully explicit knowledge that the state of oppression hurts the oppressor group as well as those oppressed.

Post-colonial criticism might here claim that – just as in some other poems by Hewitt, e.g. 'Those Swans Remember' with its inventory of symbols from different cultures or in 'Two Irish Saints', Patrick and Colmcille, – Irish/Gaelic legends are appropriated in Hewitt's reference to Lir's children who are banished but turned homewards, longing and listening for the bells calling them back from their exile. This is, however, also part of Hewitt's personal myth.

The charms of exile, yet longing for home

A slightly different attitude is shown in a long descriptive poem called 'A Country Walk in May' (1960). Hewitt looks back summing up:

> [...]
> My wife and I meet our fourth summer here,
> where my trade prospers, in an atmosphere
> more friendly to my independent mind
> than that brusque canton we have left behind,
> and, through the months, we've grown to like the scene
> where the clay is redder and the grass is green.
> *(Coll. Poems* 519)

He further marks his ambivalence in the words 'our exile-home' (519) and as his eyes sweep over the surroundings he acknowledges – with clear reservations:

> a comfortable landscape, certainly,
> known from the paintings, sober, nurtured, rich,
> yet never mine at heart. (520)

We may note on the last line the ambivalence inherent in the exilic condition. The adjectives are appreciative but with their hard vowels and steady pace somehow more rational than emotional and in sharp contrast to the dancing music of his Irish homeland in

> [...] The whin-bright ditch
> across the sloping moss of the long hill;
> the twisty trout-brown stream, from sill to sill
> of gleaming rock, that jostles chattering;
> [...]
> this is my landscape [...] (520)

The nostalgic tone is also unmistakable when in 'Suburban Spring in Warwickshire' (1968) something reminds him of his 'grandmother's garden, / in another country' (*Coll. Poems* 165). Exile is, however, not only a movement away in a geographical sense, it also takes place in language, in the differences between dialects, as in 'The Search' (1966).

> We left the western island to live among strangers
> in a city older by centuries
> than the market town which we had come from
> where the slow river spills out between green hills
> and gulls perch on the bannered poles.
>
> It is a hard responsibility to be a stranger;
> to hear your speech sounding at odds with your neighbours';
> remembering that you are a guest in the house.

Note that a word like 'stranger', 'the other' of certain theories, is applied on the first line to their new neighbours but later to themselves, to Hewitt and his wife. The longing tone in the description of his home town expresses the conflicting feelings even about an appreciated exile. Accordingly:

> Often you will regret the voyage,
> wakening in the dark night to recall that other place
> or glimpsing the moon rising and recollecting
> that it is also rising over named hills,
> shining on known waters.

Again he refers to the hills surrounding Belfast, the waters of the river Lagan and the Belfast Loch[1]. The key defining words here are 'named' and 'known'. Then his double allegiance comes to the fore:

> But sometimes the thought
> that you have not come away from, but returned,
> to this older place whose landmarks are yours also,
> occurs when you look down a long street remarking
> the architectural styles or move through the landscape
> with wheat ripening in large fields.

The issue of allegiance to first or second home become further complicated, however, – just as in that early poem 'Ireland':

> Yet you may not rest here, having come back,
> for this is not your abiding place, either.

> The authorities declare that in former days
> the western island was uninhabited,
> just as where you reside now was once tundra,
> and what you seek may be no more than
> a broken circle of stones on a rough hillside, somewhere.
>
> > (*Coll. Poems* 160)

In the long historical perspective the issue of home and exile has become an existential issue, calling the very essence of home in question. Or perhaps this could be seen as that 'plurality of vision [...] an awareness of simultaneous dimensions' that Edward Said proclaims in his *Reflections on Exile* (186). Yet another way of looking at it might be to apply Kiberd's reading of Goldsmith's situation: 'Goldsmith discovered that nobody really migrates: people simply bring their native landscape and personal baggage with them wherever they go' (111). Playing on the expression 'sent to Coventry' Eamonn Hughes declares that in Hewitt's case 'Coventry is not just a real place, it is also a condition' (264).

With the eruption of the Troubles at the end of the sixties, however, Hewitt's belonging to his native province becomes a burning issue. He brings out a whole collection about it, mainly in the sonnet form, *An Ulster Reckoning* (1971). Whereas earlier he

spoke in terms of 'An Irishman in Coventry' the poems are now
entitled 'A Belfastman Abroad Argues with Himself' or 'An
Ulsterman'. In the latter poem we can see clearly the affirmation
of his origin and at the end hear the passionate tone of the
marginalized and dehumanized Shylock's argument:

> This is my country. If my people came
> from England here four centuries ago,
> the only trace that's left is in my name.
> Kilmore, Armagh, no other sod can show
> the weathered stone of our first burying.
> Born in Belfast, which drew the landless in,
> that river-straddling, hill-rimmed town, I cling
> to the inflexions of my origin.
>
> Though creed-crazed zealots and the ignorant crowd,
> long-nurtured, never checked, in ways of hate,
> have made our streets a byword of offence,
> this is my country, never disavowed.
> When it is fouled, shall I not remonstrate?
> My heritage is not their violence. (*Coll. Poems* 132)

As Hewitt is nearing his retirement we then hear him doubtfully
asking himself in 'Exile':

> Although it is my native place
> and dear to me for many associations,
> how can I return to that city
> from my exile among strangers?
> These people I now live among
> are friendly in the street
> and quiet in the evenings
> around their own hearths.
> And I grown old
> do not wish to shuffle
> through the rubble of my dreams
> and lie down in hope's ashes:
> the Phoenix is a fabulous bird. (*Coll. Poems* 141-42)

The crushing of his hopes in fire, however, gives him the idea of the Phoenix rising out of the ashes as a symbol of rebirth and wonderful renewal.

At the end of his fifteen-year-long exile Hewitt wrote the important article 'No Rootless Colonist' in Coventry. It deals with the issue of identity among people living like him in England but being of Planter stock from Ireland:

> In my experience people of Planter stock often suffer from some crisis of identity, of not knowing where they belong. Among us you will find some who call themselves British, some Irish, some Ulstermen, usually with a degree of hesitation or mental fumbling. ('No Rootless' 90)

Referring to William Allingham, a 19th century poet from Ulster and a friend of Tennyson's, he speaks about him in terms that could just as well describe his own situation: 'For in England he readily found the companionship of literary people and a congenial atmosphere of liberal concerns with the arts' ('No Rootless' 90). By contrast he refers to 'the general feebleness of toleration for opposing views' (91 a) back home and how he had felt 'set apart from the majority of people in my native country' due to his educated background in English literature and history. At the same time he also notes the prejudice on the other side: 'when I first came to live here in England I found that it was automatically assumed by my new colleagues or acquanitances that, since I had come from Ireland, I must be a Catholic' (91 b), i.e. belong to the majority in Ireland. His sense of home and belonging is thus always problematized. Claiming the great Irish writers of the early twentieth century and also the younger men of the Irish Literary Revival as well as the best American writers of the time as models he points out further on in the essay that 'Dublin was our literary capital' (92 a). Even so his museum work led him to research into notable men of Ulster stock and he gradually became 'equipped with a local imaginative Mythology' (92 b). During the war he had found that 'lecturing in army camps broadened my experience of the six partitioned counties of the North. And walking in the Rosses I felt myself no stranger' (93b).

It was at this time, in 1943, that he wrote 'Conacre', mentioned above. Moving towards the end of the essay he declares: 'I have so far no more than outlined the chart of a highly personal journey to a point of self-realisation' (95a), concluding:

> I have experienced a deep enduring sense of our human past before the Lion Gate at Mycenae and among the Rolright Stones of the Oxfordshire border, but it is the north-eastern corner of Ireland where I was born and lived until my fiftieth year, where the only ancestors I can name are buried:
> > Grain of my timber, how I grew,
> > my syntax, cadence, rhetoric,
> > grammar of my dialect. (95 b)

Another poem, '1957-1972' sums up his years in exile in a comparison with Dante's situation:

> […]
> No Florence his sick town.
> Yet there was exile once after a defeat,
> and years spent walking through an alien place
> among bland strangers kinder than his kin,
> and then there was return –
> as some translated poet wrote –
> to this betraying violent city
> irremediably home. (*Coll. Poems* 221-22)

Exile, nationality and identity

In this context the relation of identity to exile has to be discussed. To be an exile you have to have some sort of home identity while living in other surroundings. It can even be maintained that it is being away that creates the emotional understanding of what home is. Exile, thus, has to do with the identity of your home but likewise with the identity of the alien place. Part of the problem might even be the clash between these two identities. Or, from a different perspective, as Andrew Gurr claims about the colonial exile, 'the search for identity and the construction of a vision of home amount to the same thing' (qtd in Ward 239). Applied to

Hewitt this can, at some other time, be traced in the development of Ulster landscapes in his poems, but here I can only briefly indicate the difference exile made to his autobiographical writing. In the early fifties he started to write on his childhood, the country from which at that age he could be said to be exiled. His chronicle of a quarter-century working in the Ulster Museum was, however, not tackled until he was away in Coventry looking back from his exile, assessing his professional home in the province he had wanted to devote his efforts to.

Another aspect that Hewitt looks into is the issue of nationality, as we have seen in other contexts above. Among his autobiographical papers written while he was in Coventry is a section or chapter called, with reference to the Irishman in Shakespeare's *Henry V*, 'What is my Nation?' To a twentieth-century Ulsterman it is, of course, an even trickier question. Hewitt remembers that during the war it was much easier to get from his part of Britain to Dublin than to his own capital, London, which was almost inaccessible. Over the years he gave much thought to his national identity and it can be claimed that this is what led him on to his views on regionalism.[2] Another question in this autobiographical chapter is: 'At what point in the generations does an immigrant's sense of new nationhood begin?' He goes on arguing:

> So, as I set out the names and factors as known to me, I found myself believing that, while land is important, and language important, and religion important, the single factor of greatest moment which may include, do without or transcend any or all of these, can best be called the Myth of the Nation, the clustering together of the images of men or events, legendary or historical, of the unexamined ideas of places, beliefs, memories which have suddenly or gradually set in a recognisable body, maybe like a nebula, dense at the centre, tenuous round the edges.

He then considers Irish myths, both those shared and those belonging to the different sections of Irish society, concluding, '[...] a person born in the Northern Province of Ireland has his loyalties clearly marked: first to his native province, secondly to the whole island, thirdly to what, for tact's sake, I termed the British Archipelago and fourthly to Europe'. Since the 60's when this was written, his views have become remarkably modern, some might even call them post-national.

Dissent as exile

The chapter 'My Generation' in 'A North Light' accounts for the meetings and other activities of the Left Book Club, the Progressive Bookshop and other socially radical associations for a relatively small circle of friends.[3] At times it even led to their being suspected as enemies of the state. With Hewitt dissent, whether political or cultural, in the sense of keeping firmly to his convictions against the dominant opinion was of the utmost importance, a matter of self-respect and honour. He grew up in a Methodist family but maintained his stance as an atheist, moving 'beyond the creeds' ('No Rootless' 91a). Politically he distinguished himself from the predominantly conservative views of the Protestants in power by being staunchly of the left. He was open to friendship with bohemian artists and actors in a way that was not socially accepted. Above all in his thinking he ardently defended radical, egalitarian and socialist ideas. His models and heroes were to be found among dissenters such as John Ball, the Diggers, the Levellers, the Chartists, Paine, Cobbet, Morris – 'these epitomise for me the British democratic tradition' ('No Rootless' 91b). In the poem 'Roseblade's visitants and mine' (1975) he added John 'Toland the Irish deist' (1670-1722) and 'Gerrard Winstanley (1609-c.1660), leader of the Diggers or True Levellers' (*Coll. Poems* 646), characterizing them as

> the sturdy folk, the nameless and the named,
> the vertical men who never genuflected,
> the asserters, the protesters (*Coll. Poems* 332)

Thus creating what he calls his personal myth he finds his home in it while at the same time drawing up sharp lines of demarcation for his symbolic exile in distancing himself from the majority.

Conclusion

In Seamus Heaney's review from 1972 of Hewitt's first *Collected Poems* he distinguishes a pattern showing first 'an early period when he examines himself against his native community', a period of conflicting expressions to do with home, identity and alienation. Then 'after his shift to England in 1957, he sets his lonely present against a rooted past, in terms of a lost community and family', a period that ended with painful assessments of the conflict back home and in his own mind. At the end of the collection 'his sensibility surrenders to an inundation by the far but half-remembered world of Greece. This is an accumulation of honesty and craft, with its beautiful pointed moments of definition and its inevitable realizations of development' (209). This is then the pattern of the book Heaney is reviewing, a pattern created when Hewitt arranged the order of the poems. We may note, however, that it is not always the chronological order and, as we have seen, rootedness and feelings of being at home overlap with alienation long before his actual exile which did not only mean a lost community but also a new one. In addition, feeling at home, the sense of recognition, of belonging, presents itself also when over the years he is travelling in Greece, Sicily, in Warsaw and Vienna, in many different places, something that does not prevent him from feeling a stranger in other respects, no part of that context.

Reading Hewitt, then, has demonstrated a considerable breadth of the concept of exile, of leaving home, due to migration or colonization as with his forefathers, to economic hardship and expectations for a better future abroad as with his uncles, for family reasons as was the case with his parental grandparents, or cultural exclusion as with himself. He gives ample evidence of inner or symbolic exile and, thus, a longing and need for a home in this respect, at the same time as he emphatically proclaims his deep roots in the soil of his Northern Irish landscape. This landscape in combination with an eclectic personal myth of Irish legends, Ulster folklore and, especially, a collection of role models among rebels and protesters forms his lasting refuge when he settles back in Belfast again after his retirement to an unprecedented period of creativity.

Notes

¹ For a more extensive account of the role of Belfast in Hewitt's work
  see my essay on the subject.
² This is further developed in Hewitt's essays 'The Bitter Gourd: Some
  Problems of the Ulster Writer' (1945) *Ancestral Voices* 108-21,
  'Regionalism: The Last Chance' (1947) *Ancestral Voices* 122-25, but
  also e.g. in John Wilson Foster's 'Radical Regionalism' *Colonial
  Consequences* 278-96.
³ Cf. Longley 18 and Cunningham 27-33.

References

Brown, Terence. 'John Hewitt: an Ulster of the Mind' in *The Poet's
    Place: Essays in Honour of John Hewitt, 1907-87*. Ed. Gerald Dawe
    and John Wilson Foster. Belfast: Institute of Irish Studies, The
    Queen's University of Belfast: 1991. 299-311.
Cunningham, Valentine. *British Writers of the Thirties*. Oxford,
    New York: Oxford University Press, 1988.
Foster, John Wilson. *Colonial Consequences: Essays in Irish Literature
    and Culture*. Dublin: The Liliput Press, 1991.
— '"The Dissidence of Dissent"' in *Across a Roaring Hill: The
    Protestant Imagination in Modern Ireland*. Ed. Gerald Dawe &
    Edna Longley. Belfast: Blackstaff, 1985. 139-60.
Heaney, Seamus. *Preoccupations: Selected Prose 1968-1978*. London:
    Faber, 1980.
Hewitt, John. 'A North Light' in manuscript, University of Ulster
    library at Coleraine. One of the 38 chapters published in
    Ancestral Voices along with two chapters of similar nature but
    not included in this autobiography.
— *Ancestral Voices: The Selected Prose of John Hewitt*. Ed. Tom
    Clyde. Belfast: Blackstaff, 1987.
— Introduction to *The Poems of William Allingham*. Ed. John
    Hewitt. Dublin, 1967. 7-19.
— 'No Rootless Colonist', *Aquarius* No.5. (1972): 90-95. Also in
    Ancestral Voices 146-57.
— 'Planter's Gothic'. The parts which were published in *The Bell*
    (1953) reprinted in *Ancestral Voices* 1-33.
— *Rhyming Weavers and Other Country Poets of Antrim and Down*.
    Ed. and introduced by John Hewitt. Belfast: Blackstaff, 1974.

— *The Collected Poems*. Ed. Frank Ormsby. Belfast: Blackstaff, 1991.

Hughes, Eamonn. 'Sent to Coventry: Emigrations and Autobiography' in *Returning to Ourselves: Second Volume of Papers from the John Hewitt International Summer School*. Ed. Eve Patten. Belfast: Lagan Press, 1995. 261-75.

Johnstone, Robert. Review of *The Collected Poems of John Hewitt* in *The Irish Times* 25 January 1992.

Joyce, James. *A Portrait of the Artist as a Young Man*. 1916. London: Heinemann, 1964.

Kiberd, Declan. *Irish Classics*. London: Granta Books, 2000.

Longley, Edna. 'Progressive Bookmen: Left-wing Politics and Ulster Protestant Writers' in *Returning to Ourselves: Second Volume of Papers from the John Hewitt International Summer School*. Ed. Eve Patten. Belfast: Lagan Press, 1995. 16-40.

Olinder, Britta. 'John Hewitt's Belfast' in *The Irish Writer and the City*. Ed. Maurice Harmons. (Irish Literary Studies. 18) Gerrards Cross, Bucks.: Colin Smythe, 1984. 144-52.

Said, Edward. *Reflections on Exile and Other Essays*. Cambridge, Mass.: Harvard University Press, 2000.

Vance, Norman. *Irish Literature. A Social History: Tradition, Identity and Difference*. Oxford: Basil Blackwell, 1990.

Ward, Patrick. *Exile, Emigration and Irish Writing*. Dublin: Irish Academic Press, 2002.

The Celtic Ray:
Representations of Diaspora Identities in Van Morrison's Lyrics

Bent Sørensen

This paper is an examination of representations of Celtic roots and Irish diaspora identities in three 1980s albums by Belfast born singer/songwriter, Van Morrison.

Although Morrison originates in Ulster, he has spent the bulk of his life in self-imposed exile in North America, England and Europe. His music is based on a mixture of North American forms (rhythm and blues/jazz and folk/country) and traditional Irish folk inspiration. His main fan base has always been located in the USA and in continental Europe, and for many years Morrison lived in homes in Woodstock, New York, coastal California, and rural England, residences interspersed with lengthy sojourns in various European countries, such as France and Denmark. The 1980s saw him return more explicitly to Irish roots, and a trilogy of albums from that period contain songs whose lyrics and tunes express Celtic longings, culminating in a full-length album collaboration with The Chieftains (*Irish Heartbeat*, 1988), which features 7 traditional Irish songs (one a Patrick Kavanagh poem set to a traditional Irish air), a Scottish song, and two self-penned Van Morrison songs, which were re-recordings of songs originally appearing on *Beautiful Vision* (1982) and *Inarticulate Speech of the Heart* (1983).

This paper shows how these two songs ('Celtic Ray' and 'Irish Heartbeat') thematise tensions between longing and belonging in a conflict typical of diaspora texts. The songs propose a revival of a utopian brotherhood of peoples once (and again in the future) living on the 'Celtic Ray'. As the songs reappear in full Celtic-style

Re-Mapping Exile: Realities and Metaphors in Irish Literature and History, ed. Michael Böss, Irene Gilsenan Nordin and Britta Olinder, *The Dolphin* 34. © 2005 by Aarhus University Press, Denmark. ISBN 87 7934 010 5.

arrangements on the 1988 album, they form a seamless part of a whole suite of songs on migration (usually figured as 'roving') and exile, describing an arch in the singer's personal development of identity, both as a journey from painful courtship to joyous marriage (embodied in the first and last songs, 'Star of the County Down' and 'Marie's Wedding'), and as a journey through loss and death (referenced in almost all the songs in the middle sequence of the album). This arch symbolises an Irish journey into exile, through hardship and potential death, to a homecoming and 'settling' in Irish climes once more.

The paper contextualises this analysis with a discussion of Morrison's notions of Celtic brotherhood as a hybrid between American New Age philosophies and Irish identity positions (both identity constructs oscillate between collectivist messages and individualist realisations of them). Morrison's quest for enlightenment became more and more explicit throughout the eighties as witnessed by album titles such as the already cited ones from 1982 and 1983, as well as *Sense of Wonder* (1985), *Avalon Sunset* (1989), and finally *Enlightenment* (1990). Only on a surface level did an intervening album title from 1986, *No Guru, No Method, No Teacher*, appear to contradict the singer-songwriter's quest for esoteric knowledge, since that album title is in fact a quote from Krishnamurti, the mystic messiah trained by the Theosophical Society (founded by Madame Blavatsky) to enlighten the world (Heylin 393). Morrison songs from the 1980s are glosses of teachings from a number of esoteric, New Age or occult beliefs, including Scientology, whose founder L. Ron Hubbard, is explicitly thanked in the liner notes to *Inarticulate Speech of the Heart*. The richest vein mined by Morrison in those years is, however, the writings of Alice A. Bailey, whose theories concerning illusion, glamour, maya, and the strange entity known as 'The Dweller on the Threshold' – all obstacles to true enlightenment – can be traced on several Morrison albums.

The postulate here is that this hybrid of esoteric knowledge, Irish identity longings, and a cross-cultural musical style and performance, creates the only viable recipe for life for Morrison whose character reflects a contradiction between an extremely shy and private persona, and an extroverted performer persona whose only existence is in the public gaze. Morrison is thus seen to be 'Hiding in the Light', to gloss Dick Hebdige's 1980 book of the same title, which details the narcissistic paradox of hiding and exposure inherent in subcultural deviance, which seems apt to characterise Morrison's desires as well. This duality is further mirrored in Morrison's own internal and external exile positions, and partly explains his continuing quest for identity, figured as a battle between revelation in the form of enlightenment and concealment in clouds of mysticism.

Stuart Hall's identification of two separate ways of conceptualising 'cultural identity' is useful here to understand the unsolvable tensions of Morrison's project of 'homecoming'. Hall writes: 'The first position defines "cultural identity" in terms of one, shared culture, a sort of collective "one true self", hiding inside the many other, more superficial or artificially imposed "selves", which people with a shared history and ancestry hold in common.' (Hall 234). This is precisely the type of cultural identity Morrison has been frustratedly searching for throughout his diaspora life, whether as ethnically defined or esoterically displaced onto New Age collectivism. Hall's second type of cultural identity, in reality fits Morrison's life situation better, but has never presented itself to Morrison as a viable alternative, which is all the more tragic as it might hold the key for Morrison to conceptualise his alienation more fruitfully:

> This second position recognizes that, as well as the many points of similarity, there are also critical points of deep and significant *difference* which constitute 'what we really are'; or rather – since history has intervened – 'what we have become' [...] Cultural identity in this second sense is a matter of 'becoming' as well as of 'being'. It belongs to the future as much as to the past. It is not something which already exists, transcending place, time, history and culture [...] Far from being grounded in mere 'recovery' of the past, which is waiting to be found, and which when found, will secure our sense of ourselves into eternity, identities are the names we give to the different ways we are positioned by, and position ourselves within, the narratives of the past. (Hall 236)

This constructivist, historicist credo is the antithesis of the esoteric, pan-Celtic identity quest project of Van Morrison.

Origins and Displacements

In numerous songs spread out over his whole recording career, Morrison references his origins, childhood and youth in Belfast, where he was born in 1945. He grew up on Hyndford Street in a lower middle class neighbourhood in Protestant dominated East Belfast. However, his parents were not typical Ulster Protestants: Morrison's father, George, came from a family with Scottish, Presbyterian roots, and was an electrician by trade, but really more interested in his passionate hobby of collecting American blues, bluegrass, country and jazz records. Morrison's mother, Violet, unexpectedly developed an intensely religious zeal at the time when Morrison was around 10, but contrary to the norm she channelled her beliefs into Jehovah's Witnesses activities (hence Morrison's tribute 'Kingdom Hall' on his 1978 album *Wavelength*). This combination of a worldly father, whom Morrison has repeatedly described as an atheist, and a spiritual mother, would immediately seem to have set Morrison on his subsequent path of vacillation between belief and doubt. The parents seem to have embodied the same polarity of personality facets that Morrison himself exhibits: The father an introverted uncommunicative non-believer, ultimately disappointed with his life in Belfast; the mother an extrovert, performative personality, eager to communicate her views to people even to the extent of trying to convert them religiously.

What remains of Morrison's childhood memories – at least when one bases such reconstructions on the lyrics of his songs – is a melange of snapshots of spiritual moments of intense but confusing insight (referenced in early songs such as 'Cyprus Avenue', 'Into the Mystic', 'It Stoned Me') and lists of instances of musical and literary exposure and influence, such as may be heard in 'Cleaning Windows', 'On Hyndford Street' and as late as in 'The Meaning of Loneliness' on Morrison's most recent album *What's Wrong with This Picture?* (2003). The presence in his mind of these images of origin and home has however continued to be strong and haunting. It is possible that Morrison left Belfast long before he ever possessed the spiritual and mental resources to understand his ambivalent feelings of belonging and displacement through difference, and that this has caused him to associate Belfast and his family with traumatic and frustrating experiences, which he only worked through 25 years after first leaving Ulster to pursue a life as a wandering troubadour.

The modes of transmission of Morrison's remembrances of his early years are such that only speculation can be forwarded. He has never accounted explicitly for his mystical experiences, or at least only in poetical terms via his songs. Morrison has long toyed with the idea of writing his autobiography, but a manuscript has never materialised, so one is forced to rely on the work of unauthorised biographers. While a great number of such titles exist, none are particularly well written, and all draw so extensively on the previous ones that a number of factual errors are bound to be perpetuated through them like a daisy chain. The matter is exacerbated by Morrison's notorious distrust of journalists and biographers alike (going to such extreme lengths as writing a song titled, 'New Biography' (*Back on Top*, 1999), which lampoons all biographical activity as being merely a part of 'the fame game'), which means that interviews are rare and usually confrontational rather than informational. This habit of course irritates biographers no end, and biases almost all portraits of Morrison against him. The one exception seems to be Steve Turner's 1993 book *It's Too Late to Stop Now* (borrowing its title from Morrison's superb live album from 1974), which grows out of a trusting relationship between biographer and subject and forms perhaps the most reliable source to Morrison's spiritual quest. The proceeding sketch of Morrison's roving years is based largely on Turner and the most recent, but rather vengeful biography, *Can You Feel the Silence: Van Morrison, A New Biography* (2002) by Clinton Heylin, whose subtitle, alluding to the aforementioned Morrison song, illustrates the quarrels he had to go through with Morrison's representatives before he could publish what is the hitherto longest work on Morrison's career. Heylin's work is particularly useful because of its many interview excerpts with Morrison's collaborators and associates, and we shall draw mainly on this book in our examination of Morrison's Celtic mysticism of the 1980s.

Irish Rover

A performer from a very young age onwards, Morrison soon found Belfast too small for his ambitions and talent. After a number of band experiences, he established a slightly more stable constellation of musicians known as *Them*, and rapidly began accepting lengthy gigs rather far away from home: Glasgow, several German cities, and eventually London. By the time Morrison turned 20 he was a seasoned musician and traveller. His first extended tour of America had taken him to San Francisco and Los Angeles as early as May 1966, after which he had recorded in New York City, before taking up residence in Cambridge, Massachusetts. In February 1969 he relocated to Woodstock, in up-state New York, where he lived with his wife, Janet Planet, until April 1971, by which time Woodstock had become a major locus for hippie pilgrimage in the wake of the 1969 festival. Morrison's quest for the unspoiled rural setting which he and Janet Planet required to live out their (or in actuality his) dream of a quiet country life continued when he relocated to Marin County, California where he set up a long term residence that even outlasted the marriage to Janet.

In the mid-1970s Morrison gradually began leaving the American continent, increasingly dividing his time between California and various homes in Britain. He set up offices and residence in London in 1976, and from 1978 spent a lot of time in the village of Epwell in Oxfordshire. The early 1980s marked a culmination of 'roving' between villages and cities: 1982 saw the establishment of a long-term home in Holland Park, London, where Morrison was at his most accessible to friends and fellow musicians. The tenure in Holland Park in fact lasted till 1991, although the offices relocated to Bath as early as 1988. In the meantime, however, Morrison still kept up his California ties, residing part-time in Mill Valley, right up till 1983. The stay in California was prolonged due to the fact that Morrison's parents both had emigrated there in the 1970s and had been set up in homes and a business (a small record shop for his father) by

Morrison. Complicating the residence situation even further, Morrison began a long-term relationship with a Danish woman and apparently spent ample time with her in the suburbs of Copenhagen in 1981-82, and on tour where colleagues described her as a calming and anchoring influence on Morrison (The Danish connection is manifested in the song 'Vanlose Stairway' on the 1982 *Beautiful Vision* album). The sojourn in Europe was never particularly permanent, however, and England's rural setting exerted the strongest pull on Morrison throughout the early 1990s. This was marked by a move from Holland Park, London to the village of Little Somerford in Wiltshire in 1991. (Information collated from Turner, Heylin and Hinton)

During the 1970s references to Ireland were relatively rare in Morrison's songs. While 1968's *Astral Weeks* had glossed some of the foundational visions associated with home, which Morrison was to return to in the 1980s with his rediscovery of Irish landscapes and myths, the 1970s can be seen as a dormant period in Morrison's Irishness. Only sporadic returns to Ireland itself to tour (but never to Belfast, to the resentment of his hometown fans) occasionally sparked longings to return out of exile. One such instance could arguably be red into the lyrics of the title song on *St. Dominic's Preview* (1972). This is one of Morrison's most enigmatic songs, effortlessly blending images of the Notre Dame Cathedral in Paris with images of garbage outside 'Safeway supermarkets in the rain' and with '52nd Street apartments'. Among the many localities the songs whirlwinds through are some that can be construed as Irish (perhaps including St. Dominic's itself), none more clearly so than the reference to 'freedom marching' and how 'the chains, badges, flags and emblems' are a 'strain on every brain and every eye'. These references would appear to gloss some of the best-known public manifestations of the division of Ulster into Protestant and Catholic groups, each marking their allegiances with colours, flags and emblems and commemorative marches.

Political references in Morrison's songs are rare, but not unique. Certainly the lines from 1971's 'Tupelo Honey' can be glossed as political, even with their displacement back into chivalric time: 'You can't stop us on the road to freedom/You can't keep us 'cause our eyes can see/Men with insight, men in granite/Knights in armour bent on chivalry'. It was, however, not until Morrison's appearance at a 1996 peace rally, featuring Bill Clinton (who wanted to play sax with Morrison, but was not allowed to go on by his own security people), that Morrison became publicly associated with the peace efforts in (Northern) Ireland.

The most overtly Irish of Morrison's 1970s albums was *Veedon Fleece* (1974), which has cover art featuring Morrison and two Irish wolfhounds (a theme revamped on the cover of 1995's *Days Like This* where the two hounds have been supplemented with Morrison's then fiancé, former Miss Ireland, Michelle Rocha, sending a rather more domesticated signal of Irish belonging). This album details a quest for a Celtic equivalent to the Golden Fleece pursued by Jason and the Argonauts in Greek mythology. Consistently underrated, the album contains overtly Irish themes both lyrically and musically in gems such as 'Streets of Arklow' and 'Country Fair', which eerily prefigures the Irish ballads to appear on the Chieftains collaboration *Irish Heartbeat* 14 years later.

Glamour and the Dweller on the Threshold

The context of Alice A. Bailey's esoteric work and other mysticist sources is crucial for the understanding of Morrison's 1980s production, and therefore a detour into this context ('Into the Mystic' as it were, glossing the early Morrison song of that title from his 1970 album, *Moondance*) is necessary at this point. The book, *Glamour: A World Problem* – like several other works signed by Bailey – are in fact presented as dictated to her by 'The Tibetan', who also prefaces *Glamour* explaining that he is 'a Tibetan disciple of a certain degree [living] in a physical body like other men, on the borders of Tibet' (Bailey v). The books are thus a kind of telepathically guided automatic writing by Bailey, much in the vein of Yeats' notions of poetic visions, which we know inspired Morrison from an early age.

Morrison cites *Glamour: A World Problem*, on the record sleeve of *Beautiful Vision* (1982) as having inspired the lyrics of two of the songs appearing on that album, 'Dweller on the Threshold' and

'Aryan Mist'. Bailey and the Tibetan's thesis in the book is, briefly told, that human beings in the current age of the world, where what they refer to (in unpleasant sounding phrasing) as the 'Aryan race' (32) is dominant, suffer from degrees of illusion preventing them from further spiritual development and enlightenment. This illusion comes in four degrees, one of which is 'glamour'. In this esoteric parlance 'glamour' is thus negatively charged and part of the greater illusion of mankind about its role in the universal (astral) scheme of things. 'Glamour has oft been regarded as a curious attempt of what are called the "black forces" to deceive and hoodwink well-meaning aspirants' (Bailey 20) '*The Problem of Glamour* is found when the mental illusion is intensified with desire. It is illusion on the astral plane' (Bailey 21). Glamour is thus the result of vanity and temptation to glorify oneself and one's spiritual progress. Morrison refers to 'glamour' in the lyrics of no less than four songs throughout his career, two of which are the ones mentioned above as explicitly inspired by Bailey.

The fourth and ultimate stage of illusion, according to Bailey, is mysteriously personified into 'The Dweller on the Threshold'. Bailey says about this entity that:

> '[It] is usually regarded as presenting the final test of man's courage, and as being in the nature of a gigantic thoughtform or factor which has to be dissipated, prior to taking initiation. Some regard it as the sumtotal of a man's faults, his evil nature, which hinders his being recognised as fit to tread the Path of Holiness'. (21)

Further she comments: 'It is in reality a vitalised thoughtform – embodying mental force, astral force and vital energy'(27). This avatar is therefore the essential foe all disciples must wrestle with to progress spiritually.

Thus, when Morrison refers to himself as that evil entity in the song titled 'Dweller on the Threshold', he is dramatically suggesting his shortcomings as a spiritual being, but after this initial identification with evil, he drives on toward a 'higher ground' (later specifically Christian in 'Whenever God Shines His

Light on Me' on *Avalon Sunset*), where he might fuse with the Dweller's antithesis, the 'Angel of the Presence': 'I'm a Dweller on the Threshold/And I'm waiting at the door/And I'm standing in the darkness/I don't want to wait no more//Feel the Angel of the Presence/In the mighty crystal fire/Lift me up, consume my darkness/Let me travel even higher'. The cataclysmic event, where light and dark meet, will 'consume my darkness' and prepare the way to cross the Threshold. On the album this leads to a progression in the song titles: 'Beautiful Vision', 'She Gives Me Religion', the ascent up the 'Vanlose Stairway', the lifting of the 'Aryan Mist' ('The fog of illusion/The fog of confusion/Is hanging all over the world'), and leads 'Across The Bridge Where Angels Dwell'.

To return to Bailey's esoteric programme we should note that the guidance for the Dweller in his project of fusing with the Angel and crossing the Threshold takes the form of a number of Rays. Of these there are seven, none of which are specifically Celtic in Bailey's terminology, but all of which help the seeker overcome specific temptations, and which in different measures make up people's personalities in the 'Aryan Race', as we move toward the 'Aquarian Age' (Bailey 156-157). Thus, it seems clear that the whole of Morrison's album is deeply inspired by Bailey's esoteric system, from the invocation of the brotherhood of Celtic peoples following the Ray in the opening track, and at least till the penultimate track's crossing of the bridge into Heaven: 'Ahead where home awaits the heart/Ahead where home is waiting/Ahead where home awaits the heart/Peace is near'. This longing for home is already ripe for a coupling with the ending of exile and reversal of the exodus that created the diaspora.

1983's *Inarticulate Speech of the Heart* continues the musical style of the previous album. It also addresses issues of homecoming and brotherhood, as for example in the extremely simplistic mantra of the lyrics of 'River of Time': 'Brother of mine/Sister of mine/Heart and soul/Body and mind/Meet me on the river of time'. Similar sentiments are signalled by the titles of 'Cry for Home' and 'Irish Heartbeat', and thoroughly borne out by the lyrics' childlike longings for home: 'I'll be waiting on that shore/To hear the cry for home/You won't have to worry anymore/When you hear the cry for home'. Morrison is ready for return, but still lacks a specific direction and an end goal.

Bailey's influence is less obvious on this record, but the explicit reference to Scientology, could surely be examined and reveal similar translations from Hubbard's cosmology to Morrison's. It is clear, however, that the project of seeking for an esoteric identity is not over. On the 1983 album the figure of John Donne is evoked to stand for the quester who seeks 'down through the ages' for various esoteric teachings. At some point he is then replaced by a man 'out of Ireland', W.B. Yeats: 'Rave on let a man come out of Ireland/Rave on Mr. Yeats/Rave on down through the Holy Rosey Cross/Rave on down through theosophy, and the Golden Dawn/Rave on through the writing of *A Vision'*. Yeats is for a while the perfect figure for Morrison's quest through the Rosicrucian and other esoteric teachings, not least because he was Irish (though never an exile), but also because his emphasis on automatic writing and belief in the creative inspiration of visions, mirrors Morrison's own so exactly.

The esoteric thought system provides a context for understanding Morrison's longing for 'home'. If the external exile is a continuing condition of life in the diaspora, the internal healing that might occur under the guidance of the 'Celtic Ray'[1] holds out a promise at least of providing an inner sanctuary, or a spiritual home. The problem with the esoteric understanding of belonging is, of course, that it involves a construction of cultural identity which is extremely a-historical and non-specific, and while the esoteric solution promises a collectivist paradise the road each seeker walks toward this dream is exclusively individualistic.

Irish Heartbeat

The two New Age[2] albums of the 1980s, *Beautiful Vision* and *Inarticulate Speech of the Heart* each contained one song specifically preoccupied with Irish identities. 'Celtic Ray' (in its 1982 version) proposes a unity between the Celtic peoples and territories of Britain and Ireland, and this unity is figured as a shared origin symbolised by a mother's voice calling to her scattered children to reunite in the light of the Celtic Ray. This evocation of the diaspora of an original Ur-Celtic race is underscored by the setting, consisting of (stereo)typical morning scenes where other voices, those of working men (McManus, the fish monger and the coal-brick man) trigger the memory of the mother(land)'s voice, summoning the children, who among themselves agree: 'Listen Jimmy! I want to go home/I've been away from the Ray too long'. 'Irish Heartbeat' contains both a marshalling of Irish forces to remain true to the homeland: 'Don't rush away/Rush away from your own ones/Just one more day/One more day with your own ones', and a welcoming back of the prodigals who despite this urging may have gone the diaspora route anyway: 'There's a stranger/And he's standing at your door/Might be your best friend, might be your brother/You may never know'. This stranger is immediately revealed to be a figure for the song's speaker himself: 'I'm going back/Going back to my own ones/Come back to talk/Talk a while with my own ones'. Ultimately the vision of the song is that only 'with your own ones' can you find your own soul.

These two songs are enhanced on their original albums by some instrumentation from the Celtic register, such as flutes and pipes, but emerge radically more potent when rendered fully Celtic by the Chieftains' arrangement of them on *Irish Heartbeat* in 1988. This album can be seen as a geographical tour of Ireland containing songs from both North and South, and referencing the full Celtic geography of the Emerald Isle and beyond. A transformation of the lyrics of 'Celtic Ray' on *Irish Heartbeat* is also of significance. The Celtic Ray brotherhood has been emended to exclude England, and instead the verses reference first Brittany and then Cornwall as part of the list of the Ur-Celtic nations and peoples. This political act of excising England from the cradles of the Celts flies somewhat in the face of Morrison's yearlong residence in the English countryside. One might guess that Cornwall is proposed as a compromise way of referencing an English territory without uttering the dreaded name of England herself.

Morrison and Moloney chose the traditional songs on the album, apparently via a consensus process. Each had a shortlist of songs they wished to include on the album, and through a number of sessions, no doubt eased by libations of Guinness and whiskey, the set list was agreed upon by the two, after which Moloney worked up 'shapes' for the arrangements. It seems clear that several songs were childhood favourites of Morrison's. His father was partial to Irish tenor John McCormack, and from his repertoire one must surmise came 'Star of the County Down' and 'She Moved Through the Fair'. Morrison's mother taught her granddaughter, Shana, songs such as 'I'll Tell My Ma', a typical teasing song for children, and again 'Star of the County Down', so it seems feasible that at least those titles came from Morrison's list (cf. Heylin 417).

The theme of the County Down as a grounding geographical presence was actually already present in another Morrison song which appeared on *Beautiful Vision*, namely 'Northern Muse (Solid Ground)' – a title very suitable also for the traditional ballad of a vision of the 'brown colleen' who, muse-like, will make any man cease from roving and settle down in marriage. 'Northern Muse' contains these lines: 'And she moves on the solid ground/And she shines light all around/And she moves on the solid ground/In the County Down'. Her grounding presence is the remedy for the weariness of exile, as we learn later, but paradoxically this is an exile she herself induced in the young man: 'When I was young she made me roam from my home/In the County Down/She lifts me up/She fills my cup/When I'm tired and weary, Lord/And she keeps the flame'. This prior preoccupation with Irish geography and ground lends further weight to the speculation that Morrison wished to include 'The Star of the County Down' on the album.

I believe that Morrison is also responsible for the inclusion of 'On Raglan Road', the Patrick Kavanagh poem, both because of the many kinships between Kavanagh and Morrison[3], and because of the liberties Morrison takes with Kavanagh's text, reinterpreting the poem when performing it as a song in a completely transcendent way. (Morrison had in fact performed the song with Derek Bell prior to the recording of it with the full Chieftains line-up.) The poem's thematics of the relationship between artist and muse also places it as a perfect companion piece to 'Northern Muse'. The artist is figured as an angel who falls for the temptation to 'woo [...] a creature made of clay', and having transferred his ability to create onto her ('I gave her gifts of the mind, I gave her the secret sign that's known/To the artists who have known the true gods of sound and stone/And word and tint'), allowing her to speak poems 'with her own name', he subsequently loses 'his wings at the dawn of day'. The punishment for succumbing to the temptations of the flesh/clay muse is dramatic, yet the muse's newfound capabilities are similar to the ones of the 'Northern Muse'.

The appropriation of the poem into Morrison's own song is typical of his approach to 'covers' of other artists' material, and strongly underscored by the performance practice he adds to the works. On many of the tracks on *Irish Heartbeat* Morrison brings his trademark scat singing techniques to bear, in very sharp contrast to folk singing conventions. The jazzy riffing which can be heard in many endings on songs on the album ('Irish Heartbeat', 'Raglan Road', 'She Moved through the Fair', 'Celtic Ray', 'My Lagan Love'), caused the Chieftains great difficulties in live concert situations, since their performance practice did not involve the use of prolonged, improvised coda segments. Audiences consisting of folk purists were also offended by these jazzy mannerisms on Morrison's part, which they saw as showy, self-serving and self-promoting techniques disrupting the collectivist ethos of folk performance (stronger in Ireland through the *ceilidh* tradition for open sit-ins than anywhere else). The paradox here is that the only other open sit-in music traditions, jazz and blues, were exactly the ones Morrison was drawing upon in his vocal style on the album, so for him there was no contradiction in this cross-musical practice. One might also usefully point out that certain Irish folk traditions such as keening also draw on melisma and prolonged improvised coda techniques, and that in fact for the unbiased listener it sounds like Morrison is drawing as much on this tradition as on the scat techniques. At least Moloney contextualises Morrison's practices in this way: 'Long cadenzas, very traditional west of Ireland keening, long warbling endings' (Heylin 416), and Kevin Conneff, the Chieftains' vocalist even attempts an Irish scat himself on 'I'll Tell Me Ma'.

172 Böss, Nordin and Olinder

The other trademark Morrison technique is related to the coda practice and consists of repetition of key words and phrases from the lyrics. This is typical of gospel and blues lyrics and performance practices, but again antithetical to purist folk delivery. Morrison uses riffing on repeated lyric snippets to enter a zone of performance where his projection comes from a 'trancelike vision' (as Morrison refers to in 'Ancient Highway' on *Days Like This* (1995)), induced by the use of lyrics as mantra to meditate on during performance. Such transcendence is unheard of in folk performance in Western (including Irish) cultures, but common in First Nations musical performance practices where the ritualistic origins of music have not been displaced completely. Again 'Raglan Road' is the prime example on the album of this practice.

It is now time to substantiate our hypothesis that *Irish Heartbeat* as a whole is constructed as a celebration of Ireland and of Irish identity whether in exile or at home. Certainly, Arty McGlynn, a Morrison collaborator in the early 1980s suggests: 'At that stage Van wanted to make an Irish-identity album. It was part of wanting to be Irish in some way' (qtd in Heylin 415). We may thus expect the songs on that album to reflect various aspects of Irish identity, and indeed the lyrics abound with references to places inside Ireland: 'Star of the County Down' glosses Ireland 'From Bantry Bay up to Derry Quay and/From Galway to Dublin Town', *'Ta Mo Chleamhnas Deanta'* walks 'Cork, Dublin and Belfast towns', 'On Raglan Road' refers to that street and other Dublin scenes, 'I'll Tell Me Ma' describes 'the Belle of Belfast City', 'Carrickfergus' glosses Ballygrand and Kilkenny, too, and of course 'My Lagan Love' limns 'a lily fair' 'where Lagan streams sing lullabies'. The songs consistently couple place with personality and personal identity. The diaspora outside Ireland haunts most of the songs, too, chiefly in the theme of personal loss: The singer in *'Ta Mo Chleamhnas Deanta'* has a love who has 'crossed the ocean' and himself vows to 'go roaming the wild woods (Morrison actually sings 'wide world') all over'. 'My Lagan Love' and 'She Moved through the Fair' both treat the subject of unattainable love, and are open for interpretations that suggest that these 'loves' are lost as they have died or become disembodied entities, while in 'Carrickfergus' and 'Raglan Road' it is the speaker who is dying before he can reach his home, or is being left behind as his love is 'walking now away from me/So hurriedly'. All of these losses can be glossed as metaphors for the separation from love and land in the diaspora.

However, the overall structure of the album is optimistic, as the courtship that is vowed to be unrelenting in 'Star of the County Down': 'No pipe I'll smoke, no horse I'll yoke/Till my plough turns rust coloured brown/Till a smiling bride, by my own fireside/Sits the star of the County Down'. It can thus be seen to culminate in the joyous romp of 'Marie's Wedding', which closes the album, with the celebration of a bride: 'Bright her eyes as any star' and no less fair than the 'Star' the cycles of songs commenced with. The middle songs have primarily glossed love and loss, with the exception of the childish tease of 'I'll Tell Me Ma', but the loss has been tempered by the promise of brotherhood and return from exile held out by Morrison's own two songs, offering the common Ray and the shared Heartbeat as healing presences for the diaspora. The album therefore begs to be read as a celebration of Celtic resilience and determination in the face of hardship and exile, and posits the earthy values in 'Plenty herring, plenty meal/Plenty peat to fill her kreel/Plenty bonnie bairns as well/That's the toast for Marie' as the ultimate saving grace. However, ending the Irish identity project with a Scottish song, as Morrison and the Chieftains do here, could be argued to put a question mark against the happy ending for the Irish sufferer, whose more relentless diaspora emotion then ends with the words of 'My Lagan Love': 'No life have I, no liberty'…

The Beauty of the Days Gone By
The arch of entry into, passage through, and return from the diaspora, indicated by the *Irish Heartbeat* album was ultimately not a fulfilment of Morrison's own twisted identity project. We conclude with a cursory examination of later developments in Morrison's oeuvre.

As already hinted at the almost obsessive listing of street names, and Irish place names in general is a recurrent feature of Morrison's 1980s and 1990s oeuvre, as witnessed for instance by numerous songs on the two-record set *Hymns to the Silence* from 1991, which features the song 'On Hyndford Street'. The visions which left Morrison tongue-tied and shaking 'like a leaf on a tree' in 'Cyprus Avenue' in 1968 are constantly linked with specificity of place, and the only hermeneutics that might offer an analysis of the visionary force is gathered from arts and literature. Debussy and Kerouac are mentioned here, alongside blues- and jazz-men such as Jellyroll Morton – closing the circle back to Morrison's father's record collection. The awaited interpretation is, however, always deferred, always ends in (hymns to the) silence – or remain 'cloud hidden, whereabouts unknown', as Morrison's 1987 'Alan Watts Blues' (from *Poetic Champions Compose*) puts it, with reference to one of Watts' books. The list of common names of writers, philosophers, artists and composers in 'On Hyndford Street' is only one of many found in Morrison songs from the 1980s and 1990s.

In the 1993 song 'Too Long in Exile', Morrison generated another hermeneutic catalogue of figures he attempts to understand himself and his exile-positions through. The list is familiarly literary to begin with, referencing James Joyce, Samuel Beckett and Oscar Wilde, only to culminate with two scandal plagued, alcoholic Irish exiles from the world of sports, footballer George Best and Alex Higgins, the snooker player. These exile role models all share Morrison's own conflictedness. They sought exile to pursue freedom and fame, only to be caught up in exactly the tension of fame providing a new prison house for their creative efforts, often quite literally as in the case of Wilde. These exiles all failed to come home again, or if they did they returned as cripples, having paid too high a price for experience. Morrison's own exile seemed over in the late 1980s, but demons acquired along the road to fame and fortune have come back to Ireland with him, and continue to haunt him as they did the figures he sees as his predecessors and peers.

After 1993 the literary glosses gradually disappear from Morrison's new songs, although Yeats and Blake both return, and occasional references to new figures such as Kenneth Grahame (*Wind in the Willows*) do occur. The esoteric references continue to appear, and the quest this reflects takes in new dimensions from masculinity studies and other related fields of a therapeutic nature ('Fire in the Belly', from *The Healing Game* (1997) in an example of this). Similarly the references to popular music and popular culture continue to proliferate in Morrison-lyrics, culminating with full-fledged tribute albums in 1997 to Mose Allison, in 2000 to skiffle music, and also in 2000 to rock'n'roll and country and western via a collaboration with Linda Gail Lewis, the sister of Jerry Lee Lewis.

Morrison finally comes to terms with the figure of his father in a moving *homage* to him in the song 'Choppin' Wood' on the 2002 album *Down the Road*, where that song is immediately followed by Morrison's last comment on the Irish exile experience so far. The father's own exile experience, and homecoming is touched upon for the first time in Morrison's work: 'You wired the trains and went back home to St. Claire's shores/Before you became a spark down at the yard/You were passing through those hungry years alone/You were just trying to make a living out in Detroit'. The exile's homecoming is figured as a sacrifice, glossed through the famous phrase of Thoreau's *Walden*: 'And you came back home to Belfast/So you could be with us like/You lived your life of quiet desperation on the side'. It is clear that Morrison contemplates a similar fate for himself.

In 'What Makes the Irish Heart Beat', a title glossing his previous Irish explorations of collectivist brotherhood, Morrison instead focuses exclusively on the individual experience of inner-compelled exile as a quest for adventure: 'Just like a sailor out on the foam/Any port in a storm/Where we tend to burn the candle at both ends/Down the corridors of fame/Like the spark ignites the flame/That's what makes the Irish heart beat'. The economies of exile and diaspora living are clearly set out in these two songs. The necessity of exile is the young man's driving force, and the loss of belonging is the dear price he pays. The necessity of homecoming and shouldering of responsibility is the mature man's compelling force and the price is the closed-in life of a dreamer wishing himself away to other shores and greater freedoms. And yet that seems to be the ultimate choice – to return: 'All that trouble all that grief/That's why I had to leave/Staying

away too long is in defeat/Why I'm singing this song/Why I'm
heading back home/That's what makes the Irish heart beat'.

The diasporic dichotomies just refuse to go away, but perhaps
the overt treatment of the dichotomy of having to leave, yet not
being able to stay gone, is the beginning of an entry into Hall's
second understanding of cultural identity as incorporating past as
well as present into your construct of belonging.

Notes

1 Cf. Alan Pert's explanation given in the Glossary portion of the Van
   Morrison website: 'In esoteric teachings, each planet is associated
   with a particular Ray or type of consciousness. The Celtic or Green
   Ray is the Ray of Beauty and of the artist. It is symbolised by the
   planet Venus. "The Greeks with their art and the Celts with their
   music and dance were the true initiates of the Green Ray, and the
   influence of the astral contacts can be clearly seen to this day in the
   temperament of the Celtic races" (Dion Fortune, *Applied Magic*)'.
2 This epithet is triggered both by the lyrics, as discussed above, and
   the synth-ambience of much of the music, including several
   instrumental tracks.
3 See Paul Durcan's explanation in *Magill,* May 1988: 'Both Northerners
   – solid ground boys. Both primarily jazzmen, bluesmen, *sean nos.*
   Both concerned with the mystic – how to live with it, by it, in it; how
   to transform it; how to reveal it. Both troubadours. Both very
   ordinary blokes. Both drumlin men – rolling hills men. Both loners.
   Both comedians. Both lovepoets. Both Kerouac freaks. Both
   storytellers. Both obsessed with the hegira – from Monaghan to the
   Grand Canal, from East Belfast to Caledonia. Both originals, not
   imitators. Both first-time cats, not copycats. Both crazy. Both sane as
   sane can be. Both fascinated by at once their own Englishness and
   their own Irishness. Both obsessed with the audience and with the
   primacy of audience in any act or occasion of song or art. Both
   fascinated by the USA. Both Zen Buddhists. Both in love with names
   – placenames as well as personal names: Cypress Avenue, Inniskeen
   Road; San Anselmo, Islington; Boffyflow and Spike, Shancoduff; The
   Eternal Kansas City, The Rowley Mile; Madame George, Kitty
   Stobling; Jackie Wilson, Father Mat; O Solo Mio by McGimpsey, John
   Betjeman on Drumcondra Road.' (56)

References

Bailey, Alice A. *Glamour: A World Problem*. New York & London: Lucis, 1950.

Braziel, Jane Evans & Anita Mannur, eds. *Theorizing Diaspora*. Malden, Oxford, Melbourne, Berlin: Blackwell Publishing, 2003.

Durcan, Paul. 'The Drumshanbo Hustler: A celebration of Van Morrison' in *Magill*, May 1988.

Hall, Stuart. 'Cultural Identity and Diaspora', in Braziel and Mannur 233-246.

Hebdige, Dick. *Hiding in the Light*. London: Routledge, 1980.

Heylin, Clinton. *Can You Feel the Silence? Van Morrison: A New Biography*. London: Viking/Penguin, 2002.

Hinton, Brian. *Celtic Crossroads: The Art of Van Morrison*. London: Sanctuary Publishing, 1997.

Pert, Alan. Glossary entry on 'Celtic Ray', <http://www.harbour.sfu.ca/~hayward/van/glossary/celticray.html>

Turner, Steve. *Van Morison: Too Late to Stop Now*. London: Bloomsbury, 1993.

'Between the Dark Shore and the Light': The Exilic Subject in Eiléan Ní Chuilleanáin's *The Second Voyage*

Irene Gilsenan Nordin

One of the most striking elements in the poetry of Eiléan Ní Chuilleanáin is the use of the journey motif, where images of interior and exterior space are juxtaposed as the boundaries between self and world are brought together in a fluid and contrastive world of stability and instability. This juxtaposition is seen in the constant movement between images of fixity and flux, suggesting the constant crossings between conscious will and unconscious desire, which expresses the metaphorical journey that the speaking subject makes into language. Associated with the motif of the journey used regularly in Ní Chuilleanáin's poetry are the metaphors of separation and exile, which, in existentialist terms, can be understood as an expression of the experience of the speaking subject as s/he makes the journey in language, to emerge as a speaking and thinking being. This transitional, exilic state is what Kristeva calls the subject-in-process, where the speaking subject is seen as a split subject, situated at the intersections of language and the unconscious, in the space between the symbolic and the semiotic, between word and flesh (7). In other words, the speaking subject is constantly in transit, in a state of exile, moving between contrasting states of homelessness and home. The philosopher Rosi Braidotti refers to this type of subject as a 'nomadic subject', one that constantly moves across 'established categories and levels of experience: blurring boundaries without burning bridges' (4). Thus the idea of exile that I am concerned

Re-Mapping Exile: Realities and Metaphors in Irish Literature and History, ed. Michael Böss, Irene Gilsenan Nordin and Britta Olinder, *The Dolphin* 34. © 2005 by Aarhus University Press, Denmark. ISBN 87 7934 010 5.

with here is exile in poststructuralist terms, exile as an existential state of being, as an expression of the essential human condition.

This essay will explore the idea of existential exile and the related metaphors of homelessness and home associated with the motif of exilic subject, in Eiléan Ní Chuilleanáin's *The Second Voyage*. It will also examine how the exilic journey becomes an expression of liberation and empowerment, experienced on the speaking subject's entry into language. Exile in this sense is expressed in the poetry in the constant movement between contrasting images of fixity and flux, such as that between the conscious and the unconscious, the visible and the invisible, the spoken and the unsaid. The experience of liberation and empowerment associated with the transitory, threshold state of the in-between is expressed in moments of perception, like sharp flashes of epiphany, moments that are associated with exile and estrangement, experienced when the speaking subject is unsettled in his/her customary dwelling-place (Smith 5). This sense of estranging perception can be compared to Heidegger's idea of the experience of the 'Nothing' (93-110).[1] This is a state of homelessness reached by a 'fundamental experience' of the marvellous, which shakes us from our preoccupation with the everyday and offers a new conceptual sense of being that enables us to see things differently (Caputo 19, 29).

In Ní Chuilleanáin's poetics, such moments of estranging perception are very often associated with semiotic images of water, especially the sea, and are firmly anchored in the bodily experience of the speaking subject. For Ní Chuilleanáin, these moments of perception are situated not in any transcendental entity but in the site of the body itself, expressed metaphorically as the speaking subject travels in space, often through water, alternating between states of fixity and flux. We see an example of this in the poem 'Ferryboat':

> Once at sea, everything is changed:
> Even on the ferry, where
> There's hardly time to check all the passports
> Between the dark shore and the light. (34)

Here, the speaker is on a ferryboat at sea, in a state of temporary transit, or exile. S/he is in a semiotic state of flux, in the in-between space between the juxtaposing forces of darkness and light: 'Between the dark shore and the light'. The image of homelessness suggested here is developed in the lines which follow, where the transitory, exilic state is described as being 'officially nowhere', a state where 'in theory [one] may also drown / Though any other kind of death is more likely', suggesting the 'possibility' open to one in such a suspended state. The idea of suspension is continued in the first line of the next stanza, where the 'tables and chairs / Are chained down for fear of levitation', and the fixed, solid state of the furniture is juxtaposed with the contrasting image of possible 'levitation'. In the lines which follow, we see the speaker again in a state of semiotic transit, expressed in the image of the lifejacket, as follows:

> And a deaths-head in a lifejacket grins beside the bar
> Teaching the adjustment of the slender tapes
> That bind the buoyant soul to the sinking body,
> In case you should find yourself gasping
> In a flooded corridor or lost between cold waves. (34)

Thus, we are reminded of the homeless, in-between state of the speaking subject, suspended in time and space, between 'buoyant soul' and 'sinking body', between life and death, expressed by the speaker in the idea of struggle involved in the 'gasping' for breath, in 'a flooded corridor or lost between cold waves'.

In the poem entitled 'A Midwinter Prayer', we see the figure of the wanderer setting out on a journey, or as the speaker puts it 'the exile takes the road', on a journey which is undertaken in spite of the dangers that lie ahead. This setting out suggests the idea of conscious estrangement, and the accompanying sense of heightened awareness as the exile embarks on his unfamiliar and dangerous journey:

> In winter's early days, the exile takes the road —
> Dangerous nights with ghosts abroad:
> The eve of Samhain in the High King's hall

Fionn stood all night, his eyes open
For well-armed demons, for fire, music and death.

The wanderer catches light from chapel doors.
[. . . .]
The final Sunday after Pentecost the priest
Announced the Last Day, when the dead will spring
Like shrubs from quaking earth.
Against that spring the dark night sways
Swelling grey plumes of smoke over the edge of the world.
(45)

Here the exile wanders through a mythical landscape in time and
space. The scene moves from Samhain, the Celtic feast, literally
meaning 'summer's end' — one of the two great festivals of the
Celtic calendar, which celebrates the waning of the sun and the
coming of winter when the powers of the underworld and of
darkness grow strong[2] — to the final Sunday after the Christian
feast of the Pentecost, when the priest announces the Last Day:
'when the dead will spring / Like shrubs from quaking earth'. We
see in these lines the image of death, in the 'dark night' that 'sways
/ Swelling grey plumes of smoke over the edge of the world',
juxtaposed with that of life in the idea of the resurrection,
suggesting the promise of regeneration and new things to come.
The 'dark night' of the wanderer as he takes to the road is
counteracted by the light caught from 'chapel doors', and a sense
of promise and hope is evoked by the seed that in winter lays
waiting below the soil to emerge as new life in the spring. Thus the
wanderer in his marginalised position takes on the role of a
liminal figure, one who is outside society but who has access to a
heightened sense of perception and awareness which his liminal
status of exclusion and estrangement makes him privy to.[3] The
idea of the liminal figure of the exile is further suggested in the
remaining lines of the stanza:

(He sees, westward again, the islands
Floating lightly as bunches of foam
Alongside the neat schooner. There

> Yellow apples constantly in season
> Bend high branches, and the exile
> Is comforted in an orchard.) (45-6)

Here the image of the wanderer looking westward, towards the orchard with the yellow apples evokes a mood of escapism, reminiscent of Yeats's lines at the end of 'The Song of the Wandering Aengus' where the wanderer longs for a visionary end to his quest, when he will 'pluck till time and times are done / the silver apples of the moon / the golden apples of the sun'. The sense of fluidity, suggested in the image of the floating islands, is associated with that of insight, seen in the idea of orchard, which becomes an imaginary paradise-like space of supreme happiness. The orchard thus becomes a threshold liminal space, a semiotic source of sustenance and comfort, where the wandering subject is restored and strengthened, where 'Yellow apples' are 'constantly in season'.

As the description of exile's journey continues, he is depicted in biblical terms as 'a wise man with a star and stable', an outsider, who from his vantage point of estrangement is in a position to see things clearly: 'He is an unpeopled poet staring at a broken wall. / He sleeps in a cart by the river / Blocked by old barbed wire and dead dogs' (47). The sense of homelessness and estrangement is further developed in the next stanza, in the lines: 'He shelters in the ruined house / Where in dead silence the plaster falls / From ceilings, hour by hour' (47). In the final stanzas of the poem the idea of rebirth, echoing the mention of Pentecostal promise earlier in the poem, is further developed in the suggestion that '[w]hen February stirs the weeds / He'll start again moving to the west' (47). This idea of promise of fulfilment, or renewal, is again suggested in the final lines of the poem:

> The seed laid in the dead earth of December
> May yet grow to a flowering tree above ground.
> He will sail in a ring of welcoming islands —
> Midwinter, he can only pray to live that long. (47)

The contrasting images of homelessness and home that occur in *The Second Voyage* can be seen against the background of the mythic homeward journey — one of the best known of which is the return of Odysseus, the tale of the returning hero, who, in overcoming the many trials on his epic voyage, shows how the subject comes to consciousness and self-realization. In 'The Second Voyage', the title poem of the collection, we see the meeting of the semiotic body and the symbolic word expressed in the story of Odysseus, as he plans his second voyage (26). We see how he battles, on the one hand, with his sense of order and propriety to 'go back and organise' his house, and, on the other hand, his conflicting desire to return to the sea. In the first line of the poem, the returning hero is depicted, as he — with a certain degree of agitation — surveys the unruly and disorderly waves, which have caused him many trials during his long journey: 'Odysseus rested on his oar and saw / The ruffled foreheads of the waves / Crocodiling and mincing past' (26). This image of the dangerous and menacing waves is evoked further in the remainder of the line, as the hero: 'rammed / The oar between their jaws', suggesting the threatening force of the disorderly sea that is being battled against. The picture of the seething water is again expressed in the image of the unpredictable sea which follows, as Odysseus looks down into 'the simmering sea where scribbles of weed defined / Uncertain depth, and the slim fishes progressed / In fatal formation'. Odysseus's irritation with the resilient and uncontrollable waves is seen further in the following lines, as he thinks to himself:

> If there was a single
> Streak of decency in these waves now, they'd be ridged
> Pocked and dented with the battering they've had,
> And we could name them as Adam named the beasts. (26)

The waves, which can be understood to represent the semiotic forces of unconscious desire, threatening to disrupt the conscious order of things, will not allow themselves to be named, as 'Adam named the beasts'. This shows the uncontrollable force that the semiotic sea represents for Odysseus. The waves and the sea cannot be named because in their fluidity and absence of order they defy naming, just in the same way as the semiotic cannot be named. This imagery suggests the power of the unconscious drives represented in the semiotic image of the sea, and the difficult task that symbolic language is faced with in trying to do justice to these forces of the unconscious. Odysseus's striving symbolises the situation of the speaking subject, continually reaching out for language to give voice to experience.

In the next stanza, in keeping with the prophesy given him by the shade of Teiresias, whom he meets in Hades in Book XI of the *Odyssey* (Homer 130-1), Odysseus is told that after returning to Ithaca, he will leave the dark ocean and travel inland by foot, carrying his oar on his shoulder:

> I know what I'll do he said;
> I'll park my ship in the crook of a long pier
> (And I'll take you with me he said to the oar)
> I'll face the rising ground and walk away
> From tidal waters, up riverbeds
> Where herons parcel out the miles of stream,
> Over gaps in the hills, through warm
> Silent valleys. [. . .] (26)

The peaceful picture of the pastoral hills and the 'warm / Silent valleys' is contrasted with that of the stormy 'tidal waters' that Odysseus plans to walk away from. In the lines which follow, we see how he continues his inland journey, which — in further accordance with the prophesy — will be signalled by his meeting a man on the road, who mistakes the oar upon his shoulder for a winnowing-fan. Odysseus then plants the oar in the ground and goes back home to organise his house:

> [. . .] and when I meet a farmer
> Bold enough to look me in the eye
> With 'where are you off to with that long
> Winnowing fan over your shoulder?'
> There I will stand still
> And I'll plant you for a gatepost or a hitching-post

> And leave you as a tide-mark. I can go back
> And organise my house then. (26)

That Odysseus plants the oar for 'a gatepost or a hitching-post' suggests the idea of the oar as a mark, a symbolic act that signifies a place of threshold. This reminds us clearly of Hermes, the messenger of the gods, and the god of boundaries, traditionally associated with the gatepost, a place that signifies the crossing of thresholds (Howatson and Chilvers 262-3). Thus, the oar can be seen as a boundary mark between sea and home, between the forces of unconscious desire that Odysseus leaves behind and the stability of the land to which he turns. It is a metaphor for the unconscious forces of language itself which drive the speaking subject onwards. Leaving the oar, and the sea, behind him, Odysseus turns instead to the solid land to organise his house. In this way a dialectic tension is set up between the two forces of fixity and flux: the land, in the form of the house, which represents conscious will, and the sea, which represents the forces of unconscious desire. This juxtaposition of forces is seen in the last two lines of the poem, where unconscious desire prevails. While Odysseus's reasoning mind tells him that he should stay at home and organise his house, he feels the unconscious desire that still draws him to the sea: 'But the profound / Unfenced valleys of the ocean still held him' (26). The inner conflict that Odysseus faces in choosing between his house and the empowering forces of the sea represents the conflict between the two forces of homelessness and home, in the case of the speaking subject, the two forces of the semiotic and the symbolic, between which s/he is constantly in transit. For the time being, the forces of the symbolic house win, but the poem suggests that unconscious desire draws the speaker back to the semiotic sea.

Apart from the metaphors of water, expressing the image of homelessness, or exile, and the contrasting images of fixity, associated with the stability of home, are the many spatial metaphors used throughout the collection, where the interior semiotic world of the subject is juxtaposed with the exterior material world of objects and things. The image of the house is frequently used in Ní Chuilleanáin's poetry to express the tension between the stability of home, representing the internal world of the subject, and the contrasting world beyond the house, representing the external, outward world. In the very first poem of the collection, 'The Lady's Tower', the house appears in the form of the tower, where a paradoxical twist is given to the conventional phallic, symbolic image of the tower. Here, it becomes a symbol of the interior world of the subject as it is juxtaposed with the exterior natural world, expressed in the following evocative terms:

> Hollow my high tower leans
> Back to the cliff; my thatch
> Converses with spread sky,
> Heronries. The grey wall
> Slides downward and meets
> A sliding flooded stream. (11)

Throughout the poem, the fluctuating, transitory moods of the speaking subject are expressed in the contrasts between states of homelessness and home. This is seen, for instance, in the images of stability evoked in the possessive voice of the female speaker, as she symbolically names fixed objects around her: 'my high tower', and 'my thatch', which are contrasted with images of fluidity, as in the seemingly fluid wall which 'slides downward and meets / A sliding flooded stream'. The water, in the form of the stream, once more can be interpreted as a metaphor for the semiotic unconscious. This juxtaposing of the contrasting forces of homelessness and home is seen further in the next three-lined stanza, as the speaker contrasts the shifting 'oblique veins / Of the hill' with her damp kitchen, where the spiders are 'shaded under brown vats'. The idea of internal exile is suggested further in the voice of the speaker as she hears 'the stream change pace' and, glancing up from the stove, looks outside and sees 'the punt is now floating freely'. In the final stanza of the poem, these images of daylight activity are contrasted with those of the nocturnal, as the bodily space of the speaking subject becomes a site where boundaries are transgressed, and the unconscious and the conscious world become interchangeable in a meeting house of play:

> All night I lie sheeted, my broom chases down treads
> Delighted spirals of dust: the yellow duster glides
> Over shelves, around knobs: bristle stroking flagstone
> Dancing with the spiders around the kitchen in the dark
> While cats climb the tower and the river fills
> A spoonful of light on the cellar walls below. (11)

A moment of illumination is suggested in the final lines of the poem, where the image of the stream changes to that of a river, which − casting a transformational presence − 'fills a spoonful of light' on the dark walls of the cellar below.

Associated with the interplay between states of homelessness and home throughout *The Second Voyage* is the emphasis given to the threshold space between these two states of being. This is often expressed in Ní Chuilleanáin's poetry in the contrasting spatial metaphors of interior darkness and exterior light. This space is depicted as a place of momentary stillness in the midst of perpetual motion, a place of suspension where the body is cut off and detached from its surroundings and physically suspended in space. We see an example of this in the poem 'Atlantis', which begins as follows:

> Here I float in my glass bowl,
> Light wavering in water:
> A thread shivers binding me
> To a branching of dry pine.
> I kneel in my white nightdress
> And the watchful fish slide past. (24)

The transitory state of the subject-in-process is expressed in these lines in the floating state of the speaker, in a 'glass bowl', cut off, as it were, from his/her surroundings. The exilic state of the speaking subject is suggested in the image of the speaker 'wavering in water', yet connected by a shivering thread that binds him/her to the contrasting stability of the 'branching of dry pine', the dry anchor that keeps the 'glass bowl' of the subject afloat. This shivering thread can be compared to the 'slender tapes' of the life jacket in the poem 'Ferryboat' above, suggesting again a suspended state of being, which is juxtaposed in line five with the static image of kneeling speaker: 'I kneel in my white nightdress / And the watchful fish slide past'. As seen in 'Ferryboat', the meeting that takes place between the contrasting states of homelessness and home acts as a liminal space, a place of estrangement and perception, and, as such, it is an empowering and liberating place: 'A cold place with the spring tide', a place that is '[p]ulling out there like horses / But safe' (24). Like the semiotic sea is for Odysseus, it is a place of desire that one is drawn towards, a retreat that offers sanctuary. Reminding us of the antediluvian world of Atlantis, it is a sort of Utopia, an imaginary dream-world of detachment and desire.[4]

The concern with the threshold space between states of homelessness and home is seen clearly in the poem 'Letter to Pearse Hutchinson', which begins with the lines: 'I saw the islands in a ring all round me / And the twilight sea travelling past / Uneasy still' (39). A sense of movement and disorientation is expressed in the image of the sea 'travelling past', juxtaposed with that of 'uneasy stillness' of the speaker, bodily surrounded by the islands and the water. A threshold moment of timelessness, occurring in the meeting place between the fixed solid landmass of the islands and the fluid sea, suggesting the meeting of unconscious interior and conscious exterior, is seen in the lines: 'There was plenty of time while the sea-water / Nosed across the ruinous ocean floor / Inquiring for the ruinous door of the womb' (39). The sea-water, like an animal nosing its way along the sea bed, connects the contrasting 'ruinous ocean floor' with the 'ruinous door of the womb', emphasising the correlation between the juxtaposing images of the 'ruinous' and estrangement and hope, as both the ocean floor and the womb can be seen as places of darkness, or homelessness, but also of promise. Both the ocean floor and the womb represent semiotic unconscious desire, which is a liberating and empowering force. Longing, or desire, for the state of physical detachment offered by the sea, and the paradoxical position of estrangement and heightened visionary power that it affords, is further suggested in the final line of the poem: 'Do not expect to feel so free on land' (39).

The association of transitory moments of homelessness with moments of perception, and also with danger, is seen in the poem 'Lost Star', where a clear sense of exile is explicit in the following lines: 'The lonely pilot guides / The lost star, its passengers the crowd / Of innocents exiled in winter' (42). The solitary state of the pilot, as he guides the exiles, is linked with that of impending danger in the lines which follow: 'Sometimes, letting the vessel drift / Into danger he pauses / To feed them at his miraculous breast' (42). Here, the wandering exilic state of the travellers is interrupted or suspended, and the temporary state of homelessness that is suggested in the image of the drifting vessel is followed by a moment of wonderment, in the evocation of the comfort and nourishment of being fed at the 'miraculous breast'. The sense of estrangement of the exile is again suggested in the next stanza of the poem, as follows:

> Distant as the spirit imprisoned
> In a bronze vase buried in shingle
> At the clean edge of the sea,
> Floating like instantaneous foam or an island,
> Sealed off like a womb. (42)

Thus, the transitory state of the exilic subject is associated with a moment of enforced estrangement, or separation, in the image of the 'spirit imprisoned', floating at the 'clean edge of the sea' and 'sealed off like a womb', images of latent nourishment and safety.

A strong sense of exile and feeling of estrangement is expressed by the speaker in the poem 'Ardnaturais', where the sea is again used as an empowering agent:

> The steel edge of water shuts
> My close horizon, shears off
> Continents and the courses of ships.
> An island in a saucer of air
> Floats in the tight neck
> Of the bay, sealing

An intimate coastline. (31)

The isolated position of the speaker is clearly outlined in the 'close horizon' that is shut off by the water shearing off '[c]ontinents and the courses of ships'. This mood of isolation is continued in the lines which follow, with the image of the island hovering 'in a saucer of air', as it floats in its transitory, yet confined, space 'in the tight neck / Of the bay, sealing' the 'intimate coastline'. In the next movement of the poem, the idea of fluidity is developed in the image of the water as it explores 'the branching algae', where the transitory nature of the speaking subject is stressed, and the speaker's hair is spread out 'like John the Baptist's in a dish' (31). The allusion to John the Baptist introduces an element of shock, which, in the following lines, is further developed to that of disconcertion and fear, as it becomes a moment of heightened awareness and perception:

> Shouldering under, I feel fear
> As I see them plain: the soft anemone,
> Bladdered weed, the crouching spiked urchin, rooted
> In one clutch of pebbles, their long strands
> Shivering under the light. (31)

The wonderment of the moment of perception, associated with an estranging feeling of fear experienced by the speaker is seen in the lines: 'I feel *fear* / As I *see*' (emphasis added), followed by the list of hidden treasures which are revealed to view: 'the soft anemone', the '[b]laddered weed', and 'the crouching urchin'. All of which now become visible below the water, attached by their 'long strands', as they lie 'rooted / In one clutch of pebbles', in a careful moment of disclosure '[s]hivering under the light'. This picture of shock perception is followed in the final stanza of the poem with a further impending moment of revelation, associated with a sense of isolation and estrangement expressed in the following lines:

> Alone in the sea: a shallow breath held stiffly:
> My shadow lies

> Dark and hard like time
> Across the rolling shining stones. (31)

In the poem entitled, 'More Islands', the sea is juxtaposed with the 'dry / Moonlight shoulders' of the stationary islands, which have a frightening and estranging effect on the speaker of the poem. The poem can be read as an exploration of the imaginary world of the child:

> A child afraid of islands, their dry
> Moonlight shoulders, sees in a deep gutter
> A stone, a knot in the stream,
> She feels the gasping of wrecks,
> Cormorants and lighthouses. (40)

The images of the 'deep gutter', the 'gasping of wrecks', and the '[c]ormorants and lighthouses' all suggest an element of fear of the unknown, a sense of estrangement experienced by the speaker, while the stone suggests a sense of solidity, a point of reference, like the lighthouses in the last line, which acts as a contrasting element of rescue and light. In the next stanza, the fear of islands is echoed in the dislike of airports, which – like the lighthouses – is another paradoxical symbol of both transitory estrangement and of the fixity of the land. This is contrasted with the fluid sea, which the female subject feels 'in the waves of her hair', suggesting a sense of belonging and the known that is situated in the semiotic body itself: 'She grows up to detest airports / But feels the sea in the waves of her hair / And icebergs in a storm of lemonade' (40). The idea of heightened perception is expressed in the last stanza of the poem, in the lines: 'She knows there are some islands the sea avoids. / Boats leaving the coastline are led far astray / By strong currents, long mackerel shoals' (40). Throughout the poem, the sense of journey to understanding taken on the part of the child is emphasised in the stress given to the different states of physical experience encountered, associated with separation and insight: she is 'afraid', she 'sees', she 'feels', she 'grows up', she 'knows'. The poem ends on a note of liberation, as the transitory experiences of the speaking subject described throughout the poem are brought together in the castaway in the final lines of the poem, as the lighting of a fire 'cuts the darkness / Liberating silence'.

To conclude, I have argued that a central theme in Eiléan Ní Chuilleanáin's *The Second Voyage* is the sense of physical separation, an experience of existential exile and estrangement which is often associated with transformational moments of perception, or insight. Ní Chuilleanáin's poetry describes the human situation of existential exile, which is that of the split subject, torn between states of fixity and flux, the familiar and the unfamiliar, the mundane and the wondrous. The constant movement between these two contrasting forces can be compared to the situation of Odysseus, torn between the conscious duties to organise his house and his desire to return to the sea. But unlike the story of the returning hero, who eventually arrives safely at his destination, and according to Homer remains there, the journey that the exilic subject makes is a continual journey. The speaking subject is a body in exile, always in a state of transit, or becoming. In this way s/he never arrives at any fixed identity, but is constantly looking beyond the known fixity of the self to explore new unknown semiotic spaces — expressed especially by Ní Chuilleanáin, as we have seen, in images of water and the sea. And while these semiotic spaces may cause a sense of fear and alienation, they also afford a sense of discovery and wonder; they act as a threshold space of the in-between, where the subject in exile both suffers and rejoices. This is a place where the infinite possibilities of language exist as a liberating and empowering force, where the subject is freed from linguistic, psychic, and social networks. When it comes to existential exile, there is no returning stage for the wanderer, because for the body in space of the exilic subject — as the speaker in 'The Second Voyage' points out — 'the profound / Unfenced valleys of the ocean' always have a holding force.

Notes

[1] For Heidegger, it is only when we enter a state of nothingness that we experience the strangeness and wonder of being and beings. Thus

one becomes open to the other, or, as he expresses it, 'Only on the ground of wonder - the revelation of the nothing - does the "why?" loom before us'. See Heidegger 109.

2 According to the Celtic tradition, the feast of Samhain (Hallowe'en), representing darkness, is juxtaposed with the Celtic feast of Bealtaine (or May Day), representing brightness, when the fruits of earth begin to stir with the coming of Spring, when the appearance of the sun, marking the end of the long winter was celebrated. See Squire 40, 406. The play between lightness and darkness, a central theme in Ní Chuilleanáin's poetry, occurs frequently in Irish poetry, not least in the poetry of Seamus Heaney.

3 This can be compared to what Victor Turner describes as the threshold experience, a transitional state of becoming, occupying a transformational space outside the constraints of society and the limits of designated conceptual structures, where the liminal persona attains ambiguous and indeterminate attributes that allow for the transgression of boundaries and the subversion of everyday norms (*The Forest of Symbols* 96). It is a spiritual space 'betwixt and between' the ordered, conscious world and the world of chaos, where – to quote Turner – 'the past has lost its grip and the future has not yet taken definite shape' (qtd. in Myerhoff 117).

4 This state of heightened perception associated with exilic estrangement can be compared to that suggested by T.S. Eliot in the following lines from *The Four Quartets*:
    We must be still and still moving
    Into another intensity
    For a further union, a deeper communion
    Through the dark cold and the empty desolation. (27)

References

Braidotti, Rosi. Nomadic Subjects: Embodiment and Sexual Difference in Contemporary Feminist Theory. New York: Columbia University Press, 1994.

Caputo, John D. The Mystical Element in Heidegger's Thought. New York: Fordham University Press, 1986.

Eliot, T.S. Four Quartets. 1944. London: Faber, 1989.

Heidegger, Martin. Basic Writings. Ed. David Farrell Krell. San Francisco: Harper, 1993.

Homer. The Odyssey. Trans. Walter Shewring. Oxford: Oxford University Press, 1980.

Howatson, M.C. and Ian Chilvers, eds. Concise Oxford Companion to Classical Literature. Oxford: Oxford University Press, 1993.

Kristeva, Julia. Desire in Language: A Semiotic Approach to Literature and Art. Ed. Leon S. Roudiez. Trans Thomas Gora, Alice Jardine, and Leon S. Roudiez. New York: Columbia University Press, 1980.

Myerhoff, Barbara. 'Rites of Passage: Process and Paradox.' Celebration: Festivity and Ritual. Ed. Victor Turner. Washington DC: Smithsonian Institution Press, 1982. 109-135.

Ní Chuilleanáin, Eiléan. The Second Voyage. Dublin: Gallery, 1986.

Smith, Anna. Julia Kristeva: Readings of Exile and Estrangement. New York: St Martin's Press, 1996.

Squire, Charles. Celtic Myth and Legend. Franklin Lakes, NJ: New Page Books, 2001.

Turner, Victor. The Forest of Symbols: Aspects of Ndembu Ritual. Ithaca, NY: Cornell University Press, 1970.

'The culchies have fuckin' everythin'': Internal Exile in Roddy Doyle's *The Barrytown Trilogy*

Åke Persson

In most of his novels to date, Roddy Doyle focuses on the northside of Dublin. This part of the Irish capital – historically to a large extent deeply affected by social and economic deprivation – is presented as a world apart, as a place not belonging to the rest of the city, nor indeed the rest of Ireland. Several characters are unemployed and struggle to find work which would give them a sense of belonging and improve their self-esteem, particularly in *The Barrytown Trilogy* (*The Commitments* [1988], *The Snapper* [1990] and *The Van* [1991]). Due to failed economic policies and traditional sociocultural structures, Doyle's characters living in working-class suburban Dublin are alienated and excluded from ordinary, mainstream social interaction as they do not have access to the main economy. My essay focuses on the ways in which his characters are trapped in a system that forces them to live in what could be termed geographical as well as social and economic exile in a city and a country supposed to be their own. Gerry Smyth suggests that in Doyle's works '[t]he reader must become an active part of the meaning-making process, filling in the gaps and making choices deliberately left by the narrator' (*Novel and Nation* 67). Part of my aim, therefore, is to tune into the context and subtext of the novels, which, I suggest, would help to understand the depth of Doyle's project in the *Trilogy*.

It is my argument that Doyle problematizes the notion of exile. As many scholars have shown, the phenomena of emigration and its close relative exile have a long tradition in Ireland, spanning several centuries. As Kerby A. Miller demonstrates, there has been a steady flow of people leaving for

Re-Mapping Exile: Realities and Metaphors in Irish Literature and History, ed. Michael Böss, Irene Gilsenan Nordin and Britta Olinder, *The Dolphin* 34. © 2005 by Aarhus University Press, Denmark. ISBN 87 7934 010 5.

other countries, especially North America and Britain. Perhaps it is not surprising that a country so marked by emigration has also perceived this departure as involuntary, that is, as banishment from one's country, in short, exile. It has been argued that the main cause of emigration has been the oppression of Ireland by a foreign land. However, according to Miller, although British oppression has of course been responsible for a portion of the involuntary departure, this notion is also, at least partly, a version constructed by nationalist forces for their own purposes. He convincingly argues that in the late nineteenth century dominant Irish groups and institutions at home – the Catholic Church, landowning farmers and conservative nationalists – conveniently exploited the exile motif in order to foment Irish hatred of the British, while obscuring deep socioeconomic divisions which the Irish themselves were instrumental in creating and sustaining. Indeed, there clearly appears to have been a systematic exclusion of certain groups, as other strong groups protected their social and economic interests. Miller outlines the situation: '[T]he social forces – [of] strong-farmer family type, church, and nationalism – specifically perpetuated the exile motif in ways which justified and promoted their social and cultural authority' (128). As importantly, he goes on to argue that their authority went beyond the cultural level as it also secured economic power, excluding, alienating or forcing into emigration those who did not have the means or possibility to contribute to the economy. 'Thus', he concludes, 'emigration, albeit lamented, could continue without challenging either the relevance of the old worldview or the hegemony of the very forces which helped impel departures (129).

Significantly, the disadvantaged and those not conforming to ideals set up and promoted by dominant (nationalist) groups have either been forced to leave or, if they have chosen to stay, have not been allowed to partake in the decision-making process. According to recent historical and sociological accounts, due to severe economic crises these socio-economic divisions grew even deeper after 1921. In my reading of post-Independence socio-economic and cultural structures, large segments of the population have been forced to live in exile in their own country, unemployed long-term, banished from and excluded by official

Ireland, that is, those forces in control of ideology, land and capital. In one of many sharp analyses of Irish culture, Fintan O'Toole points out that '[p]art of this estrangement is the alienation of the young from the images and icons of official Irish culture, now seen as repressive and exclusive' (*Ex-Isle* 176). To many young Irish men and women, he goes on, Ireland has become 'a set of questions and contests rather than a given landscape waiting to be read. The relevant difference is no longer that between home and abroad, but that between the Irish themselves. Exile becomes a prism through which the diverse social forces within Ireland are separated and revealed' (178). Moreover, significantly he holds that Ireland 'has become, in a sense, a foreign country for many of its people', creating in many a feeling of 'internal exile' (178). That sense of banishment is particularly true, I would suggest, for the characters in the Dublin represented in Roddy Doyle's *Trilogy*.

Discussions of the *Trilogy*, though, seem to be dominated by its comic aspects, and there is an agreement that these three texts manage to convey a sense of humour that few texts do. Brian Donnelly, for example, refers to the *Trilogy* as 'hilarious comic novels' (17), and Christina Hunt Mahony's assessment of *The Commitments* is that it is 'vulgar and extremely funny' (247). Interestingly, many commentaries also seem to be at a loss as to where to situate the texts and whether or not they engage with any serious issues in Irish life. Donnelly, for instance, suggests that '[t]he metropolis of the older novelist is a place firmly rooted in contemporary social and political realities', while 'the location of Doyle's early fictions exists outside of the immediacy of Irish public history' (19). Ian Haywood, too, although generally sympathetic to the *Trilogy*, argues that 'his fiction contains no explicit engagement with the "general way of life" in contemporary Ireland' (160). Seemingly dismissing the *Trilogy*, and reducing it to trivial popular art, José Lanters goes even further, contending that 'Doyle's early novels, *The Commitments* (1987), *The Snapper* (1990), and *The Van* (1991), were consciously a-historical and a-political in their reflection of the ephemera of contemporary North Dublin pop-culture' (245).

However, even if the texts may not offer much *explicit* commentary on Irish history and politics, it is my argument that far from being a-historical and a-political and existing outside of Irish public history, the novels in the *Trilogy* invite readings in which an understanding of the social, political and cultural context from which they spring is fundamental in order to open up the works, particularly regarding the systematic socioeconomic exclusion Doyle's characters face; without some understanding of the 'hegemonic forces' in Ireland, to lean on Gramsci, Doyle's texts arguably lose much of their radical edge and remain simply entertaining. Gerry Smyth, for example, firmly holds that the texts are attempts at engaging with traditional Irish pieties. As he states: 'His work has crystallised with great insight and force many of the significant themes and debates of contemporary Irish culture' (*Novel and Nation* 66).

It seems fruitful, then, to place Doyle's texts within a wider framework, that is the web-like systems of norms and values, or ideologies that, according to the Russian theorist Mikhail Bakhtin, are in dialogue with and indeed contest each other. This dialogue, or contest, seems particularly relevant and heated in an Irish context, where in the discipline of Irish Studies in the last two decades or so there has flourished a controversial activity known as 'revisionism'. Revisionism, as the term indicates, seeks sceptically to revise, or re-examine, received wisdoms regarding Irish history, culture and identity. Central to this strand of thought is the notion that the Irish past has been interpreted to fit a particular myth, or narrative, which in turn, as Graham and Proudfoot suggest in *A Historical Geography of Ireland*, 'is used to justify political demands, and aspirations and justify contemporary events' (7). It is a myth, they go on, that is anchored in three principal characteristics: one, it is Gaelic; two, it is Catholic; and three, it is rural. If everything, revisionists argue, is made to fit such a myth crucial to define an Irish identity, it follows that other interpretations and experiences are suppressed and stifled, 'impoverishing Irish nationality and its sense of identity' (8). In other words, the official version of Irish history, a corner-stone in Irish identity, is seen as exclusive in that it refuses to accept plurality, or 'the diversity from amongst those who can be included within the definition of Irishness' (8). This diversity and plurality has to be taken into account, they hold, and if it is, it forces a re-interpretation of what Ireland is. In such a project, experiences and groups previously ignored, for example the urban working-class, insist on being heard.

My starting-point is a quotation from Doyle's first novel, *The Commitments*, the first part in the *Trilogy*. Barrytown is a fictional, working-class suburb in north Dublin, and in the *Trilogy* we follow the Rabbitte family. In *The Commitments*, the focus is on the oldest son in the family, Jimmy Jr., and his attempts at starting a soul group as a way out of unemployment. On several occasions in the novel, he tries to raise the members' awareness as to the aims of the group, and we come to realise that many of the novel's concerns are voiced by him. In the initial stage of their (as it turns out brief) career, the following much-quoted exchange takes place:

Wha' about this politics?
-Yeah, politics. –Not songs abou' Fianna fuckin' Fail or annythin' like tha'. Real politics. (They weren't with him.)
-Where are yi from? (He answered the question himself.) – Dublin. (He asked another one.) –Wha' part o' Dublin? Barrytown. Wha' class are yis? Workin' class. Are yis proud of it? Yeah, yis are. (Then a practical question.) –Who buys the most records? The workin' class. Are yis with me? (Not really.) –Your music should be abou' where you're from an' the sort o' people yeh come from. –Say it once, say it loud, I'm black an' I'm proud.
They looked at him.
-James Brown. Did yis know – never mind. He sang tha'. –An' he made a fuckin' bomb.
They were stunned by what came next.
-The Irish are the niggers of Europe, lads.
They nearly gasped: it was so true.
-An' Dubliners are the niggers of Ireland. The culchies have fuckin' everythin'. An' the northside Dubliners are the niggers o' Dublin. –Say it loud, I'm black an' I'm proud. (13)

It would be easy enough to focus on the post-colonial concerns that this quotation invites, that is, Ireland being the victim of colonial oppression by the British, as Africans and Afro-Americans have been oppressed and enslaved by colonial forces. However, what has frequently been forgotten, or conveniently ignored, and in Alan Parker's much celebrated film adaptation actually removed completely, are the comments on Fianna Fáil and on a group Jimmy calls 'the culchies'. The band, Jimmy proudly declares, will not play 'songs abou' Fianna fuckin' Fail or annythin' like tha''. Instead, they will play music with 'Real politics'. And in a fairly confrontational tone, he states that 'The culchies have fuckin' everythin''. Significantly, Fianna Fáil has been the leading political party in Ireland more or less since the founding of the state, or at least since the 1930's. It has been explicitly nationalist in its programme, the ultimate goal being a United Ireland, although this aim has been toned down in recent years. The term 'culchies' is a derogatory epithet given to people living on the countryside and in small rural towns, a demographic category that has had a crucial role in Irish society. What the text does here, I suggest, is that it opens up to a socioeconomic structure based on a whole set of rigid values.

Rather than insisting on making his characters into post-colonial victims as part of international politics, then, Doyle quickly moves to the local, to the northside of Dublin; in doing so, Jimmy's comments, I would argue, are directed not at foreign oppression of the Irish but at forces *within* Ireland systematically excluding large parts of the population. In a way, he writes *through* the post-colonial concerns and instead zooms in on what could be termed a post-nationalist situation, that is the harsh social and economic realities which are the consequences of Irish nationalist ideals and failed domestic policies.

In order to realise the depth of the cultural and socioeconomic realities behind Doyle's concerns – and indeed the anger and frustration beneath the surface – in his *Trilogy*, and in order to establish the nature of exclusion – or banishment – and at what levels it operates, it seems necessary to draw on insights put forward by disciplines outside the realm of literature, for example socioeconomic and historical geography, sociology and history.

Most historians, sociologists and cultural commentators now agree that the first six decades after Irish Independence were generally characterised by a conservatism that cherished stasis rather than reform, which, according to Terence Brown, resulted in 'repressiveness' and 'deprivation of Irish life in general' (36). Defining itself against its former oppressors, Ireland eagerly advocated ideals that were aimed at uniting the nation, giving it a clear sense of identity and glorifying the new state. What Fintan O'Toole refers to as 'official ideology' (*Ex-Isle* 94) sought to recreate old, Gaelic Ireland, language, mythology and way of living. Central to that way of life was the idea that farming and a rural economy were superior to industry, urbanisation and city life.

Crucial, too, in that nationalist project was the Catholic Church which, Máire Nic Ghiolla Phádraig suggests, 'became a powerful ethno-national marker' (594). As most commentators also agree, the Catholic Church has had an extremely powerful position and has been able to control decisions and institutions at all levels. Two areas in which the Church has been extremely influential are education and health. As Nic Ghiolla Phádraig informs us, the Church has until recently been responsible for the education of Irish children, particularly at primary and secondary levels. Moreover, she goes on, '[n]ational school teachers' education is entirely a church-run affair with intake on a denominational basis' (603). Not surprisingly, perhaps, '[t]he Catholic Church regards this system as an extremely vital part of its overall pastoral strategy' (603-04). Another area that has been important for the Church to influence is health. Hospitals, many of them private, have been run by the Church and religious orders for a long time, securing the control of matters physical and intimate. Significantly, and most pertinent to my overall argument, Nic Ghiolla Phádraig argues that in both these areas, the Church and religious orders, by running private schools and hospitals, actively 'contribute [...] to the reproduction of inequality' by catering more for the affluent in Irish society than the poor and needy (601-05).

Related to education and health is the Church's influence on morality, most notably the issue of sex. In order to protect the purity of Irish citizens, the Censorship of Publications Act was passed in 1929, which meant that it was possible to 'prohibit any work it considered "indecent or obscene", as well as all literature advocating birth control' (Lee, 158). It meant that not only pornographic material was banned, but also works by writers who tried to question established structures as well as books giving advice on health and family. This 'cultural exclusivism' (Brown 58) was to last for approximately 50 years and resulted in an impoverishment of Irish cultural and spiritual life; in *Banned in Ireland*, Julia Carlson alerts us to the fact that as late as in the 1980's works by, for example, Roland Barthes, Susan Sontag and Angela Carter fell victims to the law (18).

Interestingly, not only books were targeted, but also popular music from abroad, 'the dance music of the time, often dismissed under the generic name of "jazz"'. In intense campaigns throughout the 1930's and 1940's, and later in the 1950's, this type of 'alien' dance music, it was eagerly argued, awakened 'sin and lustful desire' around Ireland. Also, 'the more this music was played, the less time there was for Irish traditional music and song' (McLoone 26-7). In the light of the dominant atmosphere at the time, it does not seem particularly strange that these campaigns were cheered on by the Church as well as nationalist groups and politicians.

The Church, then, has been a tremendously powerful force, but it has to a large extent been supported by the farming community. It is important to point out that the relationship between Church and farmers has been close and they have been an extension of each other. In fact, this close relationship has arguably been the most crucial component in the perpetuation of the rigidly conservative sociopolitical and religious structure so intriguing to observers. It seems fair to argue that the clergy and the farmers have taken care to protect each others' interests at many levels. Nic Ghiolla Phádraig observes that for decades

> Irish parishes were staffed by priests of middle class/strong farmer background which added weight to their superiority over their parishioners and drew them to associate with better-off sections. Juniorates, in some orders, took in

aspirants as young as twelve years – to the financial relief of their parents. [...] the minute socio-economic distinctions of society were faithfully reproduced in the intake of aspirants to the priesthood and religious life. In this way inequality in society was legitimated. (614-15)

In this system, the father remained the head of the farm until very old age. The farm was passed on to the eldest son, while other sons either moved on to become priests or emigrated. In order to protect the land, they married very late, even so opposing pre-marital sex, because if children were born outside of wedlock, the land was threatened. Therefore, morality and economic interests were interconnected, creating a strong web of power that excluded those without means and those who did not live up to the official ideals, for example, many groups living in the city.

Thus, rural life and a rural economy have been part and parcel of Irish identity after Independence, and the image of Ireland as a rural paradise was consciously exploited by nationalism and used for its purposes. As Martin McLoone suggests: 'In its fundamental principles, cultural nationalism defined Gaelic Irish identity as essentially rural in character and the culture of nationalist Ireland was correspondingly anti-urban and anti-industrial in its imaginings' (18). In the popular mind, this meant that city life was perceived as harmful and decadent and that the further away you got from the east of Ireland – the big city of Dublin and the geographical closeness to England – the more genuinely Irish you were. The image of Ireland as a country where time has stopped because of the slow pace of country living is one that has been exploited both politically and economically, within Ireland and abroad. Thus, until very recently the famous John Hinde postcards depicted an Ireland with carts, horses, turf, and thatched cottages. Films, too, perpetuated the image of Ireland as a primitive and charmingly backward country, for example in John Ford's memorable film *The Quiet Man*, starring John Wayne and Maureen O'Hara (Connolly 7). In books for tourists, as well, such as coffee-table books, these images prevailed well into the 1980's, showing pictures of, among other things, quiet village life, old men talking outside a village pub, or old women feeding animals at a small farm (e. g. Löbl-Schreyer and Schröder). The rural world, then, has been crucial in the construction of Irish identity, at the expense of urban realities.

On the political arena, the rural mythology and Catholicism have had staunch defenders and partners in the political party Fianna Fáil, which has been in government for long periods since Independence, even if its main opposition, Fianna Gael, has also been in power at times. Fianna Fáil's close ties to the Church are well-documented by now, and in most areas, the party has stayed close to the teachings of the Church, creating a solid power structure clearly patriarchal and nationalist in nature. If it stayed close to the Church, it also envisioned, in true nationalist fashion, Ireland as a rural Eden. In his 1943 St. Patrick's Day broadcast, the leader Eamon de Valera made his famous declaration:

> That Ireland which we dreamed of would be the home of a people who valued material wealth only as a basis of right living [...] a land whose countryside would be bright with cosy homesteads, whose fields and villages would be joyous with sounds of industry, the romping of sturdy children, the contests of athletic youths, the laughter of comely maidens; whose firesides would be the forums of the wisdom of serene old age. (qtd. in Brown 113)

However, the reality has been different from the one dreamt of by de Valera and when in power the party has shown great reluctance to alleviate the vast socio-economic needs of those segments of the population that do not have capital, land or respectable middle-class professions. Instead, as Terence Brown points out, there has been 'a social order in which church, farmer, grocer, and gombeen publican comprise a corrupt and corrupting alliance, intent on social advancement' (27); indeed, the protection of private property was written into the 1937 Constitution (MacLaran, *Dublin* 69). The economic conservatism emanating from such an order resulted in economic stagnation, in which social and economic reform had little or no place, since together with industrialisation and city life it represented modernity, so eagerly rejected as it was perceived as a serious threat to the existing structures. For a long time, few serious attempts were made to solve the poverty caused by a rapidly increasing unemployment, nor to take care of the immense housing problems of the capital's inner city, which was left to deteriorate into what could only be referred to as slum-like tenements (Brown 159). Perhaps the clearest evidence of the economic inactivity and neglect by the state was the fact that the socio-economic system relied on emigration to solve many of the economic problems. In other words, rather than trying to cater for its citizens' needs, the system managed to get rid of large parts of the population that could not contribute to the economy, thus being a burden. With the exception of brief periods, this type of systematic exclusion lasted until the 1990's.

Those city dwellers in meagre circumstances that decided to stay faced yet another type of exclusion, namely what is referred to by geographers and urban planners as 'dispersal'. New areas were built aimed at catering mainly for the relatively humble demands of the working-class, many of whom were more or less coerced, or at least very strongly encouraged, to move to places like Crumlin and Kimmage and, later, Finglas and Cabra, when bad inner-city housing was demolished – 'slum-clearance', as Punch terms it ('Transformation' 41) – to create space for the development of, for example, offices (e. g. O'Toole, *Black Hole* 118; Punch, 'Transformation' 42). As MacLaran argues, many of these areas were developed at minimal costs, resulting in poor quality (*Dublin* 112-13; 204) as well as emphasising the notion that they were deliberately constructed to segregate the under-privileged working-class from the affluent classes, which in turn arguably enhances the feeling of internal exile (Bartley and Saris 82). Importantly, space and social class are closely linked, as Gregory affirms: 'Spatial structure is not [...] merely the arena in which class conflicts express themselves, but also the domain within which and, in part, through which class relations are constituted' (qtd. in MacLaran, *Dublin* 84). That the environment forms part of the socio-economic structuring in society, including social divisions and injustice, is further contended by Jennifer Wolch and Michael Dear in *The Power of Geography*:

Inequality and poverty are endemic to capitalism, and the facts of geography facilitate their reproduction through generations. Central to this thesis is Hagerstrand's notion of a "daily-life environment," composed of residence and/or workplace, and defined by the physical friction of distance plus the social distance of class. Every social group operates within a typical daily "prism," which, for the disadvantaged, closes into a "prison" of space and resources. Deficiencies in the environment (for instance, limitations on mobility, and the quality of social resources) clearly limit an individual's potential, or market capacity; and poverty limits access to more favorable environments. (6)

More recently, similar acts of dispersal have taken place, including the creation of north Dublin suburbs, such as Ballymun, in which Doyle's *Trilogy* is set. Indeed, in his later work, *Paddy Clarke Ha Ha Ha* (1993), the construction of new Dublin Corporation estates forms an important part of the novel's concerns. Drudy and MacLaran hold that the factors 'influencing dispersal of population to the periphery of Dublin' were what they call 'market-induced' or 'policy-induced' ('Demographic Change' 10). The former would include high land prices and '"high value" uses such as offices' (10), while the latter would include 'both Central and Local Government policies play[ing] a significant role in influencing the movement of population to the periphery' (11).

In the late 1950's and 1960's, there were attempts by Fianna Fáil to think in new ways, especially in economic policies. Through mainly foreign investors there was a temporary improvement in the Irish economy, resulting in some basic social change. But the optimism felt in the 1960's and early 1970's slowly turned into a recession in the latter part of the decade. This was largely due to 'heavy dependence on foreign borrowing' (Brown 249); the national debt rose from £78 million in 1977 to a staggering £6,703 million in 1983. As Terence Brown puts it, 'the winds of recession (blew) with devastating force' (250). He further alerts us to the rapidly increasing unemployment rate at this time:

> Between 1979 and 1982 unemployment rose by 77 percent and
> at 160,000 people in the latter year seemed dangerously high.
> By December of 1984, however, it would reach 208,000, which
> represented 16.4 percent of the work force (well ahead of the
> overall EEC figure of 10.3 percent). [...] And almost a third of
> the unemployed were under 25 years of age. (250)

The capital, and particularly its working-class areas, were badly
affected, and it was recorded that in some parts of north Dublin
52 % of heads of households 'were on the live register of
unemployed, a figure that increased to 70 % in 1986' (Moore 140).

However, while unemployment rose rapidly in Dublin, the
situation was not quite as bad in other regions; Drudy and
MacLaran establish that in the period 1971-1991 '[t]he numbers
unemployed [...] increased significantly in all parts of Ireland [...]
but Dublin [...] increased by a factor of five compared to a factor
of three in the rest of the country' ('Output' 21). One might expect
serious efforts to be made to improve the situation for those living
in the capital, for example by schemes encouraging businesses
and industry to create jobs. Yet, as Christopher T. Whelan claims,
the government's 'regional policies distributed industrial jobs
from urban to rural areas' (333). According to Drudy and
MacLaran, these policies 'influenced the location of industries and
services over the last few decades', and since 'Irish industrial
policy has contained a strong "regional" orientation', due to the
notion that 'the twelve counties along the western seaboard [...]
were widely perceived to be at a disadvantage when compared to
areas such as Dublin', it is concluded that 'Dublin thus lost out
heavily during the 1980s and this is reflected in the significant rise
in unemployment [in this period]' ('Output' 19; also Punch,
'Economic Geographies' 37). This means, then, that economic
policies systematically favoured rural areas at the expense of
areas such as north Dublin mainly inhabited by the working-class.
Thus, Jimmy Jr.'s indignant comment that 'the culchies have
fuckin' everythin'' could be read as an astute political assessment.
Moreover, these policies were largely responsible not only for
mass unemployment, but also for creating an unusually high level
of long-term unemployment, the consequences of which are,

among other things, marginalisation and exclusion; in fact, it went so far that these groups, according to Sheelagh Drudy, are now referred to as 'the underclass' (311), a category for which there is little or no hope of returning from what could be termed internal exile.

I have spent some time outlining what many see as the dominant features of traditional Ireland and the failure of Fianna Fáil, the devoted custodians of nationalist ideals, to cater for the needs of large groups of the population. Of course, one may be justified in asking what relevance all this has to a novel dealing with a group of unemployed trying to form a soul band in 1980's Dublin, or to a young pregnant woman, or to a man selling burgers from a van. But it is my argument that the features I have described form the backdrop against which Doyle's *Trilogy* could fruitfully be read and which, I suggest, form the subtext of the works. Most importantly, perhaps, the very fact that he focuses on segments of the Irish population that have been largely ignored, that is the socially and economically excluded in deprived urban suburbs, is in itself an intervention in the socio-political debate. He insists on treating an area which few tourists would come into contact with; in fact, some critics even implied that the life represented in Barrytown is a falsification of what Ireland really stands for, as if Doyle's main aim was to somehow 'tamper [...] with the tourist industry' (qtd. in Smyth, *Novel and Nation* 111) rather than challenging the popular images of Ireland I mentioned earlier.

It would be safe to suggest that much of the appeal of *The Commitments* and *The Snapper* can be found in the sense of optimism and transformation that they convey, arguably inverting the Censorship Act from 1929 and its strict guidelines regarding the humour, the irreverent language, the growing skills which in turn boost their self-confidence, the sexual freedom, the foreign-type music (in *The Commitments*), the moving father-daughter relationship and Jimmy Sr.'s growing awareness of the female body (in *The Snapper*). Nevertheless, in the first two novels the darker undercurrents are not far beneath the surface and come to the fore at times. In *The Van*, on the other hand, a far bleaker representation of unemployment and the state of affairs in this particular part of Dublin is offered.

While there is a contagious energy in *The Commitments*, the text frequently insists on reminding us of the harsh realities and social divisions the characters encounter. From the very beginning, music is exploited as a vehicle to voice the social divisions they meet on a daily basis. In a kind of mapping of the popular music at the time, Jimmy, Derek and Outspan assess what various groups and genres represent in order to decide the right genre for them. In that assessment, Jimmy dismisses the music of Depeche Mode as being 'art school stuff', 'the way their stuff, their songs like, are aimed at gits like themselves. Wankers with funny haircuts. An' rich das' (10). Later in the novel, jazz, too, is dismissed in a similar fashion, as Joey the Lips passionately holds that jazz is for 'middle-class white kids with little beards and berets' and 'hip honky brats and intellectuals' (108-09). Admittedly, these two types of music are foreign, yet the comments signal a strong awareness of socio-economic division and exclusion, a clear social difference between the haves and the have-nots. This difference is further emphasised in Jimmy's advertisement for auditions, which specifically states that 'Rednecks and southsiders need not apply' (15). South Dublin historically represents much of the wealth and political power in Ireland. Generally, here reside the middle and upper middle classes, and demographically this part differs quite significantly from the northside in that many of the social ills found in the north have had far less impact on the southside. Therefore, the advertisement makes a statement pointing out the underlying socio-economic division within the city.

Rather than wanting to play what they perceive as middle class music, they wish to play soul, which is later defined, among other things, as 'the people's music. Ordinary people making music for ordinary people' (107). Significantly, the novel's use of soul as a metaphor highlights the ways in which the group members have previously been denied an identity in contemporary Ireland. Indeed, the novel seems to suggest that they have not even existed prior to the band and that their voices have not been heard by official Ireland. In what I read as a central scene, the members are given stage names by Jimmy. For example, James Clifford becomes James the Soul Surgeon Clifford, Dean Fay becomes Dean Good Times Fay; the female singers Imelda, Natalie and Bernie are given the names Sonya, Sofia and Tanya respectively, The Commitmentettes. The novel points out that this night 'was one of the best' (40), and it is so, it is implied, because they are transformed from being ordinary into being special, as Jimmy puts it. In other words, in that act, they are named into existence.

The notion that until now their existence and experiences have largely been unacknowledged by official Ireland is further suggested when they have their first gig in the local Community Centre, where, the novel significantly states, 'Dublin Soul was about to be born' (92). Instrumental in that birth is a song called 'Night Train' and in the American original several American stations form part of the lyrics. Significantly, however, they rewrite the lyrics and instead use the stations situated on the northside of the commuter line called the DART: Connolly, Killester, Harmonstown, Raheny, Kilbarrack, Howth Junction Bayside and Sutton stations. Furthermore, as part of the audience gets up on stage to form the train with the band and in fact sing along with the band, it becomes a collective attempt at voicing their existence. Through that song, the novel goes on, 'Dublin Soul had been delivered' (92). The altered lyrics as well as the collective response, then, could be read as an insistence on writing their particular geography, space, experience and reality, in short their identity, into mainstream Dublin. Judging from the audience's reaction – 'The cheering went on for minutes' (93) – it becomes a metaphorical journey through ignored and neglected Dublin, where exclusion is temporarily turned into inclusion.

Through their music, then, the group seeks a way into Irish/Dublin society. However, they fail in their aspirations, largely due to internal conflicts but also, it is speculated, because soul isn't right for Ireland at this time, which implies that they are up against strong forces unwilling to let them in. That a kind of gatekeeping exists, as part of a system of exclusion, is anticipated earlier in the novel, when Jimmy is looking for commercial venues for the band's performances. The manager of one pub, for instance, makes clear that his pub 'only did heavy metal groups', because 'the heavy metal crowd was older and very well behaved, and drank like fish', while another 'only booked groups that modelled themselves on Echo and The Bunnymen because they were always reviewed and the reviews usually included praise for the manager and his pioneering work' (113-14). In the light of this resistance, their lack of success does not seem surprising. At the end of the novel, Jimmy echoes his earlier statement about the culchies: 'You've got to remember tha' half the country is fuckin' farmers'. But even if at the level of the story their attempt fails, the text itself is part of a questioning of what kind of ideals Ireland represents. It would seem, though, that the text's message is ultimately a pessimistic one in that it offers little hope that their exclusion will end.

While, as I argue, *The Commitments* invites a reading that has to take into account the social and economic divisions within Dublin, it may be more difficult to place *The Snapper* within the same sphere. Nevertheless, similar to the former text, the reader is regularly reminded of the characters' hardships, struggles and exclusion at various levels, as they are constantly part of their lives, always present. The novel focuses on the Rabbitte family's everyday life and responses to the pregnancy of the twenty-year-old daughter Sharon, unmarried and still living at home. Such an unwanted pregnancy out-of-wedlock, and with a much older, married man, may in itself pose a challenge to views in an Ireland where such subjects have been taboo. There are plenty of tragic real-life stories with these ingredients, often hushed down, and every year several thousand Irish women, many of them very young, go to England to have an abortion. The fact that the neighbourhood has many more young women in similar circumstances highlights a hidden problem that has been ignored by the authorities, thus, indeed, revealing a hidden Ireland in the capital. A reluctance to alleviate the plight of unmarried mothers, then, is one type of marginalisation that Irish society is guilty of, it is implied, a situation further reflected in the attitudes of her boss towards Sharon's pregnancy. He seems unable to appreciate her predicament, forcing her to do physically demanding work (230) and actually making sexual jokes at her expense (317-18), which ultimately results in her leaving her job, despite the fact that, as her mother tells her through Tracy, 'jobs don't grow on trees' (171).

Throughout the novel there are frequent references to economic hardships through unemployment. For example, the second oldest son, Leslie, is no longer in school and is therefore available on the job market. There are no jobs, though, and the text lets us understand that this constitutes a considerable problem not only for the family's financial situation but also for their general well-being, since, as is shown by Leslie's staying in bed in the mornings, unemployment generates passivity. Moreover, they seem to be at the mercy of employers who may or may not have temporary and badly paid jobs some time in the future. As Jimmy Sr. says of his boss:

> Cummins said he might have somethin' for Leslie in a few weeks.
> -I'll believe it when I see it, said Veronica.
> -[...] He said he'll ask round an' see if anny of his pals have annythin' for him. Yeh know, the golf an' church collection shower.
> -You wouldn't want to be relying on them.
> -True. (235-36)

Leslie, we are told, signs up for an unemployment scheme at ANCO, a state institution aimed at helping unemployed gain certain skills that will make them attractive on the market. However, it is suggested that this and similar institutions fail to do what they are supposed to do since they are seriously out of tune with their clients' needs; in fact, by treating them as inferior, second-class citizens, ANCO even seems to be part of the state's systematic exclusion of the unemployed, again reflecting socio-economic division within the city. Bertie, a friend of Jimmy Sr's, is enrolled in a scheme called Jobsearch. '-Don't talk to me abou' Jobsearch [...] I speet on Jobsearch', he tells his friends in the pub and goes on:

D'yis know wha' they had me doin' today, do yis? Yis won't believe this.
-Wha'? said Bimbo.
-They were teachin' us how to use the phone.
-Wha'!?
-I swear to God. The fuckin' phone.
-You're not serious.
-I am, yeh know. I fuckin'am. The gringo in charge handed ou' photocopies of a diagram of a phone [...] A fuckin' phone [...] It's true, I'm tellin' yeh. I was embarrassed for him, the poor cunt. He knew it was fuckin'stupid himself. You could tell; the poor fucker tellin' us where to put the tenpences. One chap told him where he could stick the tenpences an' then he walked ou'. [...] It was the greatest waste o' fuckin' time, said Bertie. (247-48)

This type of activity, it is suggested, leads nowhere and only perpetuates a feeling of inadequacy and a strong sense of never-ending alienation.

If the first two novels of the *Trilogy* to a large extent exploit comedy to deal with serious contemporary issues in Ireland, the third novel, *The Van*, is different in that the tone is generally darker. Comedy, it may be implied, is ultimately too limited a tool by which to adequately capture the deep effects and severe consequences of long-term unemployment for the individual as well as for society at large. It can be noted that Doyle's subsequent works – *Paddy Clarke Ha Ha Ha*, *The Woman Who Walked into Doors* (1997) and *A Star Called Henry* (1999) as well as his TV series *Family* – do not return to the comedy of the first two novels. In *The Van*, we again meet the Rabbitte family, and this time, too, much of the focus is on the father, Jimmy Sr. However, rather than trying to open up to new ways of thinking, and move closer to his daughter and his wife, as he tries to do in *The Snapper*, he is increasingly alienated from his wife, children and friends. The cause is unemployment.

In his generation, his identity as a man is based on and linked to the notion that the man, as the head of the family, is the main wage-earner. Therefore, when he is unable to provide for the

family, his identity and sense of self-worth are slipping away.
Time and again in the early parts of the novel we see Jimmy Sr.
alone in an empty house, trying to find something useful to fill his
time with, while his wife attends classes in adult education. As
one critic argues, he becomes a 'passive object rather than an
active agent' (Smyth, *Novel and Nation* 74). In some bitingly
moving passages, we feel his humiliation. For example, in a
gesture to show sympathy for his father, Jimmy Jr. hands him a
fiver for the pub, showing the father's vulnerability; in another
scene, the family having dinner together, his son Darren
ruthlessly undermines the father's position as bread-winner:

> What abou' you? said Darren to his da. –Look at the state o'
> you.
> Jimmy Sr looked at Darren. Darren was looking back at him,
> waiting for a reaction. Jimmy Sr wasn't going to take that from
> him, not for another couple of years.
> He pointed his fork at Darren.
> -Don't you forget who paid for tha' dinner in front of you,
> son, righ'.
> -I know who paid for it, said Darren. –The state. (440)

In Jimmy Sr's eyes, relying on hand-outs from the state is failure
and the scene further erodes his self-respect, making him a loser
in front of his family.

The tone changes somewhat when he gets together with his
friend Bimbo and repairs a van in order to start selling burgers.
The monotony is turned into activity, pessimism into optimism,
and temporarily he regains his self-confidence. Still, even in this
seemingly happy situation, the deprivation in the area, one of the
consequences of chronic unemployment, insists on raising its ugly
head. In one of the novel's darkest passages, Jimmy Sr. meditates
on gangs of teenagers roaming the streets causing trouble and
committing crimes. He refers to them as 'The Living Dead',
implying that a whole generation runs the risk of being lost,
arguably betrayed by the authorities and their economic neglect,
as the only future the young can look forward to is a bleak one
dominated by hopelessness, unemployment and crime: 'The way

they behaved, you could tell they didn't give a fuck about anything', he thinks and continues: '[T]hey didn't do anything for a laugh [...] They were like fuckin' zombies. When Jimmy Sr saw them, especially when it was raining, he always thought the same thing: they'd be dead before they were twenty' (519-20).

The public dimension of social and economic marginalisation is further highlighted when after a row Jimmy Sr. and Bimbo try to rescue their friendship by going for a night out to Leeson Street, a street notorious for its many nightclubs. The vast distance between Jimmy Sr's struggle on the northside and the affluence of the southsiders, who are able and willing to pay 20 pounds for a bottle of bad wine, places his situation in a broader socio-economic context and suggests that not enough is being done by those in power to create jobs and reduce unemployment. Earlier in the novel, as Jimmy goes into town to kill time, he has noted this wealth on the southside, especially among young people; 'there was money in this town' (409), he observes, but it is also made clear that he will never gain from it, even less have access to it.

Significantly, the official attitude toward Jimmy's and Bimbo's humble enterprise is shown when a representative from the Eastern Health Board comes to inspect the van. Not surprisingly, perhaps, their business is ordered to close down by the authorities, as it does not meet the required standards of hygiene. What makes the event more humiliating, however, is the inspector's comments on their personal hygiene and appearance, as if they were a lower type of humans, which underlines the feeling that they are second-class citizens. For official power, it is suggested, to close them down is not enough; they also have to be humiliated so that they know their place.

The novel ends with the destruction of the van, in what could be read as an act of doing away with their last hope of making a living. There is no optimism, Jimmy Sr. is still unemployed, a victim of the larger, impersonal force of a system which does not approve of their efforts and whose interests seem to be protected by official bureaucracy. At the personal level, there are no signs that his damaged relationship with family and friends will improve in the future. Exclusion, alienation and a sense of internal exile are, it would seem, permanent.

In the 1980's and early 1990's, Ireland went through severe economic recession, one consequence of which was, among other things, mass unemployment in Dublin and particularly in northside suburbs. This recession, many economists hold, was mainly due to the fact that dominant groups held on to traditional structures and attitudes that did little to support those worse off, which in turn helped to maintain the vast socio-economic divisions in the capital. In Roddy Doyle's *The Barrytown Trilogy*, what I read as a systematic exclusion of the working-class finds artistic expression. His characters, I have argued, are excluded at several levels: social, economic, geographical and cultural. Consequently, they are forced to live in what could be termed internal exile. Although *The Commitments* and *The Snapper* are predominantly comic in nature, they insist on reminding the reader of the harsh socio-economic realities which the characters have to cope with on a daily basis and which deeply affect their lives. In *The Van*, the long-term unemployment encountered by Jimmy Sr. results in hopelessness and degradation, as he is forced to continue his internal exile in northside Dublin, a victim of failed economic policies and banished from mainstream society.

References

Bakhtin, Mikhail. *The Dialogic Imagination*. Trans. Caryl Emerson and Michael Holquist. Austin: Texas UP, 1981.

Bartley, Brendan and A. Jamie Saris. 'Social Exclusion and Cherry Orchard: A Hidden Side of Suburban Dublin'. *Dublin: Contemporary Trends and Issues for the Twenty-First Century*. Ed. James Killen and Andrew MacLaran. Geographical Society of Ireland, Special publication 11. Dublin: The Geographical Society of Ireland and The Centre for Urban and Regional Studies, Trinity College Dublin, 1999. 81-92.

Brown, Terence. *Ireland: A Social and Cultural History, 1922 to the Present*. Ithaka and London: Cornell UP, 1985.

Carlson, Julia, ed. *Banned in Ireland: Censorship and the Irish Writer*. London: Routledge, 1990.

Clancy, Patrick et. al., eds.. *Irish Society: Sociological Perspectives*. Dublin: Institute of Public Administration in association with The Sociological Association of Ireland, 2001.

Connolly, Claire, ed. *Theorizing Ireland*. Basingstoke and New York: Palgrave Macmillan, 2003.

Donnelly, Brian. 'Roddy Doyle: From Barrytown to the GPO'. *Irish University Review* 30.1 (Spring/Summer 2000): 17-31.

Doyle, Roddy. *The Barrytown Trilogy* (*The Commitments*, *The Snapper*, *The Van*). London: Secker and Warburg, 1992.

Drudy, P. J. and Andrew MacLaran. 'The Built Environment'. *Dublin: Economic and Social Trends*. Vol. 1. Dublin: Centre for Urban and Regional Studies, Trinity College Dublin, 1994. 23-36.

— 'Demographic Change and Structure'. *Dublin: Economic and Social Trends*. Vol. 1. Dublin: Centre for Urban and Regional Studies, Trinity College Dublin, 1994. 7-12.

— 'Output, Employment and Unemployment'. *Dublin: Economic and Social Trends*. Vol. 1. Dublin: Centre for Urban and Regional Studies, Trinity College Dublin, 1994. 13-22.

Drudy, P. J. and Leona Walker. 'Dublin in a Regional Context'. *Dublin: Economic and Social Trends*. Vol. 2. Ed. P. J. Drudy and Andrew MacLaran. Dublin: Centre for Urban and Regional Studies, Trinity College Dublin, 1996. 7-19.

Drudy, Sheelagh. 'Class Society, Inequality and the "Declassed"'. *Irish Society: Sociological Perspectives*. Ed. Patrick Clancy et. al. Dublin: Institute of Public Administration in association with The Sociological Association of Ireland, 2001. 295-323.

Graham, B. J. and L. J. Proudfoot. *An Historical Geography of Ireland*. London and San Diego: Academic Press, 1993.

Gramsci, Antonio. *Selections from the Prison Notebooks of Antonio Gramsci*. Ed. and trans. Quintin Hoare and Geoffrey Nowell Smith. London: Lawrence and Wishart, 1971.

Haywood, Ian. *Working-Class Fiction: From Chartism to Trainspotting*. Plymouth: Northcote House, 1997.

Hunt Mahony, Christina. *Contemporary Irish Literature: Transforming Tradition*. New York: St. Martin's Press, 1998.

Lanters, José. 'Demythicizing/Remythicizing the Rising: Roddy Doyle's *A Star Called Henry'*. *Hungarian Journal of English and American Studies*. Irish Issue 8.1 (Spring 2002): 245-58.

Lee, Joseph J. *Ireland 1912-1985: Politics and Society*. Cambridge: Cambridge UP, 1989.

Löbl-Schreyer and Schröder, Dieter. *Irland*. Trans. Edward Brehmer. Stockholm: Bokorama, 1988.

MacLaran, Andrew. *Dublin: The Shaping of a Capital*. London and New York: Belhaven Press, 1993.

— 'Inner Dublin: Change and Development'. *Dublin: Contemporary Trends and Issues for the Twenty-First Century*. Ed. James Killen and Andrew MacLaran. Geographical Society of Ireland, Special publication 11. Dublin: The Geographical Society of Ireland and The Centre for Urban and Regional Studies, Trinity College Dublin, 1999. 21-33.

McLoone, Martin. *Irish Film: The Emergence of a Contemporary Cinema*. London: British Film Institute, 2000.

Miller, Kerby A. *Emigrants and Exiles: Ireland and the Irish Exodus to North America*. New York and Oxford: Oxford UP, 1985.

Moore, Niamh. 'Rejuvenating Docklands: The Irish Context'. *Irish Geography* 32.2 (1999): 135-49.

Nic Ghiolla Phádraig, Máire. 'The Power of the Catholic Church in the Republic of Ireland'. *Irish Society: Sociological Perspectives*. Ed. Patrick Clancy et. al. Dublin: Institute of Public Administration in association with The Sociological Association of Ireland, 2001. 593-619.

O'Toole, Fintan. *The Ex-Isle of Erin: Images of a Global Ireland*. Dublin: New Island Books, 1997.

O'Toole, Fintan. *A Mass for Jesse James: A Journey through 1980's Ireland*. Dublin: Raven Arts Press, 1990.

O'Toole, Fintan. *Black Hole, Green Card: The Disappearance of Ireland*. Dublin: New Island Books, 1994.

Punch, Michael. 'Economic Geographies of the Urban System: Top-down/Bottom-up Trajectories of Development and Change in Dublin's Inner City'. *Journal of Irish Urban Studies* 1.2 (2002): 31-53.

— 'Inner-City Transformation and Renewal: The View from the Grassroots'. *Dublin: Economic and Social Trends*. Vol. 3. Ed. P. J.

Drudy and Andrew MacLaran. Dublin: Centre for Urban and Regional Studies, Trinity College Dublin, 2001: 38-51.

Ryan, Ray (ed.). *Writing in the Irish Republic: Literature, Culture, Politics 1949-1999*. London: Macmillan, 2000.

Smyth, Gerry. *The Novel and the Nation: Studies in the New Irish Fiction*. London: Pluto Press, 1997.

— 'The Right to the City: Re-presentations of Dublin in Contemporary Irish Fiction'. *Contemporary Irish Fiction: Themes, Tropes, Theories*. Ed. Liam Harte and Michael Parker. London: Macmillan, 2000: 13-34.

Ward, Patrick. *Exile, Emigration and Irish Writing*. Dublin and Portland, OR: Irish Academic Press, 2002.

Whelan, Christopher T. 'Class Transformation and Social Mobility in the Republic of Ireland'. *Irish Society: Sociological Perspectives*. Dublin: Institute of Public Administration in association with The Sociological Association of Ireland, 2001: 324-57.

Wolch, Jennifer and Michael Dear, eds. *The Power of Geography: How Territory Shapes Social Life*. Boston: Unwyn Hyman, 1989.

'Washed up on Somebody Else's Tide': The Exile Motif in Contemporary Poetry by Women

Britta Olinder

'I am a stranger in your country', 'Unlike anyone else', 'I was taken from my [...] land, / Washed up on someone else's tide, / A pale corpse: "cordially hated by the natives."'
'Now I have not the least sense of place', 'as if I don't exist', 'there is no safe haven / For settler or dispossessed'.

These extracts – to be discussed later – from a poem by Louise C. Callaghan sum up a variety of experiences and feelings of what it means to be in exile. To be a stranger, 'the other', marginalized, suffering the pain of being separated from one's home, dispossessed, losing one's sense of direction, having a sensation of total alienation and lack of security – these are words to describe the exilic situation, notably from a woman's point of view. In accounts of Irish literary works on the subject, the story of male exile is predominant. The seminal texts were 'authored out of male psychologies' (Ward 232). Thus a writer like Kate O'Brien is misrepresented in accounts of Irish exiles, as pointed out by Patrick Ward who observes her 'evident refusal to acknowledge the [male] patterns of exilic sentiment', something that 'raises intriguing issues regarding female representation and authorship in the discourse of exile' (9).

My aim here is to investigate the concept of exile and its uses in some poems by women primarily taken from the section on 'Contemporary Poetry', edited by Nuala Ní Dhomhnaill in the fifth volume of *The Field Day Anthology of Irish Writing*: *Irish Women's Writing and Traditions*. My first question   after having

Re-Mapping Exile: Realities and Metaphors in Irish Literature and History, ed. Michael Böss, Irene Gilsenan Nordin and Britta Olinder, *The Dolphin* 34. © 2005 by Aarhus University Press, Denmark. ISBN 87 7934 010 5.

studied John Hewitt's views on exile (see article above) is: To what extent and how do women see exile in a different light compared to men? We realize that, dependent on fathers or husbands in a patriarchal system, they can be forced away into exile from the world known to them. An issue here is whether marriage itself can be experienced by women as exile?

As has become apparent in the other contributions to this collection, exile seems almost to be part of the Irish condition. When it comes to literature we need only mention classical writers like Shaw, Wilde and, of course, Joyce who spent most of his life outside Ireland writing exclusively about his home country and who treats the topic explicitly in his only published and staged play entitled precisely *Exiles* (1918). We can also observe that practically every Irish writer deals with borderlines in society, between religious or ethnic groups or between social classes; divisions that force people into exile.

As a literary motif exile is, therefore, evident in many ways. To take some random examples from the latter part of the twentieth century: Brian Friel with his breakthrough play *Philadelphia, Here I Come!* (1964)[1], and for the present purpose especially *The Loves of Cass McGuire* (1966). It is about a woman who emigrated to the US, living there most of her life but returning to Ireland only to discover that, more than ever, she is in exile in her own home country, where her family dispose of her in a home for the elderly. What a woman playwright like Christina Reid adds to the usual political, social or economic reasons for going into exile is the issue of children, notably extramarital ones who would keep their mothers in exile, away from the moral judgments in Ireland. With another dramatist, Anne Devlin, the need to get away from patriarchal structures becomes explicit, witness Frieda, one of the main characters in *Ourselves Alone* (1986). She rebels against the habits and limitations that men impose on women, apparently no less in their common fight for human rights. That is why it is not really her lover Frieda leaves but Ireland in the sense of the political situation of struggles between factions, social conflicts and, not least, harassment and exploitation of women.

So much for drama. In the area of poetry it was discovered that, after long and shameful neglect of women in Irish

anthologies, even *The Field Day Anthology of Irish Literature*, so
eagerly awaited and finally appearing in the early nineties,
included only four women poets among thirty-seven male ones.
This raised such an outcry of protest that not only one but two
volumes had to be added to the previous three. These additions
devote about a hundred double-columned pages to contemporary
women's poetry. Of about two hundred poems some ten seem to
shed some light on the issue of exile. It is, however, worth
mentioning that even after the strong reactions to gender
imbalance the situation is not much better among critics, witness
Declan Kiberd in his *Inventing Ireland* – in spite of his section on
early feminism. Thus of the poets dealt with below only Eavan
Boland made it into the randomly chosen works by Kiberd and
Goodby. My purpose here is just to sketch a map of similarities
and possible differences between male and female attitudes to
exile and treatments of this concept as found in this important
anthology, complemented by other material within easy reach on
and by the poets.

One poem by **Angela Patten, 'The Country of Belonging'** (1390)
caught my attention with the words 'exiled in Babylon', here
applied to Daniel of biblical history, contrasting him as dream-
interpreter with the plural first persons' inability in interpreting
the lines of the new-born's foot-soles. 'Your lined foot-soles are a
hieroglyph / we cannot yet decipher.' Looking more closely at the
poem we can distinguish the different stages of development. The
way I follow the logic of it, 'the country of becoming' of the title
and the last line of the poem is the land of exile from the 'other
worlds' which are still sending messages etched also on the palms
of the baby. This land of exile is further described in the first
stanza as 'the human episode / in all its troubled loveliness'. The
earlier stages, which would presumably represent the home from
which the child is exiled, are evoked in the shapes of 'foetus, fish,
amphibian'. After swimming 'through a tunnel / whose walls
were shaken by earthquake' and feeling the roof pressing in on all
sides the person-to-be wakes up to the experience of peace, which
is really just the absence of pleasure. The newly arrived exile first
has to try on 'space, exploring theories / of connection and

detachment' but is warned that 'it takes / a long time to become human', i.e. to adapt to the new country. Even so this little being is comforted: 'You have reached / the place where it all happens.'

The poem is, thus, focussed on the newborn baby seen as a messenger from other worlds. What is, after all, not quite clear is whether it is now really exiled in this life or has come home from exile in the earlier existence. Is 'the human episode / In all its troubled loveliness', 'the country of becoming' to which the newborn is welcomed, home or exile? In any case the idea of exile has acquired existential dimensions to be related to religious ideas about being a stranger, a pilgrim in this life, longing for the celestial home.

It is, finally, to be noted that Angela Patten (b. 1952) emigrated to the USA in 1977 and, thus has her own experience of exile (O'Breen 222).

Evangeline Paterson's 'Dispossessed' (1387) tells us straightforwardly in a very spare, simple and concentrated way of a forced exile for economic reasons, what can be recognized as a colonial situation – it seems to describe conditions in Africa in the colonial period. It is as if we were looking at photographs:

This man is called Obed. His surname
is in another language. You do not need
to know it.

This is his room.He lives here
by himself. He does not have
enough food.

These are his wife and children.
They live a long way off. He sends them money.
They do not have enough food.

The rest of the poem describes how he goes home once a year, longed for and welcomed by his family who run to meet him. Then he has to go back to his lonely room in the city. The question is raised concerning his feelings about the kind of life he and his

wife and children are forced to live. He does not seem to show
any emotions. In any case he is not rebellious, he neither throws
bombs nor breaks windows. The important thing is to send home
money and not forget his duties. The very bareness of the style
illustrates the poverty of the poem's characters. We cannot be
certain that it concerns exile to another country; only that the
man's family 'stay / in the hard land where nothing grows' while
where he works ' his surname / is in another language', he is a
stranger. They are 'a long way off' from one another. The
restrained feelings are mentioned indirectly as the children run to
meet him. They would seem to have a lot to cry for in their
destitution, but we are told that it is for happiness they cry when
seeing the father of the family at home. Since they are not allowed
where the father works and lodges, there is a hint that remaining
at home but separated from a family member also equals some
sort of exile, especially in these poor circumstances. Their poverty
is emphasized as the reason for the man's exile. Neither he nor his
family have enough food. They are dipossessed as the title
proclaims.

Along with this Paterson (b. 1928) conveys a feeling of exile in
several other poems in her collection *Lucifer, with Angels*. In
'Leaving for Hospital' (27) Mrs Kavanagh departs from her home
to go to the dreaded hospital as if she were going into exile:

> She looked once at the house in the grey light,
> and looked away, and did not look again,
> but oh how her thoughts and fears and wishes clung
> like straw to the hedges as she went down the lane.

Paterson's clearest example of the exile theme is 'Elegy for
Madeleine' (54) about Madeleine of France who married James V
of Scotland. Her exile to Scotland is, however, all too soon
followed by one to the life beyond.

Colette Ní Ghallchóir (b. 1950) also indicates the forces behind
exile in **'Farewell to the Glens'**, originally in Irish (1372). It is
about the need to get away from sorrow and curses, from poor
food, from the cold and the dark, from dead cows, death and

'battles / over boggy bad wetlands'. This part of the home country has, thus, become 'The Glen of emigration'. In the poem's repetitions and qualifications of the Irish glen we perceive the desillusionment with the glorification of history, with songs and stories of heroic fighting. The word 'glen' itself is to be noted, always written with a capital letter, reminding us that it is usually found in descriptions of romantic beauty and mystery. The very repetition of it in various constellations from sorrow to battles and death expresses the bitterness felt about the falshood of these recurrent elements of patriotic discourse heard in traditional songs and legends which have turned into a shared life lie. At the same time the repetitions are evidence of the strong oral tradition alive in Ní Ghallchóir's work.

The connection of exile with banishment and emprisonment is brought out in **Caitlín Maude's** (1941-82) **'Captivity'** (1352) which was originally written in Irish and translated by Nuala Ní Dhomhnaill. The subtext is Blake's 'Tiger', here 'a wild animal / from the tropics / famous and renowned / for my beauty.' But this wild animal who used to be as fierce as Blake describes him, shaking the forest trees with his roar, no longer embodies the question how God could create something so fearful and potentially evil. He is now reduced to captivity, a passive victim, utterly powerless in his enforced dislocation to a foreign country far away. There is a gulf here between north and south, between captivity behind bars and freedom outside, between power and powerlessness. It has been read as a metaphor for the poet's feelings of emprisonment in her last year of illness, but was in fact written in the mid 1960's (McBreen 138).

In **'The Leaving'** (1355) **Paula Meehan** (b. 1955) speaks about the decision or non-decision to leave and go into exile. It is the story of a man who seems paralysed and out of reach of his woman who does everything to arrange for their escape. He just keeps himself apart and busy with his manuscripts and family photos. We get the impression of a dangerous political situation with soldiers around and many neighbours already in prison. The question is whether to dare the flight through the forest under the protection of the dark in order to cross the frontier to safety.

The ambivalence between staying or leaving is emphasized. The man is apparently tied to what has been his life so far. While his reluctance to leave makes up the drama of the poem, the woman feels exile is the only hope for safety, needed for the sake of the child she is bearing. She is not leaving her home and man with an easy heart but once she is in safety, she is grateful for it.

I have not found much explicitly on exile in Paula Meehan's poems, but one other, 'Return and No Blame' (23-24) in *The Man who was Marked by Winter* tells us of homecoming 'after the long seasons away', of someone driven 'down unknown roads / where they spoke in different tongues'. This exile has had its geographical run but seems still, after the return, to loom in family relationships:

> Yes, father, I will have more tea
> and sit here quiet in this room of my childhood
> and watch while the flames flicker
> the story of our distance on the wall. (24)

Captivity and issues of freedom and power / powerlessness are central in two poems on seal-women, using the old legends as metaphors and myths of home and exile within the state of marriage. A footnote informs the reader that in the West of Ireland and Scotland there is a belief

> that seals are 'the people of the sea', and at judicious times, like at the full-moon, they shed their grey sealskin cloaks and dance like men and women. If you can steal the shedded sealskin cloak the seal must follow you forever. Various myths of men who married seal women are based on this story. (1321)

Just as exile is Janus-faced, turned both back to the old home and forward to the new one in exile, the seal woman in **Moyra Donaldson's** (b. 1956) **'Songs for Bones'** (1321-22) is both seal swimming and woman dancing, 'both magnificent'. She is drawn into marriage by the man who had seen her dancing and stolen her sealskin and by his promises to let her go in seven years, promises that are not kept. Her being ill at ease is concretely described as loss of power, of physical health. Her skin gets dry and pale, her eyes darken and her legs are so weak she can neither dance nor walk properly. But her husband refuses to let her return. It is her daughter who saves her. She hears her mother weeping with weakness and despair and, 'loving her mother more than she feared to lose her', she brings her the sealskin. After a tender farewell sealwoman slips into the water and disappears. She has returned to her home after her exile to married life.

This poem, too, could have been entitled 'captivity', but it is not so much the emprisonment as being away from her home, not being allowed into her right element that is the primary thing about the sealwoman's condition; thus rather to be defined as exile endured in her marriage. Whether captivity or exile, it weakens and changes her. The final moral of the poem, however, is that it is in our own power to make that return from exile to our true home.

Katherine Duffy's (b. 1962) '**Questioning Seal-Woman**' (1325-26), published in the same year (1998) as Donaldson's, seems more comfortable with her role and it is not at all certain that she will have the courage or the capacity 'to seek her road to the sea'. Even so there is something unsatisfactory about her life in the exile of her marriage. She forgets herself, who she is, and there is pain even if she allows it to dwindle, 'deep in your back, a lost pool' or 'a faint tinkle of scales / in the air, when you turn your head suddenly'. In this case the child, a boy, does not know about her past and it seems impossible to communicate to him her experiences from a life in the sea, about things like 'the peril of nets [...] the opulence of jellyfish'. In short, the poem asks questions about the state of exile within marriage away from the woman's original home, even when she has everything a woman could desire of material satisfaction. This poem poses questions not only about home and exile but also whether material goods, comfort and consumerism are enough to keep you happy, about what is really valuable in life, the full moon 'above / immoderate pastures of water' and – not least – questions about your skill, or 'stealth / to seek the road to the sea', and especially, your courage in taking that road back to your true home.

Something similar can be seen in **Moyra Donaldson's 'Poem Found in a Castle'** (1321). This marriage exile is defined by the cold, by summer as never ending winter. The woman is objectified, led into the chamber by her husband, who 'placed a torc of silver on my neck', seemingly as an adornment but, we understand, also to mark his possession and power; then 'called me his wife'.

It was only in her dreams that she could get back home to her sisters. Later the alienation and separation from her own sons is complete; she is 'their cold and foreign mother'. There is no way out. Her dreams now are of herself in the shape of the swift and agile bird of prey, the falcon, trained to have no will of its own but only to obey the falconer. Thus she has no longer any other home than this marriage, exiled even in her dreams. She is cut off from everything else, reduced to being the toy of her husband.

'The Palatine Daughter Marries a Catholic' (1311-12) is the poem quoted from in the beginning. In the first place this is emigration to, not from Ireland. In addition **Louise C. Callghan** (b. 1948) presents two kinds of exile, first the daughter having to move with her family and then having to marry into the new country. This is, indeed, an illustration of Said's description of exile: 'Exile is the unhealable rift forced between a human being and a native place, between the self and its true home. The essential sadness of the break can never be surmounted' (49). The passive form demonstrates her unwillingness in 'I was taken from' while the possessive pronoun in 'my Rhine-watered land' denotes her true belonging. The increased hopelessness is expressed in 'washed up on someone else's tide' with the distancing effect in the genitive 'someone else's' in contrast to the intimacy of the previous 'my [...] land'. Being exiled has even taken her life in some sense; she is just 'a pale corpse'. It has deeply affected her identity, her 'sense of place', her sense of belonging. Alienation and estrangement from everything around her is painted in a series of situations: She reads is as if she did not exist, in a landscape changing with the seasons without effect on her; she is not fully there.

And then again in the passive form, as a court order: 'I'm summoned / by marriage like a piece of furniture'. She is just an object with no will of her own. 'Our bibles are all buried now' indicates that the distinguishing feature of her Protestant faith, which was part of her identity, is no longer there to support her in her new life in a Catholic marriage. What is then left for her husband to love? The hopeless 'land of no return'? An empty shell, 'patches of blue haze'? Or just her belongings, 'the grey canvas shoes / beneath my strange palatine bed' along with odd habits from overseas? As the poem moves on to her response to his love, passivity is again emphasized, reluctance to take part or take sides because of her total lack of security, the feeling of not being at home, of not having a home, the situation, in other words, of somebody who has been uprooted, a settler which is what she became when she had to move with her family, losing her home in Rhineland Germany and feeling a stranger in the new country and even more dispossessed, further from any recognizable home in her marriage to someone with a different background.

In Callaghan's *The Puzzle-Heart* there is another poem, 'Letters to America' (12-16) dealing with a very different aspect of exile, the feelings of emptiness and 'love's bitter mystery' experienced by the mother left behind when her son has emigrated to the USA.

In '**Mise Éire'**, finally, **Eavan Boland** opposes and corrects Patrick Pearse's view of Ireland. No longer, as in the earlier poem, is the personification of the country 'older than the Old Woman of Beare' but 'a sloven's mix'. The glory of having born 'Cuchulain the valiant' is turned into the picture of the woman 'holding her half-dead baby to her'. When Pearse speaks of the shame of her own children selling their mother, Boland's woman is quite capable of that transaction herself. As to being left 'lonelier than the Old Woman of Beare', Boland's woman is prepared to mingle her immigrant voice with people speaking differently, to adjust to the new conditions in a foreign country and struggle on.

The exile in Boland's poem distances herself from her home country, from its old language, old style of writing, from its history that is bandaged up by songs and crime made beautiful by rhyme and rhythm. She was, in a sense, in exile at home, in Ireland, as an outsider, a prostitute. Going into exile is an act of rebellion – not as it is usually seen, 'a punishment imposed by an oppressive imperialism' (Ward 231). The persona turns her back on Ireland, concluding the chapter of emigration by not even wanting to go back. Her immigrant speech – not without sounds of homesickness – is perceived as 'a kind of scar' which 'heals after a while / into a passable imitation / of what went before.' Displacement is moved from the exiled person to the Irish nation. It is Ireland that is displaced 'into dactyls, /oaths made / by animal tallows / of the candle'.

Apart from the fact that she gave her first collection of poetry the suggestive title of *New Territory* (1967) Boland (b. 1945) has remarkably many poems explicitly on exile. 'After a Childhood Away from Ireland' (24-25) in *Night Feed* is about homecoming with the conclusion: 'What I had lost / was not land / but the habit / of land, / whether of growing out of, / or settling back on, / or being defined by.'

The Journey explores several different aspects of exile. In 'An Irish Childhood in England' (50-51) the misery of being among strange people in an alien environment is strongly underlined: 'In a strange city, in another country, / on nights in a North-facing bedroom, / waiting for the sleep that never did / restore me as I'd hoped to what I'd lost'. And later: '[…] when all of England to an Irish child / was nothing more than what you'd lost and how'. Another poem 'Fond Memory' (52), however, contains some comfort as her father is playing the piano and singing 'the slow / lilts' of Tom Moore. It makes her think: 'this is my country, was, will be again, /This upward-straining song made to be / Our safe inventory of pain.' Comparing her own situation to that of 'The Emigrant Irish' (54) she realizes how much worse off they were. 'They would have thrived on our necessities'. The difference was, of course, also that they had nothing to lose. And in their hardships, patience and long-suffering they still had 'all the old songs. And nothing to lose.' The use of this poem by Mary Robinson, when she was inaugurated as President, to remind people of the diaspora overseas, has been pointed out by Declan Kiberd (608).

In *Outside History* 'The Game' (16) of a rather grim imagination is framed by reactions of alienation brought on by 'an English spring' and the irony of praying 'for the King in the chapel' while 'In Exile' (40) deals with German girls coming to help her family in Ireland when she was very small. They came from 'a ruined city', there was a sense of injury and they were isolated in this environment since they did not understand either English or French. Their own language consisted of 'syllables in which pain was / radical, integral'. It makes her think, so many years later, of how her own speech in alien New England is at variance with the speech around her. In contrast to the case in 'Mise Eire' her 'speech will not heal. I do not want it to heal'. If we compare with the earlier 'An Irish Childhood in England' she had then

> let the world I knew become the space
> between the words that I had by heart
> and all the other speech that always was
> becoming the language of the country that
> I came to (*Outside History* 50)

Later on, in *The Lost Land*, language becomes 'A Habitable Grief' (29). Boland refers to her childhood in 'a strange country', learning 'a second language there / which has stood me in good stead' and calls it 'the lingua franca of a lost land'. She declares:

> This is what language is:
> a habitable grief. A turn of speech
> for the everyday and ordinary abrasion
> of losses such as this:
>
> which hurts
> just enough to be a scar.

And heals just enough to be a nation. (*Lost Land* 29)

Conclusion

The poems discussed here form only a very narrow and fairly arbitrary selection on the theme of exile. As Joan McBreen has shown by presenting almost twice as many contemporary women poets as *Field Day* V, there is much larger scope for a more thorough investigation of the theme in poems by women. Even this limited choice bears out Patrick Ward's assumption mentioned before about raising 'intriguing issues regarding female representation and authorship in the discourse of exile' (9). Along with Kerby Miller he directs our attention to the predominant 'idea of exile in the Gaelic, Catholic and nationalist traditions', observing that it thus 'excludes Protestants' which, of course, has its bearing on the Louise Callaghan poem. The concentration 'on masculine perceptions, needs and emotions', Ward argues, 'minimises and marginalises the experiences of women' (25). In fact it could be maintained that in many ways a woman's situation in a patriarchal system can be compared to that of an exile. We could ask ourselves to what extent 'the other', so often used about women, is a synonym of 'exile' (cf. Moi 150).

Some of the poems, however, do not distinguish themselves clearly from men's work on the same theme. They show colonial traces, primarily in Maude's wild animal from the tropics, now in captivity, but also Patterson's presentation of the man forced to work for his family far away from them and Ní Ghallchóir's 'Farewell to the Glen'. In the latter two poems exile is a result of hunger and poverty. Homesickness is naturally in evidence in most cases as is the bitterness of conditions that left exile and emigration as the only options. In this respect Paula Mehan's poem adds complications. The man who stays at home seems to be in inner exile, while the woman who has to leave her home, in gratefully accepting her escape into 'another state' seems to have accepted her exile as the safety of a home.

The feeling of being dispossessed is strongly expressed by Evangeline Paterson. Angela Patten adds the existential dimension with perspectives on the existence before, but also during and after life. In 'Mise Eire' Boland resembles Ní

Ghallchóir in her quite scornful dissociation from Ireland as representing a life she wants to leave far behind her to enjoy a better life in a new country. Her persona refuses even to look back but cannot help connecting her homesickness with language. This aspect is also something Boland has developed in other poems, the feeling of exile and estrangement when not speaking the same language or dialect as people around you. At the same time she seems to be able to agree with Anna Smith's impression of Kristeva's writing 'that the language of exile is the only language worth knowing [...] most especially for her own language as a woman' (5).

When we come, however, to the poems on seal-women as well as Donaldson's 'Poem Found in a Castle' and Callaghan's 'Palatine Daughter' and their speaking of matrimony in terms of exile and homelessness, this is a specifically feminine viewpoint which was the most interesting variation of the theme of exile in this material; evidence, indeed, of the 'different magnetic field'[2] of women's poetry.

Notes
[1] The dates of plays given here in the text are of the first performance.
[2] Eavan Boland quoted by Nuala Ní Dhomhnaill in her introduction to 'Contemporary Poetry' in *The Field Day Anthology* V. 1290.

References

Boland, Eavan. *The Journey and Other Poems*. Manchester: Carcanet, 1987.

— *The Lost Land*. Manchester: Carcanet, 1998.

— *New Territory*. Dublin: Allen Figgis, 1967.

— *Night Feed*. 1982. Dublin: Arlen House, 1984.

— *Outside History*. Manchester: Carcanet, 1990.

Callghan, Louise. *The Puzzle-Heart*. Cliffs of Moher, Co. Clare, 1999.

'Contemporary Poetry'. Ed. Nuala Ní Dhomhniall in *The Field Day Anthology of Irish Writing*. Vol V: *Irish Women's Writing and Traditions*. Ed. Angela Bourke et als. Cork: Cork UP, 2002. 1290-1408.

Devlin, Anne. *Ourselves Alone*. London: Faber, 1986.

Friel, Brian. *Philadelphia, Here I Come!* 1965. London: Faber, 1970.
— *The Loves of Cass McGuire*. London: Faber, 1967.
Goodby, John. *Irish Poetry since 1950: From Stillness into History*. Manchester and New York: Manchester UP, 2000.
Joyce, James. *Exiles*. 1918. London: Jonathan Cape, 1952.
Kiberd, Declan. *Inventing Ireland: The Literature of the Modern Nation*. London: Vintage, 1996.
McBreen, Joan. *The White Page / An Bhileog Bhan: Twentieth-Century Irish Women Poets*. Cliffs of Moher, County Clare: Salmon Publishing, 1999.
Meehan, Paula. *The Man who was Marked by Winter*. Oldcastle, Co. Meath: Gallery Press, 1991.
Miller, Kerby A. *Emigrants and Exiles: Ireland and the Irish Exodus to North America*. New York, Oxford: Oxford UP, 1985.
Moi, Toril. *Sexual / Textual Politics*. 1985. London and New York: Routledge, 1989.
Paterson, Evangeline. *Lucifer, with Angels*. Dublin: Dedalus, 1994.
Reid, Christina. *Tea in a China Cup*. London: Methuen, 1987.
— *The Belle of the Belfast City*. London: Methuen, 1989.
Said, Edward. 'The Mind of Winter: Reflections on Life in Exile' in *Harpers Magazine*. Vol. 269, no 161 (Sept. 1984): 49-55.
Smith, Anna. *Julia Kristeva: Readings of Exile and Estrangement*. London: Macmillan, 1996.
Ward, Patrick. *Exile, Emigration and Irish Writing*. Dublin: Irish Academic Press, 2002.

John Banville's *Shroud*:
Exile in Simulation

Hedda Friberg

Introduction

If certain postmodern thinkers are to be believed, much is
disturbing about the condition of the western world after World
War I. It is a slippery, sliding sort of world in which uncertainties
have replaced certainties and in which humanity has lost its
bearings. According to Jean Baudrillard, we have launched a
'universe of simulation, where [...] no one is represented nor
representative of anything any more' and in which we are
'simulators, we are simulacra' (152). In this world, and from
itself, humanity is in a sense exiled. Albert Camus suspected this:
humanity is a stranger in universe, the exilic condition
irremediable – *sans recours* – (*Le Mythe* 18). John Banville, too,
apparently suspects this, as, in *Shroud*, he sets the central
character adrift in exile - in the sense of banishment, as well as in
the sense of alienation, or estrangement. Reading *Shroud*, then,
through some of Baudrillard's early ideas on contemporary
culture, as he expressed them in *Simulacra and Simulation*,[1] I
suggest that Banville's protagonist is moving in a state of exile in
simulation – from the history of his people, from any likeness of a
god, and from his own self. Below, these three levels of what I
term exile in simulation will be examined in *Shroud*.

In referring, in the following, to the exilic condition of the
protagonist of *Shroud*, I have considered Edward Said's comment,
in his 'Reflections on Exile,' that exile is a defining characteristic
of modern culture: 'We have become accustomed to thinking of
the modern period itself as spiritually orphaned and alienated,
the age of anxiety and estrangement. Nietzsche taught us to feel
uncomfortable with tradition, and Freud to regard domestic
intimacy as the polite face painted on patricidal and incestuous

Re-Mapping Exile: Realities and Metaphors in Irish Literature and History, ed.
Michael Böss, Irene Gilsenan Nordin and Britta Olinder, *The Dolphin* 34.
© 2005 by Aarhus University Press, Denmark. ISBN 87 7934 010 5.

rage. Modern western culture is in large part the work of exiles, émigrés, refugees' (Said 173). Among these terms, and others, I have come to favour 'exile' over 'emigré,' or 'expatriate,' since it indicates, as suggested in Patrick Ward's recent survey of exile and Irish writing, that whereas the emigré has hopes of returning to his homeland if and when political winds turn, and while the expatriate is 'distinguished by the temporary nature' of his or her absence from home, the exile is involved in an irreversible process (Dahlie in *Ward* 14-15). Also, although external exile is the primary focus of the above study by Ward, states of internal exile, relevant to the study of Banville's novel, are also discussed:

> This twentieth-century view of exile arises no doubt, [sic] out of the experiences of Romanticism, the mass movement of populations (voluntary and compulsory) and [. . .] resistance to nationalism by many Modernist and Post-Modernist artists and intellectuals. It differs clearly from the pre-modern idea of exile in that it is looser, more ambiguous, voluntarist and concerned with distinguishing the intellectual from the masses. (Ward 184)

The kind of inner exile – not necessarily voluntary, however – suggested here is a motif in Banville's art. Thus, the exiled intellectual, although invariably male, takes various shapes in Banville's novels prior to that of the scholar and critic who is at center in *Shroud*: he is a scientist in *Dr. Copernicus* and *Kepler* and a scientist-in-spe in *Mefisto*; he is an actor in *Eclipse*; he is an intellectual outsider exiled in his criminal act in *The Book of Evidence* and *Ghosts*, those two remarkable novels about Freddie Montgomery (in the latter he is also in a Prospero-like, insular exile). Finally, the Cambridge-trained Victor Maskell, in *The Untouchable,* enters a multi-levelled exilic condition of espionage.

The formal concerns that always seem central to Banville as an artist have, in *Shroud*, been used to find forms that adequately reflect man's exilic condition in the floating, gliding postmodern world that, according to Baudrillard, is at hand. In no previous novel by Banville are the uncertainties and immeasurabilities of a decentered universe and the subject's precarious place in it, its exiled condition, more powerfully conveyed than in *Shroud*.

Prior to delving into the various levels of exile in *Shroud* it needs to be said that the novel is a work in dialogue with poststructuralist thought. For one, the articulation of Vander's exilic condition in *Shroud* rests partially on the intertextual presence of the American deconstructionist Paul de Man's life and work. Thus, a brief detour through this presence is necessary. Similarly to his method in *The Untouchable*, the method Banville uses here involves basing his central character's life on that of a historical person. In *Shroud*, it is the life and work of Paul de Man who has provided material for 'recycling.' At one point in the novel, Axel Vander is brutally blinded on one eye. His resulting one-eyed vision, or semi-blindness, gestures toward de Man's well-known idea that, for a critic, insight is achieved only through a special blindness (de Man 102-141). It is not my purpose here to unravel the strands in *Shroud* that are connected to de Man. Suffice it to say that Banville rests his tale on one salient fact – the most sinister, perhaps, and one revealed posthumously – from de Man's biography: in his youth in Belgian Antwerp, de Man published anti-Semitic articles suggesting that, since Europe would do well without contributions made by Jewish culture, people of Jewish origin should be removed to distant parts of the world. These are, as we shall see, the opinions expressed by the first Axel Vander, in *Shroud*. Commenting on Banville's reworking of de Man's life, *The Guardian*'s Alex Clark, reviewing *Shroud* on its publication in the fall of 2002, has drawn attention to the fact that Axel Vander's predicament is ceaselessly cast and recast, to shed light not only on the 'protean nature of the self-inventing fugitive, but also to question the authority of the narrative itself – the subject, broadly speaking, of de Man's writing' (Clark 2). This protean nature of Vander's self-invented identity, the identity of an exile in simulation is at the heart of my reading of *Shroud*. Another reviewer – this one for *The Observer* – found the novel apt to deconstruct itself and felt disturbed by 'a couple of passages at the midpoint of the book that take the narrative clean off its hinges' (Mars-Jones). As this reviewer suggests, the novel does not merely draw on the life of de Man, but also on his work, reenacting de Man's belief that literary texts are self-deconstructing. What is especially interesting about the use of material related to Paul de Man in *Shroud* (as with the use of the life of the Cambridge Five spy Blunt and the childhood of the poet Louis MacNeice in *The Untouchable*) is the effect of the 'recycling' itself; it brings the status of the author down from that of god[2], to the reduced status of the kind of 'cross-road' through which Roland Barthes envisioned language, with its allusions, references, quotations, and echoes, to be passing.[3] It should be added that the intertexual currents that pass through that fork in the road to which I have now reduced John Banville, as the author, also include those texts that the lives of the living and the dead constitute. In this sense, the author as conventionally conceived becomes exiled from his work.

As *Shroud* begins to pry itself open, it offers up to the reader a self-constructing and deconstructing central character who, in order to save his life during the German occupation of Belgium during the Second World War, takes on a dead friend's name. Under the cover of this name, he escapes Belgium and goes into physical exile in England. Eventually he settles in the United States, shaping a scholarly university career for himself there.[4] He becomes known world-wide. In his sun-drenched California haven, ironically called Arcady, where as the novel opens he has reached a brittle and rather monstrous old age, he is contacted by a woman who threatens to make public his hidden past. He meets her in Turin, in northern Italy, and in and through their vague and destructive acquaintance-turned-intimacy-turned-dissolution, the stories of *Shroud* unfold. One of them is about exile: I would, again, argue that the exile of the protagonist is both external and internal; it is also of a postmodern and triple-levelled kind: first, he is exiled from the history of his people in a faked record of that history; second, he is exiled from the likeness of a god; and third, he is a subject exiled in a simulated identity. He is an exile in the realm of the simulacrum.

Exiled from a History and Its Record

In *Shroud*, the protagonist's exile from the history of his people and from the record of that history, begins with the fact of his

Jewish origin. In the novel, his early life in Antwerp – 'fifty years ago, and more' – is marked by the contrast between the life of the 'civilised, handsome, amused and amusing' Vander family (204) and that of his own, unnamed, family, whose apartment 'was the opposite of where the Vanders grandly resided. Our family shared no candle-lit Saturday night dinners abuzz with lively dispute and multi-lingual jokes [. . .] We lived an underground life; I have a sense of something torpid, brownish, exhausted; the smell is the smell of re-breathed air' (205). The Jewish youth, the protagonist whose name the reader never learns, is the friend of Axel, the charming son of the Vanders, 'for whom great things were forecast' (209). As time and the war roll on, this first Axel Vander turns to writing anti-Semitic articles for the newspapers. The essence of these articles, we are told, is a suggestion (in which we, again, recognize Paul de Man), 'that nothing of consequence would be lost to the cultural and intellectual life of Europe, really nothing at all, if certain supposedly assimilated, oriental elements were to be removed and settled somewhere far away, in the steppes of Central Asia, perhaps, or on one of Africa's more clement coasts' (214-15). The young protagonist's reaction to this astounding proposal, made by his friend, is not the outrage to which his Jewish identity would entitle him, but envy and jealousy. He would, he tells the reader, have sold his soul, sold his people, for 'one sustained moment of the public's attention' (212). When the protagonist later assumes the identity of Axel Vander, after the latter's death, he does seem to sell both his people and his soul – or his self – and he certainly enters a state of exile from them both.

To use as material in a novel the experiences of the European Jews during the Second World War, would seem hazardous.[5] John Banville has commented on this, in a review of W.G Sebald's *Austerlitz:*

> For a novelist, the Holocaust is at once a safe subject and a dangerous subject. Safe, because the emotional reaction of practically all readers will be already primed; dangerous, because almost any attempt to deal imaginatively with a crime that is well nigh unimaginable is likely to result in bathos.

There is also the moral question of whether an artist has the right to turn such horrors into the stuff of art. ("The Rubble Artist")

Banville acknowledges that in *Shroud,* the description of the Jewish experience in Belgium is 'not historically accurate'; it is, however, based on 'eye witness accounts from Germany [. . .] and from Romania' (*Shroud* 407-408). Incorporated into the novel's web of historical ties and cross-ties, these experiences are then reported by the completely untrustworthy narrator posing as Axel Vander.

Apart from the Jewish identity, the personal history of the central character is never distinctly presented; it enters the story obliquely and vanishes in the haze of simulation that is the second Axel Vander's identity. For him, his personal history and the history of his people are first processed through the pressures exerted on the Jews of Antwerp by Nazi occupation. The curtailing of personal and social liberties and the deportations increase the pressure on the population:

> as the months went on, life in those mean little streets on the wrong side of the square became increasingly attenuated, until we seemed truly to be living on air. We had a sense of floating above ourselves, buffeted now this way, now that, the frail tethering lines jerking and straining with each new ordinance that was issued against us. We grew lighter and lighter as all that we possessed was taken from us, article by article. One week we were forbidden to ride on trams, the next to ride on bicycles. (217-18)

The narrator – still in his pre-Vander identity – receives signals that he is in danger, and should leave the city on a particular day. He heeds the anonymous warning and leaves; when he returns, he is met by this:

> When I got to our street it was darker than dark, not a single window lit, and all in silence, and then I knew. Three sentries with rifles were standing around a burning brazier, stamping

their feet in the cold [. . .] Frost glittered everywhere on the pavements amid the snow, but when I trod on it I found it was not frost but broken glass. The shop windows were all shattered, their doors boarded over with fresh-cut planks [. . .] The building where I lived, or at least where I had lived until now, was as dark and empty as all the others. The broken front door hung by a single hinge. Behind it, the hall was a square black hole giving on to another universe. (248-49)

Here, it is already with an exile's eyes that the protagonist regards his former home.[6] Thus, as the soon-to-be-Vander finds that he has 'escaped seizure and deportation simply by not being at home' (257), he looks around in the house in which he is not at home and finds it a copy: 'the place was ceasing to be real, was becoming a reproduction, as it were, skilfully done, the details all exact yet lacking all authenticity. Everything looked flat and hollow, like a stage set. I noted the flinty sunlight in the window, it might have been thrown by a powerful electric lamp set up just outside the casement' (254).

Here, the narrator takes his first step into an exile in simulation. Saved from a Belgian Crystal Night of sorts, he has been 'left behind' (256), and become physically removed from his people. It is at this moment, when confronted in the house by a mysterious, possibly benevolent, man by the name of Max Shaudeine, that the protagonist appropriates the name of his dead friend. When asked to identify himself, he says, 'My name is Axel Vander' (255). The appropriation is made on the spur of the moment, to save his life, but once made, the decision *becomes* his life. As he steps into the identity of Axel Vander, one tainted by anti-Semitism, the connection to the group to which he has belonged – the Jews of Antwerp – can no longer be anything but a falsification. Vander knows that were he to be exposed, his change of identity would most likely be regarded as betrayal of his 'race' and a 'cowardly attempt to throw off a past, and a people of which I was ashamed' (237). The aged Vander claims that if this had been his intention, the attempt had failed, because 'the past, my own past, the past of all the others, is still there' (237). However, the history of his people exists, in him and to him, only as it appears processed through the simulated identity which he has assumed. Thus, he becomes exiled from the history of his people.

History is processed in a second way,[7] here, through Axel Vander's narration of it, through the language of his bleak, tired monologue. Challenging his own reliability as a narrator, alternately asserting, negating and evading 'facts' as he moves through the narrative, he makes access to any kind of 'reliable' record impossible. Revealing details of
this history and of his own personal history as entwined with it, gradually and in startling, sinister and surreal fragments, he slides by the articulation of any direct knowledge of the events. Thus, the fragmented, evasive narration makes him an exile, not just from the history of his people, but from the record of that history which, then, has become a false representation, a simulacrum.

Exiled from the Likeness of a Divinity
Apart from being exiled from the history of his people and from the record of that history, the protagonist of *Shroud* is also estranged from the likeness of a god, from a divinity of any kind. He is, to speak with Baudrillard, adrift in 'a world now long desacralized' over which 'the phantom of religion floats' (Baudrillard 153). This state of estrangement is highlighted as Cass Cleave, the girl with whom Axel Vander lives in northern Italy, asks that they go see the Holy Shroud of Turin, which is on public display (*Shroud* 306). In her frenzied way, Cass has studied the history of St Veronica's shroud: 'she had made discoveries, she knew secrets' (307). In this, Cass appears to provide an impetus toward the imaginary, toward mystery and energy, entities which, as Baudrillard seems to see it, resist the reign of the simulacrum. Vander agrees to take her to the shroud, but he mocks her interest in it: 'the Shroud was a fake; he said he knew about fakes. Did she really think it was the image of the crucified Christ?' (307). Reaching the Chapel of the Holy Shroud, they find it shut. Cass is upset and agitated. She tries to ascertain why it is closed and is finally told that it is '"being shown somewhere else"'(309). Significantly, then, the shroud is not only a likely fake

– a false likeness of the son of God – but it is an absent one, unavailable for viewing. The couple persists, however, and eventually they think they have found the shroud. It seems to be on show in a 'big striped marquee set up in a grassy square between a church and a small squat palace' (310). Entering, they discover that 'the marquee [is] only an elaborate entrance to the church, or to the palace' and they are unable to tell in which one the shroud is on display. Significantly, the space under the canvas is occupied by 'ticket booths, and souvenir stalls, and upright plastic display panels that lit up when this or that button was pressed and recounted the history of the Shroud' (310). Here, then, a Shroud-land – a Disney-land of sorts – has mushroomed: it is a plastic place of copies which hides the 'original' shroud and conceals the fact that the shroud is an absent faked image of a non-existent god. When Vander tries to buy tickets, the 'man in the glass booth' indicates that the couple must return the day after. Cass is agitated, but also relieved: 'She had not been meant to see it' (310). Yet the incident appears to indicate that resistance against the reign of the simulacrum is difficult, if not impossible, and it seems to address what Baudrillard has termed a 'wager on representation': if a sign of faith can be exchanged for meaning only as long as something – God – guarantees the exchange, one might ask, as Baudrillard does, what happens if 'God himself can be simulated, that is to say can be reduced to the signs that constitute faith? Then the whole system becomes weightless, it is no longer itself anything but a gigantic simulacrum' (5-6).

The Exiled Subject in *Shroud*: 'a contingency, misplaced and adrift in time' (68-69)

As has been indicated above, in the discussion of Axel Vander and the history of his people, Vander is an unreliable narrator and an evasive, amorphous character. This does not make him unique among the anti-heroes in the production of John Banville, who as a novelist seems to have practiced tightly controlled deception from the start – on levels of form and content alike. Thus, in a letter to his editor David Farrer, Banville wrote in 1972:

you will have noticed in my three books that appearances are terribly deceptive. The characters are never what they initially appear to be, and indeed sometimes what they appear to be at the end is not necessarily what they are. More than that, and more important than that, the structures of the books are never that which the surface suggests them to be (qtd in Tarien 387)

In the thirty years that have passed since Banville wrote that letter, appearances have not grown any less tricky. In *Shroud*, Axel Vander does, as has been suggested, deceptively shift from one identity to another.

The protean nature of Axel Vander is revealed gradually to himself and to the reader. Thus, for Vander, the exact moment when the taken name becomes an assumed identity is unclear: 'I cannot say when it was exactly that I became Axel Vander, I mean when I began to think of myself as him and no longer as myself. Not when I gave his name as mine to Max Schaudeine that day when we stood together in the snow-blue light of my parents' emptied bedroom; I had no thought, then, of taking on Axel's identity' (283-84). What was initially a spontaneous, emergency decision turns into a life-long dwelling in a new identity. Once assumed, this new name has a perfect fit. Thus, to the newly-become Axel Vander, the name feels natural,

> like putting on a new suit of clothes that had been tailored expressly for me [. . .] It was thrilling, too, in a way that I could not exactly account for. Immediately I had spoken came a breathless, tottery sensation, as if I had managed a marvellous feat of dare-devilry, as if I had leapt across a chasm, in my dazzling new raiment, or climbed to a dizzyingly high place, from which I could survey another country, one that I had heard fabulous accounts of but had never visited. (255-56)

He is looking out across a deceptively promising land of exile in simulation. Years later, as he receives Cass Cleave's letter threatening to reveal his past, Vander feels thoroughly 'cloven in two [. . .] On the one side there was the I I had been before the letter arrived, and now was this new *I*, a singular capital standing at a tilt to all the known things that had suddenly become unfamiliar' (13). In stark typographical simplicity, the text here embodies first, in the juxtaposition of the twin first person pronouns, the concept of doubling and second, in the italicised *I*, estrangement.

It seems to me that Axel Vander, in stepping into a new identity has left an old one behind – 'Man and mask are one' (287) – or perhaps eradicated altogether, the underlying one. This is reminiscent of the experience of stepping into a new language, and remaining in it for life, that Julia Kristeva has described in 'Bulgaria, my suffering'. The experience of living in exile in a language other than the one she learnt as a child places her 'at the intersection of two languages, and of at least two lengths of time' (Kristeva 167). She finds her native Bulgarian an 'almost dead language' for her and continues:

> That is to say, a part of me was slowly extinguished as I learned French [. . .] and, finally, exile cadaverized this old body and substituted another for it – at first fragile and artificial, then more and more indispensable, and now the only one that is alive, the French one. I am almost ready to believe in the myth of the resurrection when I examine that bifid state of my mind and my body. I have not mourned the childhood language in the sense that 'completed' mourning would be a detachment, a scar, indeed a forgetting. But [. . .] I have built a new residence in which I dwell and that dwells in me, and in which there unfolds what one might call [. . .] the true life of the spirit and the flesh. (Kristeva 165-66)

Similarly, Vander's old identity is cadaverized and a new structure has been erected. The new one is not positively charged, however, as is Kristeva's dwelling for 'true spirit and the flesh.' For Vander, in his old age, there is no truth of spirit left, and hardly any flesh. The identity he has stepped into is a simulated subject, a dead shell for the display of an identity.

Vander escapes from Antwerp, safely reaching England and later the United States. There, he is 'not your usual hopeful refugee from a fouled and foundering Europe' (289); he is an impostor, but he runs little risk of detection. He is, rather, able to pose as an authentic survivor from the Holocaust and he is treated reverently: 'Others [. . .] regarded me with a kind of wondering respect, with a holy reverence, almost: I was the real thing, a genuine survivor, who had come walking into their midst out of the fire and furnace smoke of the European catastrophe, like Frankenstein's monster staggering out of the burning mill' (59). This is doubly ironic when one considers that not only is the protagonist successfully passing himself off as Axel Vander, without owning up to the anti-Semitism of the latter, but he is also, on an identity level just below that one, in fact the genuine survivor – the Jewish youth who barely escaped a Crystal Night in Antwerp.

In the US, he carves for himself an academic career, which actually is of his own doing: 'Axel Vander's reputation in the world is of my making. It was I who clawed my way to this high place. I wrote the books, seized the prizes, flattered those who had to be flattered, struck down my rivals' (236). Yet, the shifting, fraudulent basis of his existence initially worries him:

> Already I had made myself adept at appearing deeply learned in a range of subjects by the skilful employment of certain key concepts, gleaned from the work of others, but to which I was able to give a personal twist of mordancy or insight. In everything I wrote there was a tensed, febrile urgency that was generated directly out of the life predicament in which I had placed myself; I was fashioning a new methodology of thinking modelled on the crossings and conflicts of my own intricate and, in large part, fabricated past. (60-61)

He asks himself what he has to gain from continuing the fraud. He sees little reason to continue it, yet he does, and asks himself why. He is not, he stresses, sufficiently 'loyal' or 'largehearted' to do this as a tribute to the original Axel. He will not turn himself into a kind of living memorial to his dead friend. Rather, if exposed, he would have 'slithered out of him with the ease of a secret agent discarding his cover and stepping into another' (285-86). Thus the mystery remains: 'If, as I insist, there is no essential, singular self, what is it exactly I am supposed to have escaped by pretending to be Axel Vander' (286). Vander has traits of Mercury, 'patron of thieves and panders,' and of Harlequin, 'created by the gods in a moment of uncontrollable mirthfulness and malice' and, of course, of 'Proteus, too, now delicate, now offensive' (379). Thus, Vander is the mythical shape-changer, but also the slithering spy.

The deceptive shape-changing quality of the impersonator Axel Vander, then, clearly has traits of that variety of inner exile which seems to adhere to the practice of espionage. John Banville is known for his powerful exploration of such a condition, in *The Untouchable*. Another explorer of espionage in fiction and fact is John Le Carré, who has described himself as existing, since childhood, in what might be called a condition of exile in espionage. It is, however, not necessarily biography that is the issue here, but, Le Carré seems to think, the artists themselves: 'Artists have very little centre. They fake. They are not the real thing. They are spies' (Knopf, interview with Le Carré). Thus, Le Carré seems to see the artist, or the intellectual, as an impostor. Lacking a centre, he simulates an identity, moving as he is in a hostile territory in which he is an irremediable exile.

In a similarly hostile exilic environment, the new Axel Vander becomes an adept spy and a master of the lie:

> I became a virtuoso of the lie, making my instrument sing so sweetly that none could doubt the veracity of its song. [. . .] I lied about everything, even when there was no need, even when the plain truth would have been more effective in maintaining the pretence. I made up details of my made-up life with obsessive scruple and inventiveness, building an impregnable alibi for a case that no court was ever likely to be called upon to try. (284-85)

The pride in his virtuosity that this maestro of the fiddle of deception expresses is, however, merely the flip side of his self-contempt. Through the doubling of identity, the faking of a history and through the lies, Vander has become a subject in exile. He is in exile, not just from his people and its history, not just from a shrouded, faked and evasive image of divinity, but from his own self. He is a decentred subject:

> I am, as is surely apparent by now, a thing made up wholly of poses. [. . .] I am all frontage; stroll around to the back and all you will find is some sawdust and a few shaky struts and a mess of wiring. There is not a sincere bone in the entire body of my text. I have manufactured a voice, as once I manufactured a reputation, from material filched from others. The accent you hear is not mine, for I have no accent. I cannot believe a word out of my own mouth. (329)

He is fully aware of having used Cass Cleave to supply him with what he lacks – a core. Whereas his friend and once-lover Kristina Novak who figures rather prominently in the novel was not much more to him than 'an afternoon of mostly simulated passion' (77), his need for Cass is of a more urgent kind. He has used her to fill the space between the sawdust and the struts: 'I seized on her to be my authenticity itself. That was what I was rooting in her for, not pleasure or youth or the last few crumbs of life's grand feast, nothing so frivolous; she was my last chance to be me' (330). Cass, herself, however, is also burdened by her self: 'the intolerable difficulty of being uniquely and inescapably herself' (334). Her fragility fills Vander with 'horrified tenderness' (334) and her final suicide – a scene which has an excruciating emotional impact on this reader – brings him back a pace or two from the brink of utter monstrosity.

To dwell a little longer on selfhood, Vander has consistently denied the concept of self in his work, yet a doubt as to the existence of a core of selfhood lingers:

> I spent the best part of what I suppose I must call my career trying to drum into those who would listen among the general mob of resistant sentimentalists surrounding me the simple lesson that there is no self: no ego, no precious individual

spark breathed into each one of us by a bearded patriarch in the sky, who does not exist either. And yet . . . For all my insistence, and to my secret shame, I admit that even I cannot entirely rid myself of the conviction of an enduring core of selfhood amid the welter of the world, a kernel immune to any gale that might pluck the leaves from the almond tree and make the sustaining branches swing and shake. (27)

These doubts, the suspicions of an 'enduring core of selfhood,' colour the quest of Axel Vander. This quest, then, has not been to escape his past or his people, neither has it been to gain an identity. Rather, it has been to escape his individual self: 'I desired to escape my own individuality, the hereness of my self, not the thereness of my world, the world of my lost, poor, people' (285). In the course of his quest, he has also constructed of himself a simulacrum in relation to the 'original' Axel Vander: He cannot in the end know what is 'he' and what is 'I.' Unable to 'remember what it was like to be the one that [he] once was' and tripping himself up on the first and third person singular, he slips in the 'welter of personal, impersonal, impersonating, pronouns' (285). Vander is not merely a 'contingency misplaced and adrift in time' (68-69), he is also adrift – and exiled – in language.

Conclusion
Before concluding my discussion of the state of exile in simulation that I consider present in John Banville's *Shroud*, I would like to point to the wry description that Banville has provided of the quintessential postmodern (though the word was still only a gleam in eye of Jacques Derrida et ses amis) European novel. There would be a faceless anti-hero, trudging the great avenues and the squalid back alleys of a nameless city, following some mysteriously ordained quest which he knows he can neither complete nor abandon, and which is, anyway, merely a metaphor for the real task in which he is engaged, namely, the search for an Identity. Even the pages of this ur-roman would have a characteristic look to them: high and narrow and somehow tottery, with squeezed margins, few paragraph breaks, and no

passages of dialogue where in more conventional tales the weary
reader could pause to paddle in the shallows.

> All very earnest, all very enigmatic, and all maddeningly
> vague. And this kind of novel is still being written in
> mainland Europe. Every year it wins one of those little-known
> but highly lucrative literary prizes offered by this or that
> unpronounceable foundation with affiliations to the European
> Union. Some of these novels even deserve a prize. Some of
> them are even read, or at least bought, by surprisingly large
> numbers of people. But it is all a far, far cry from the glory
> days of the European novel, when a new work by Thomas
> Mann or Alberto Moravia or Gunter Grass would set the
> Sunday supplements humming with excitement. Fiction in
> Europe is now generally an etiolated, unassuming, apologetic
> affair, a tired voice out of what seem exhausted cisterns
> ('Through a Glass')

It seems to me that *Shroud*, on one level, is a perversion of this
ironic description of the quintessential postmodern novel. Not
that the novel lacks dialogue, or that its pages totter, but there is
in it that almost faceless anti-hero who trudges – limps – lame and
one-eyed, through the avenues and alleys of a European city, not
nameless, but Turin. He is 'very, very old' (4) and his quest is not
for an Identity, but for a way of losing it.

If not quintessentially postmodern in the sense of the above
quotation, then, *Shroud* is certainly postmodern in a
Baudrillardian sense. It is, as I have attempted to show in the
above, a text in dialogue with Jean Baudrillard's *Simulacra and
Simulation*, and it places its male protagonist in a state of exile in
simulation. Using the term exile metaphorically, I have suggested
that the novel's Axel Vander is adrift in an exile which is
postmodern and triple-levelled:

First, the unnamed Jewish youth from Antwerp takes his
initial steps into an exile in simulation by denying his origin and
assuming the name of Axel Vander, his dead friend. He becomes
exiled from the history of his people, the Jews of Antwerp, who
were persecuted during World War II and also from the record of

that history, a record which his own fragmented, unreliable narration – alternately asserting, denying and evading 'facts'– turns into a simulacrum.

Second, the man who calls himself Axel Vander exists in exile from the likeness of a god. The futile attempts that he and Cass Cleave make to gain access to the elusive Shroud of Turin reveal the existence, in the novel, of a Shroud-land, as it were, a Disney-land of religious pretense, in which copies hide the 'original' shroud and conceal the fact that it is an absent, faked image of a non-existent god. The incident is indicative of the kind of order that Baudrillard envisions, in which God, too, may be simulated and the entire system turned into a simulacrum.

On the third level, the protagonist is exiled from his own self. He is 'not so much a person as a contingency, misplaced and adrift in time.' A shape-changer and a master of reduplication, he is Jew and Gentile, European and American, young survivor and ancient lover, spied upon and spying. He is an impostor. Through the assumption of the identity of a dead friend, the youth from Antwerp has first reduplicated himself; then, as the original fades and the copy takes over and becomes dominant, he has become a copy without an original, without center or authenticity. We have seen Vander, in a brief moment of self-loathing, use the imagery of the stage to expose his hollowness; here, he lets go of himself, accepting instead the manufactured likeness of a human being, at the core of which there is nothing but sawdust, 'shaky struts and a mess of wiring.' *Shroud* opens to a vision, then, which is as chilling as it is shrouded, and in which the self, turned simulacrum, yields to an irremediable exile in a realm of simulation.

Notes

1 It should be noted, perhaps, that John Banville apparently did not have Jean Baudrillard in mind while writing *Shroud*. In an e-mail message to me, Banville has commented on his interest in Baudrillard: 'I find his ideas interesting, but I haven't read enough [...]. He is on my shelves, waiting for a rainy day.' August 4, 2003.

2 In more than one of Banville's novels, the narrator, like a Prospero on his island, draws attention to his godlike status; in *Ghosts*, for

example, the phrase 'little god' is used. Also, the last name of the protagonist of *Birchwood* is Godkin.

3 It has been pointed out that if we accept Barthes' view that the 'author is stripped of all metaphysical status and reduced to a location (a crossroad), where language [. . .] crosses and recrosses' the reader must be 'free to enter the text from any direction' (Selden, Widdowson and Brooker 157).

4 One might recall here that Baudrillard, in a chapter entitled 'The Spiraling Cadaver', claims that the university system is decaying (150) and that it is 'in ruins: non-functional in the social arenas of the market and employment, lacking cultural substance or an end purpose of knowledge' (Baudrillard 149).

5 Baudrillard, when writing about the Holocaust, claims: 'Forgetting extermination is part of extermination, because it is also the extermination of memory, of history, of the social' (49). Baudrillard seems to see the 'restaging of extermination' – especially through the medium of television – as a creation of an artificial memory, which is too far removed in time – 'late, much too late' – to profoundly disturb (49). Through this restaging, he claims, one 'no longer makes the Jews pass through the crematorium or the gas chamber, but through the sound track and image track, through the universal screen and the microprocessor' (49). Baudrillard, here as elsewhere, develops his ideas to a point far beyond the scope of this essay. What is of interest here, however, is his claim that 'we' produce the artificial memory, the simulated extermination, hoping thereby to exorcise it 'at very little cost, and for the price of a few tears'. We have all, he writes dismissively, 'trembled and bawled in the face of extermination' (49). What we do, he seems to say, is create a copy of the holocaust which in fact effaces the real holocaust from our memory. It becomes a simulacrum behind which the real is lost.

6 It may be in order to recall here Adorno's view that the fate of houses is to be thrown away – 'it is part of morality not to be at home in one's home' – and Said's apt comment on this: 'To follow Adorno is to stand away from "home" in order to look at it with the exile's detachment' (Said 184-85).

7 My view of the impossibility of direct access to the events of history is, of course, shaped by Jacques Derrida's analysis of the thrice-processed nature of history.

References

Acheson, James. *The British and Irish Novel since 1960*. Basingstoke and London: Macmillan, 1991.

Banville, John. *Birchwood*. 1973. London: Picador, 1998.

— *Eclipse*. 2000. London: Picador, 2001.

— *Frames Trilogy*. (*The Book of Evidence*, 1989; *Ghosts*, 1993; *Athena*, 1995). London: Picador, 2001.

— *The Revolutions Trilogy* (*Doctor Copernicus*, 1976; *Kepler*,1981; *The Newton Letter*, 1982). London: Picador, 2002.

— 'The Rubble Artist.' Review of W.G Sebald's *Austerlitz*. Post date 11.19.01. Issue date 11.26.01. <http://www.thenewrepublic.com/banville112601.html> (Accessed 21 December 2001).

— *Shroud*. London: Picador, 2002.

— 'Through a Glass Vaguely.' The New Republic Online. Post date 11 December 2000. Issue date Dec. 18, 2000. <http://www.thenewrepublic.com/121800/banville121800.html> (Accessed 21 December 2001).

— *The Untouchable*. 1997. London: Picador, 1998.

Baudrillard, Jean. *Simulacra and Simulation*. Trans. Sheila Faria Glaser. Ann Arbor: University of Michigan Press, 1994.

Camus, Albert. *Le Mythe de Sisyphe*. Paris: Gallimard, 1942.

— *The Outsider*. Trans. Joseph Laredo. London: Penguin, 1982.

Clark, Alex. 'Dead men talking'. Review in *The Guardian*. Saturday, 5 October 2002. <http://books.guardian.co.uk/review/story/0,,804109,00.html> (Accessed 19 February 2003).

Knopf, A.. Interview with Le Carré. <http://www.randomhouse.com/features/lecarre/author.html>

Kristeva, Julia. *Crisis of the European Subject*. Trans. Susan Fairfield. New York: Other Press, 2000.

Man, Paul de. *Blindness and Insight: Essays in the Rhetoric of Contemporary Criticism*. 1971. 2nd ed. rev. Minneapolis: University of Minnesota Press, 1983.

Mars-Jones, Adam. 'The evil that men do'. Review in *Guardian Unlimited*. Sunday October 13, 2002.

Murphy, M. 'Reading the Future'. RTE interview, 2001. <http://www.rte.ie/radio/readingthefuture/banville.html> (Accessed 12 December 2001).

Rafroidi, Patrick and Maurice Harmon, eds. *The Irish Novel in Our Time*. Villeneuve-d'Ascq: Publication de l'Université de Lille, 1976.

Said, Edward W. *Reflections on Exile and Other Essays*. Cambridge, Mass: Harvard UP, 2002.

Selden, Raman, Peter Widdowson, and Peter Brooker. *A Reader's Guide to Contemporary Literary Theory*. 1985. London: Prentice Hall, 1997.

Tarien, Kersti. 'How Much Mystifying Mystery We Need: John Banville's *Birchwood* and Editorial Intervention'. In KarenVandevelde, ed. *New Voices in Irish Criticism*. 3. Dublin: Four Courts Press, 2002.

— 'Trying to Catch Long Lankin by his Arm: The Evolution of John Banville's Long Lankin'. *Irish University Review* 31 (Autumn/Winter 2001): 386-403.

Ward, Patrick. *Exile, Emigration and Irish Writing*. Dublin: Irish Academic Press, 2002.

CONTRIBUTORS

Michael Böss is Associate Professor of History and Irish Studies at University of Aarhus, Denmark, and Head of the Centre for Irish Studies at Aarhus. His most recent book is *Engaging Modernity* (Dublin, Veritas 2003), which he co-edited and introduced with Eamon Maher. He is co-editor of *Nordic Irish Studies.*

Hedda Friberg is Senior Lecturer in English at MidSweden University College, Härnösand, Sweden. She is the author of *An Old Order and New: The Split World of Liam O'Flaherty' s Novels* (Uppsala, 1996), and is currently engaged in research on the novels of John Banville.

Irene Gilsenan Nordin is Senior Lecturer in English at University College Dalarna, Sweden, and Director of DUCIS (Dalarna University Centre for Irish Studies). She is author of *Crediting Marvels in Seamus Heaney's* Seeing Things (Uppsala, 1999), and is currently completing a book on Eiléan Ní Chuilleanáin. She is co-editor of *Nordic Irish Studies.*

Billy Gray is Senior Lecturer in English at Luleå Technical University, Sweden. He is a graduate of The University of Ulster and wrote his doctoral dissertation on the influence of Islamic mysticism on the work of Doris Lessing. He is currently working on a research project entitled 'The Aesthetics of Ageing'.

Heidi Hansson is a Research Fellow at the Department of English, Umeå University, Sweden. She is author of *Romance Revived: Postmodern Romances and the Tradition* (1998), and is currently involved in a research project on nineteenth-century Irish women's prose.

Ida Klitgård is Research Fellow at the Department of English, University of Copenhagen, Denmark. She holds a degree in

English and Translation Studies and finished her doctoral studies in English Literature at the University of Copenhagen in 2000.

Britta Olinder is Associate Professor Emeritus of English at Gothenburg University, Sweden. She has published work on post-colonial and Irish literature, the latter focusing on John Hewitt, women playwrights and poets. She is co-editor of Criss Cross Tales: Short Stories from English-speaking Cultures.

Åke Persson is Senior Lecturer in English at University College Trollhätten /Uddevalla, Sweden. He is author of Betraying the Age: Social and Artistic Protest in Brendan Kennelly's Work (Gothenburg, 2000) and is currently engaged in research on Roddy Doyle's fiction.

Bent Sørensen is Assistant Professor of English at Aalborg University, Denmark. He is currently engaged in a book project, Transatlantic - A Cultural Text Studies Approach, and a volume, provisionally entitled Postmodern Jewish Novels. His editorial work centers on a Cultural Text Studies project, which includes a monograph series and a web-based journal.